JOHN LOCKE'S
MORAL REVOLUTION

From Natural Law to Moral Relativism

Samuel Zinaich, Jr.

University Press of America,® Inc.
Lanham · Boulder · New York · Toronto · Oxford

Contents

Preface

A time-honored course on the History of Modern Philosophy taught at a liberal arts college or at a graduate school stresses the Modern canon. This means that students will be required to read portions of the Continental Rationalists, e.g., Rene Descartes (1596-1650), Benedictus de Spinoza (1632-1677), and Gottfried Liebniz (1646-1716), the British Empiricists, e.g., John Locke (1632-1704), George Berkeley (1685-1753), and David Hume (1711-1776), and if there is time (and, of course, if your students are not too exhausted), Immanuel Kant's critique of Modern Philosophy.

Although there may be others writers, e.g., Thomas Hobbes (1588-1679), that may be included, the names above represent the core figures for such a course. Unfortunately, the majority of texts dedicated to the History of Modern Philosophy often present a narrow slice of the writer's thought. This is understandable because the authors mentioned earlier were all prolific writers. But this approach leads to the following problem. Students are often left with a skewed or, in a worse case scenario, an, inaccurate account of the philosopher's outlook. For example, consider this case. When I was in college and graduate school, I was taught that John Locke's primary focus (especially in his later years) was epistemology. However, even a cursory reading of Locke's corpus will reveal that nothing could be further from the truth. Granted, Locke does address various epistemological issues, but an internal review into his works reveals that he was committed to something quite different.

My own understanding of Locke was initially in line with this traditional account. Like most of my colleagues and peers, we read though the canon focusing on the passages that we presupposed to be important, and we skimmed through those other passages that we were taught to ignore. But one day, early in my own philosophical career, one of my graduate school professors, Professor Edward F. McClennen, who was teaching a course on the History of Moral Philosophy, pointed out to me, what he called, "some strange passages in Locke's writings." He made the case that although these "strange passages" are typically ignored, when they are looked at more closely, they teach a very different story about what Locke was attempting to do.

Under Professor McClennen's direction, I began to reread Locke again in the light of these passages. What I discovered was something that I initially had a hard time believing. In fact, it turned into a real mystery because the standpoint was inconsistent with almost every traditional understanding of Locke's works. So, what was supposed to be a paper for a typical course about the History of Moral Theory eventually led me to write a dissertation to solve this mystery.

Unfortunately, although I attempted to unravel the mystery in my dissertation, it only led to more questions and, as a result, the mystery deepened. But what could be so mysterious about Locke's views? The mystery concerns how to reconcile Locke's obvious commitment to Christianity including his infatuation with theological voluntarianism, his early loyalty to natural law theory including his later claims that morality, like mathematics, can be demonstrated, and what looks like a commitment to a version of negative utilitarianism. How are all of these doctrines to reconciled? Initally, this seemed impossible; nevertheless, I undertook this project with no idea of where I was going to end up.

Even after two publications, this project still feels too big for me to manage. Nevertheless, this book represents my attempt to reconcile all these elements in Locke's thinking, and to present a coherent examination of Lock'e viewpoint. Unluckily, in order to do this, I had to do something I did not want to do. I had to break faith with most, if not all, of the traditional understandings of Locke. As I will discuss later, there are two basic approaches to interpret and to manage Locke's point of view. Of course, taking this approach puts me at a disadvantage. This is so because when a writer attempts to put forth a new understanding of one of the canon fathers, his ideas are likely to be counted as suspicious and promptly discounted unless, of course, he can make a plausible defense. But, as anyone may know, making a credible argument is easier said than done. One can always take the easy way out and write just a critical piece and argue that all the tradition standpoints are false. I do a lot of that; but, within this book I also try to articulate what Locke ended up doing. I hope that I have made such a case, but I will have to wait to see if this is so. Having said this, I trust that my readers will give my point of view a fair and even-handed reading.

Acknowledgments

No words can quite express my gratitude to all the individuals who have been a part of this book. Although the number of people are too many to mention, I will point out those who have been particularly prominent.

My first acknowledgment goes to Fred Miller, Jr., Executive Director of the Social Philosophy and Policy Center, Bowling Green, OH. Dr. Miller played a significant role in the early formation of my dissertation of which this book partly reflects. In addition to his tireless comments, Dr. Miller made arrangements for me to spend time with Dr. Michael J. Zuckert. Under Dr. Zuckert's fine direction, my awkward and ambiguous understanding of the issues discussed in this book took their present shape. I will forever be indebted to Dr. Zuckert's direction and encouragement.

Attention should also be given to Dr. Dennis Barbour, Chair of the Department of English and Philosophy, Purdue University Calumet, Hammond, IN. Dr. Barbour made recourses available to me in order to complete this project including hiring Dr. Sandra Utz. Dr. Utz' editorial expertise combed out my syntactical and grammatical problems.

Additionally, my deepest appreciation goes to my wife, Susan. Words cannot communicate my love for her strength and encouragement as I put this book together.

Finally, I would like to thank following publishers for the permission to use the following books and articles: Oxford University Press for the use of W. Von Leyden, Introduction to *Essays On the Law of Nature, together with transcripts of Locke's shorthand in his journal of 1676,* edited W. Von Leyden, 1-92. Oxford: Clarendon Press, 1954; Edinburgh University Press for the use of John Colman, *John Locke's-Moral Philosophy.* Edinburgh: Edinburgh University Press, 1983; to

Hilail Gildin, editor of *Interpretation: A Journal of Political Philosophy* for the use of Robert Horwitz. "John Locke's *Questions Concerning the Law of Nature*: A Commentary." *Interpretation: A Journal of Political Philosophy* 19, no. 3 (1992): 251-306 and Samuel Zinaich, Jr, "The Internal Coherency of Locke's Moral Views in the *Questions Concerning the Law of Nature*." *Interpretation: A Journal of Political Philosophy* 29, no. 1 (Fall 2001): 55-73; and to Professor Roland Hall, editor of *Locke Studies,* for the use of Samuel Zinaich, Jr., "Locke's Moral Revolution: from Natural Law to Moral Relativism." *The Locke Newsletter* 31 (2000): 79-114.

Introduction

After John Locke finished making a copy of his lectures on natural law in 1664, he artfully concealed each leaf of his lecture within his various notebooks and other papers. Here his lectures remained hidden for two hundred and eighty-two years until they were discovered by Dr. Wolfgang von Leyden in 1946 and later published by him in 1954.[1] Initially, this seems curious but perhaps it is understandable: maybe Locke was not entirely happy with what he had written. Or maybe he lost interest in this work?[2] These explanations are plausible, but they are ultimately dissatisfying because Locke took such great pains to hide each leaf.[3] It really appears that Locke was attempting to keep it hidden for a particular reason. But what reason could Locke have had? On a first reading of these lectures, there is nothing unusual about what Locke had written, i.e., there are no views, which are atheistic or anything that resemble Hobbes' views, which could have caused him trouble.[4] It is a work, which, for all intents and purposes, is a standard, orthodox view in the Christian natural law tradition.[5] Moreover, Locke evidently delivered these lectures to his students while he was Censor of Moral Philosophy at Christ Church, Oxford, from 1660-1664. At any rate Locke states in his Valedictory Speech of 1664 that he engaged in disputations concerning natural law with his former students, now the new Bachelors of Arts:

> [F]arewell, you too, my fellow soldiers, or should I say my masters? For having been overmastered by you so many times I acknowledge you as victors: in this philosophical arena you have so distinguished yourselves that anyone of you would be thought to be an Aristotle, since he had an intimate knowledge of nature and mankind, or an Alexander, able to conquer all. I took part this year in your disputa-

tion on such terms that I always went out at once beaten and en-
riched. Such indeed was the grace of your victory that your arguments, to which I so often yielded, added as much to my knowledge
as they detracted from my reputation. That law about which was all
our strife had often eluded my fruitless quest, had not your way of
life restored that very same law which your tongue had wrested from
me. Hence it can be doubted whether your disputations assaulted the
law of nature or your behavior defended it, more keenly.[6]

What is more curious is that roughly a year after Locke published
An Essay Concerning Human Understanding[7] in 1690, many scholars
at Oxford, having considered his account of the source of morality and
law, told Locke's life-long friend, James Tyrrell, that what Locke had
written had "come very near to what is so much cryed out upon in Mr:
Hobs."[8] Their critique of Locke's ideas in the *Essay* amounted to a
charge of Hobbesianism. Such a charge could be fatal not only for a
scholar's career, but also for a scholar's life.[9] Not surprisingly, he pro-
tested vehemently that he never read Hobbes and that his own name
should be completely disassociated from that of "the monster of
Malmesbury."[10] However, as von Leyden points out, Tyrrell, having
read the *Essays* and being thoroughly acquainted with them, suggested
to Locke something that appeared to be reasonable, at least on the surface of things, viz., that he publish these lectures to acquit himself of
these charges and resolve the ambiguities in the *Essay*.[11] Locke refused,
and as Horwitz points out:

> Whatever his ultimate intention may have been with regard to his re-
> flections on the law of nature, it is evident that he had no intention of
> publishing them early in life, certainly not while he was a tutor at Ox-
> ford, and, as one may gather, at no point during his lifetime.[12]

Although Tyrrell's intentions may have been to protect Locke,
Locke's refusal to publish his lectures was probably the most reasonable thing for him to do (especially given the kind of negative attention
that the *Essay* was receiving). One reason for this is, unlike Tyrrell,
Locke understood that there was an important difference between his
two works. If he had published his lectures, this would have only added
more fuel to their charges because his critics would have been able to
compare both works. What they would have found was that Locke's
thinking had changed in important ways. In fact, this is exactly what I
have attempted to document in this book. For example, I argue that in
the *Essay* Locke retreats from his early views, which occur in the *Es-*

says. This is so because Locke's account of the formulation of moral knowledge in the *Essay* does not resemble his formulation of moral knowledge in the *Essays*. One reason for this is Locke does not advocate in the *Essay* a natural law explanation concerning why we believe some actions are morally good or evil, or, e.g., why some of our moral claims are true or false.

By taking this position, I stand opposed to the traditional understanding of the relationship between the *Essay* and the *Essays*. Since the publication of the *Essays* in 1954, two major and mutually exclusive standpoints have emerged. The first one is called the reconcilability thesis and the other is the irreconcilability thesis. I will begin with the former.

The reconcilability thesis is the claim that Locke's theory of moral knowledge in the *Essay* is compatible with the theory of natural law propounded in the *Essays*. There are, however, three objections to this thesis: First, the *Essay* is at odds with the *Essays* because Locke rejects the essentialism of the *Essays*, and instead, accepts a corpuscular view of the world in the *Essay*. Second, Locke departs in the *Essay* from the natural law tradition in his treatment of good and evil. Third, Locke abandons the moral absolutism of the *Essays* for a version of ethical relativism in the *Essay*. John Colman, who espouses the reconcilability thesis, has offered replies to each of these objections.[13] A number of scholars tend to agree with Colman.[14] Nevertheless, I shall argue (in chapter 4) that Colman's replies fail, and that the three objections stand.

The irreconcilability thesis is the assertion that Locke's theory of moral knowledge in the *Essay* is incompatible with his theory of natural law in the *Essays*. Peter Laslett, who defends the irreconcilability thesis, argues that this is so because "The *Essay* has no room for natural law."[15] But even though I agree with Laslett on this point, I disagree with his reason for the incompatibility. Laslett argues that there is an incompatibility because of Locke's inability to manage his own views. Instead, I argue in Chapter Four that there is a better explanation for the incompatibility of the *Essay* and *Essays*. I make a case that there is a difference because Locke began both works from different starting points.

Prior to chapter 4, however, I set up in chapters 1, 2 and 3, the discussion, which occurs in chapter 4. For example, in chapter 1, I present the context and the circumstances in which the *Essays* and the *Essay* were written. I argue that Locke responded to very different concerns in the *Essays* and the *Essay*. In chapters 2 and 3, I lay out what I take to be some of the major views of the *Essays* and the *Essay*. For example, in chapter 2 I discuss three central views of the *Essays*: first, Locke's reliance upon Aristotelian essentialism; second, his view of the nature of virtue and vice; and third, his moral absolutism. In chapter 3 I discuss three of his views as they occur in the *Essay*: first, Locke's view of essentialism; second, his ideas of the nature of good and evil; and, third, his moral relativism.

Finally, in chapter 5, I discuss the ramifications of my argument for some fundamental issues in the understanding of Locke in the history of moral philosophy and of his political philosophy. For example, it is currently thought by some scholars that Locke's *Two Treatises of Government*[16] relate far more closely to the *Essays* than to the *Essay* because of the role of the law of nature in the first and second and its incompatibility with the third. However, in the chapter 5 I outline a paradoxical alternative; even though on the surface of things it appears that the *Essays* and the *Treatises* are conceptually linked by virtue of his use of the term "law of nature," when we look closer at Locke's reasoning, we see that the link is between the *Essay* and the *Treatises*.

Notes

1 John Locke's initial thoughts about the law of nature are recorded in ten different essays, which have been called both the *Essays on the Law of Nature*, ed. and trans. W. von Leyden (Oxford, 1958), and the *Questions Concerning the Law of Nature*, eds. Robert Horwitz, Jenny Strauss Clay, and Diskin Clay and trans. Diskin Clay (Ithaca & London, 1990). This work by Locke remained unpublished until 1954 when von Leyden first published it. While not much published scholarship has been devoted to the examination of the correctness of either edition, there is one notable exception. M. A. Stewart has discussed the limitations in the edition of Horwitz, et al. in his "Critical Notice," *The Locke Newsletter* 23 (1992): 145-165. References to Locke's essays will follow the standard edition, viz., von Leyden's edition (hereafter *Essays*). Additionally, all references to Locke's *Essays* are by page and folio number.

2 Von Leyden also speculates about this very point and offers five different explanations for why Locke did not publish the *Essays*. First, publishing the *Essays* would have meant the laborious task of translating them into English since writers in the second half of the seventeenth century preferred the vernacular to the Latin. Second, von Leyden points out that a good deal of what Locke wrote in the *Essays* found its way into the *Essay*. "Thus, in a sense the *Essays* were used by Locke as if they had been a preliminary draft of part of the *Essay*" (von Leyden, "introduction to the *Essays*," 14). Third, many of his views in the *Essay* as representative of his changing views "made it indeed difficult for him to adhere whole-heartedly to his doctrine of natural law" (Ibid.). Fourth, von Leyden points out that his views of law and civil authority had changed toward the vindication of individual rights and liberty. Finally, "The *Essays* were, after all, the work of youth [and] lack the maturity of his later thought and may have induced in him a feeling of diffidence" (Ibid., 15). In my estimation, reason three is probably the most correct reason.

3 Robert Horwitz, "introduction to *Questions Concerning the Law of Nature*," 45.

4 Horwitz points out an interesting example of the overall hysterical attitude toward Thomas Hobbes: "in 1676 . . . the earl of Clarendon . . . considered it an important service to the king to 'answer Mr. Hobbes's *Leviathan*, and to confute the doctrine therein contain'd, so pernicious to the Sovereign Power of Kings, and destructive to the affection and allegiance of Subjects.' The earl of Clarendon also observes: 'I would make no scruple to declare, that I never read any Book that contains in it some much Sedition, Treason, and Impiety as this *Leviathan*; and therefore that it is very unfit to be read, taught, or sold, as dissolving all the ligaments of Government, and undermining all principles of Religion.'" (Ibid., FN 18, 7-8).

5 By the term "Christian natural law tradition" I do not mean to imply that there are clear-cut criteria by which we can clearly delineate those who are and who are not a part of this tradition. There are a number of characteristics, which many Protestant and Catholic interpreters of this tradition (e.g., Aquinas, Hooker, and Culverwel) have in common. My view of this term is largely informed by Horwitz, who describes it in detail in the introduction of his edition of the *Essays* (Horwitz, "introduction to the *Questions*," 11-19). For my pur-

pose, I will merely summarize his points. Horwitz explains that at the core of this tradition is "an explicit understanding of the nature and genesis of law" (Ibid., 11). The first fundamental tenet is that the seat of law or center of all authority is God, and the highest and most comprehensive manifestation of law is God's eternal law. This point leads to the second tenet, which is that God created a perfectly structured world and gave every creature, including humans, a station and laws to operate within, which are best agreeable and conformable to their beings. Another tenet of the Christian natural law tradition is the existence of natural law. Natural law is a knowable source of moral knowledge, which is imprinted upon the minds of rational creatures, and, in virtue of this law, rational creatures derive their respective inclinations to pursue their ends and to act properly. Finally, although the law of nature is knowable by some sort of means (which is the only point common among natural law theorists) and even though what God requires of us is discoverable in virtue of this means, according to this view, humankind suffers the wages of original sin. Because of this our lives are characterized by sin and disobedience, i.e., we often resist the natural inclinations and make no attempt to discover by natural means what is right. To remedy this, God also provided another source of moral knowledge, which is divinely revealed in the Scriptures. There are, therefore, two sources of moral knowledge to provide rational creatures with needful instruction.

6 Locke, *Essays On the Laws of Nature*, 237 and 239.

7 References to Locke's *Essay* will follow the standard edition, John Locke, *Essay Concerning Human Understanding*, ed. P. H. Nidditch (Oxford, 1975), hereafter *Essay*. All references to this work are by book, chapter, and section number.

8 James Tyrrell to Locke, 30 June 1690, *The Correspondence of John Locke*, ed. E. S. de Beer (Oxford, 1979), 4:102. One such critic, as Horwitz points out, was John Edwards of Cambridge: "In his *A Brief Vindication of the Fundamental Articles of the Christian Faith* Edwards denounced Locke as gravely mistaken in his understanding of natural law, and a dangerous enemy to Christian Morality and religion altogether (Horwitz, "introduction to the *Questions*," 26-7). Even more interestingly, after Sir Isaac Newton read the *Essay*, he wrote to Locke, "I took you for a Hobbist" (Issac Newton to Locke, 16 September 1693, *The Correspondence of John Locke*, ed. E. S. de Beer [Oxford, 1979], 4:727). See also Samuel I. Mintz, *The Hunting of Leviathan* (Cambridge: Cambridge University Press, 1962) for a discussion of the attempts of seventeenth century individuals to root out and eradicate the ideas associated with the *Leviathan*.

9 Horwitz points out that in Locke's day the attack against Hobbes did not stop with mere calumny. He writes:

Locke may well have been present on the afternoon of 21 July 1683 when the last major public book burning took place at Oxford. That dire action had been deemed necessary by the university's vice chancellor following identification by the professor of divinity of "certaine propositions taken out of severall rebellious and seditious authours." It was duly proposed, and unanimously agreed that they, the books be condemned to be burned. . . . Among the heretical books burned that afternoon were "Thomas Hobs' *Leviathan* and *De Cive*, and *The Shaftesburian Association*," and works by ten other authors. (Horwitz, "introduction to the *Questions*," 9)

10 Horwitz, "introduction to the *Questions*," 7. Maurice Cranston, Locke's twentieth-century biographer, points out that although there are instances where Locke's doctrines in the *Essay* appear to be similar to some of what Hobbes had written: "at no time in his life would Locke admit his debt to Hobbes. He even came to pretend he had never read Hobbes properly" (*John Locke: A Biography* [New York: The Macmillan Company, 1957], 62). Moreover, Laslett speculates that the similarity between Locke's ideas and Hobbes may be just a coincidence, but he adds that it is more likely that Locke read Hobbes when he was young (when his tendency was authoritarian) and "having read it and forgotten it . . . he then reproduced [it] as a notion of his own" (Peter Laslett, "introduction to the *Two Treatises of Government*," by John Locke, ed. Peter Laslett [Cambridge: Cambridge University Press, 1993], 73).

11 Von Leyden, "introduction to the *Essays*," 13. It is important to understand that Tyrrell had pressed Locke to publish the *Essays* sometime even before the controversy over the *Essay*. When Locke left for Holland in 1683, he left a number of books and manuscripts in the care of Tyrrell, including the *Essays*. Tyrrell, according to Horwitz, evidently painstakingly pored over Locke's books and manuscripts (Horwitz, "introduction to the *Questions*," 42-43). J. B. Schneewind also points out that maybe one other person knew about Locke's work on natural law. See his essay "Locke's Moral Philosophy," in Vere Chappell (ed.), *The Cambridge Companion to Locke* (Cambridge: Cambridge University Press, 1994), 199. Von Leyden even suggests that Tyrrell's painstaking perusal turned into a case of plagiarism for his own works:

Several of Tyrrell's chief arguments concerning natural law, to which there is in fact no parallel in Locke's *Essay*, are so much like those in Locke's essays on natural law that there be little doubt about their derivation. Tyrrell makes no mention of the essay in his *Disquisition*, and in some places where his arguments resemble Locke's he even intimates that he is the first to set them forth. (von Leyden, "introduction to the *Essays*," 85-86)

A closer reading of Locke's correspondence reveals that Tyrrell sent to Locke his manuscript and made Locke aware of the passages that he borrowed from Locke's own manuscript. See James Tyrrell to Locke, 9 August 1692, *The Correspondence of John Locke*, ed. E. S. de Beer (Oxford: Oxford University Press, 1979), 4:493-496.

12 Horwitz, "introduction to the *Questions*," 33.

13 John Colman, *John Locke's Moral Philosophy* (Edinburgh: Edinburgh University Press, 1983).

14 For example, see Michael Ayers, *Locke* (London: Routledge, 1991), 2:189; Ruth W. Grant, *John Locke's Liberalism* (Chicago: University of Chicago Press, 1987), 42; Andrzej Rapaczynski, *Nature and Politics: Liberalism in the Philosophies of Hobbes, Locke, and Rousseau* (Cornell: Cornell University Press, 1987), 169; John W. Yolton, *Locke and the Compass of Human Understanding* (Cambridge: Cambridge University Press, 1970), 171; W. von Leyden, "introduction to the *Essays*," 60-88; and A. John Simmons, *The Lockean Theory of Rights* (Princeton: Princeton University Press, 1992), fn. 12, 19. Colman, however, offers what may be described as the most extensive attempt to show how the accounts of moral knowledge in the *Essay* and the *Essays* are reconcilable. For example, A. John Simmons writes: "Colman has convincingly defended the consistency of Locke's various efforts in moral philosophy . . . against the charges of inconsistency. . . ." (Ibid.).

15 Laslett, "introduction to *Two Treatises of Government*," 81.

16 References to Locke's *Two Treatises of Government* will follow the standard edition, John Locke, *Two Treatises of Government*, ed. Peter Laslett (Cambridge: Cambridge University Press, 1993), hereafter *Treatises*. All references to this work are by chapter and section number.

1
The Historical Context of the
Essays and the *Essay*

Introduction

W. von Leyden argues that Locke's early doctrine of natural law in the *Essays* formed the starting-point for the *Essay*; that is, the *Essay* was written as a philosophical justification for his doctrine of natural law in the *Essays*.[1] I shall argue that von Leyden's view is mistaken. Rather, the *Essays*, finished in 1664, was partly a response to the developing political crisis associated with the centralization of the Crown after the restoration of Charles II in 1660. However, I shall argue that the *Essay*, published in 1690, was a response to a different sort of crisis, viz., an epistemological crisis created by the new science of Robert Boyle. More specifically, I shall argue that the pervasive and foundational presence in the *Essay* of the metaphysical views of Robert Boyle suggests that Locke wrote in order to follow out the implications that Boyle's views had for moral and religious knowledge.

To this end, I have broken this chapter into two parts: First, I describe the context of the early 1660s when Locke wrote the *Essays*. Second, I describe the later context and contrast the concerns that may have motivated him to write the *Essay*.

The Context of the *Essays*

Locke's own hand-written manuscript of the *Essays* indicates that he finished it in the year 1664. It is thus a product of the early years of what scholars call the Restoration Period, the time immediately following the crisis period of England's civil war which lasted from roughly

1642 until 1660. That crisis ended in 1660 when the Stuart Monarchy was restored to power.

England's civil war was in part a crisis of political authority. That is, it was a crisis of attitudes over the Ancient Constitution of England.[2] Prior to the crisis, the Crown, for various reasons, sought to consolidate its power. It partly attempted to do this by giving an explanation about what it thought was the origin of its power and the proper relationship between itself and the Ancient Constitution. To sum up the Crown's view, there is evidence from primary sources that it believed that its authority and power over political, religious, and moral matters was absolute.[3] One of the reasons that the Crown gave was that God allegedly recognized the absolute authority of its power on earth since the Bible seems to report that God calls the kings on earth "gods."[4] Moreover, the Crown believed that it had absolute authority because its power and authority was above the law or Ancient Constitution, since it believed it was historically the author and giver of the Ancient Constitution.

The Crown's attitude toward the Ancient Constitution was met with opposition. Many individuals, especially those in Parliament, i.e., those in the House of Commons, remained incredulous. As the accounts go, the opposition countered by giving their own competing interpretation of the origins of the King's authority and the King's relationship to the Ancient Constitution. Many believed that the King's authority over political, religious, and moral matters was not absolute. One of the reasons given was that God never recognized the King, or any King, as having absolute earthly power. Moreover, the King was not the author and giver of the Ancient Constitution. In fact, one member of Parliament argued that the Ancient Constitution of England existed prior to the existence of the British Monarch and prior to the Norman conquest.[5] Zuckert, in a discussion on this very point about the Ancient Constitution of England, writes:

> [T]his appeal to a set of parliamentary privileges and subjects' rights "as ancient as the kingdom itself" had two aspects. First, it served to reject the very idea of an "original of political power." There was no such thing; the beginning was itself originless. Therefore, there was no original authority that ordained the constitution and the rights it embodied, and if no authority in the past to establish the constitution, then no authority in the present to disestablish or override it.[6]

Initially, the opposition to the Crown's attitude was one of uneasy toleration. But toward the 1640s the tension increased as certain actions by the Crown created a crisis attitude in the minds of the opposition in Parliament.[7] From 1642 until 1660, the opposition attempted to control the crisis they believed was taking place. For example, in 1649 members of Parliament executed the King and abolished the Monarchy. Many scholars believe that it was not until 1660 that that a resolution to the crisis took place.[8]

The years prior to and around 1660 also appear to be important for Locke. Although many individuals supported the return of the Stuarts, initially Locke was ambivalent about this. For example, in a letter written to his father in 1659, Locke said that he thought of taking up arms himself except that he did not know on which side to fight.[9] Like others, Locke wanted an end to the turmoil. However, there were abuses associated with both sides. For example, both sides seemed to be committed to an authoritarian outlook and arbitrary rule.

However, by the year 1660, although Locke never took up arms to fight for either side (as his father did), his views concerning the return of Charles Stuart changed, i.e., he favored the return of the Monarchy. In fact, there is evidence of his change of view in two pamphlets, which Locke circulated among his friends in 1660. The first pamphlet, initially written in English, is entitled, *Question: Whether the Civil Magistrate may lawfully impose and determine the use of indifferent things in reference to Religious Worship*. The second pamphlet, initially written in Latin, is translated as, *Whether the civil magistrate may incorporate indifferent things into the ceremonies of divine worship and impose them on the people: Confirmed*.[10] In the *Two Tracts* not only do we see Locke's first attempt at sustained political and ethical argument, we also see his attitude toward the political crisis he grew up with and his views about how to solve it. Once we understand Locke's attitude in these two pamphlets it will be easier to understand his views in the *Essays* and perhaps one important reason why he wrote the *Essays*.[11]

Von Leyden writes that from the internal evidence of the first pamphlet of the *Two Tracts* both of Locke's pamphlets were in response to a leaflet, which had been published in 1660 by Edward Bagshaw entitled, *The Great Questions Concerning Things Indifferent in Religious Worship*.[12] In this leaflet, Bagshaw's main argument, as I understand it, is a scriptural defense of the claim that there are religious matters which should be left up to the individual and to the individual's conscience to follow or not, and which are not subject to the magistrate's interference.

Locke responded in the *Two Tracts* by arguing in two similar but different ways. The conclusions of both pamphlets are the same, viz., that the magistrate[13] has a right to impose religious or non-religious ceremonies or any other indifferent acts[14] on his subjects. The *Two Tracts* differ in that, in the first pamphlet, Locke takes up Bagshaw's argument sentence by sentence and argues for alternative interpretations of the scriptures Bagshaw uses to defend his position, while in the second, Locke takes up the theoretical problems implicit but untreated in the first tract. In any event, in both pamphlets Locke looks to the restored monarchy as a means to settle the political and ecclesiastical crisis of England.

But why would Locke, the great defender of liberalism and toleration, defend such a view? Initially, Phillip Abrams speculates that Locke's heavy-handed authoritarian views in the *Two Tracts* were just perhaps a temporary aberration. This may be so because one year later Locke refused to allow either one of the pamphlets to be published. Additionally, it may seem plausible to assume that after the Restoration, Locke psychologically recovered from the crisis and reembraced his original liberal views. Abrams, however, points out that even though this view is not unfounded, there really is no solid evidence that Locke was a liberal prior to 1660:

> [A]ll we can say with confidence about Locke's political thinking prior to December 1660 is that he wanted to be left alone. He was skeptical and timorous: "I would be quiet and I would be safe', he writes and adds, 'but if I cannot enjoy them together the last must certainly be had at any rate." His sense of insecurity was explicitly intellectual—it is the uncertainty of knowledge, the chaos of opinions, that make him anxious.[15]

Abrams' quotation, I think, leads us to the heart of the matter. That is, at this point in Locke's life he had a suspicious view of human nature. For example, one of his reasons for giving the magistrate control over all aspects of his subjects' lives is due to the fact that without such control chaos will eventually break out:

> Grant the people once free and unlimited in the exercise of their religion and where will they stop, where will they themselves bound it, and will it not be religion to destroy all that are not of their profession?. . . Though I can believe that our author would not make this large use of his liberty, yet if he thinks others would not so far improve his principles, let him look some years back he will find that a

liberty for tender consciences was the first inlet to all those confu-
sions and unheard of and destructive opinions that over spread this
nation.[16]

Abrams points out the same thing about the *Two Tracts*:

> He starts, appropriately, from a political assumption—that men are so
> depraved and partial in their own causes that if they are not bound to
> a common order in society they will destroy one another and them-
> selves. A theory of law is the ostensible foundation of both *Tracts*.
> But it is not the rational weight of this theory that sustains and in-
> forms Locke's writing. Rather, it is an instinctive commitment to
> government as a means of order, a conviction that the free use of in-
> different things spells civil chaos.[17]

However, by 1664 there is a change in Locke's views. For example, in the *Essays*, there is an increased reliance on the concept of the
law of nature.[18] This reliance has implications for his views about the
magistrate and human nature. Whereas in the *Two Tracts* the magistrate
had control over every aspect of life, even those aspects that were indifferent, in the *Essays*, the magistrate himself, like his subjects, is under
absolute rules of duties and prohibitions contained in the law of nature,[19] and, in the cases in which the substance of an act is not prescribed by the law of nature:

> In cases like these, the 'matter' of the action is neither good nor bad,
> but the circumstances accompanying it are so determined. We are not
> bond here absolutely, but only conditionally, and it depends on our
> ability, and is entrusted to our prudence, whether or or not we care to
> undertake some such actions in which we incur obligation.[20]

Moreover, his views of human nature have also changed. This
change could well be described as a change from a Hobbesian perspective, as Abrams calls Locke's early view, to an Aristotelian perspective.[21] For example, in the *Two Tracts*, whereas human survival depends upon, first, the laying down of the right to anything including the
natural right of liberty and, then, transferal of it to him who is authorized to receive it, the *Essays* describes humans as seeking the union of
others to form societies:

> Further, he feels himself not only to be impelled by life's experiences
> and pressing needs to procure and preserve a life in society with other

men, but also to be urged to enter into society by a certain propensity of nature, and to be prepared for the maintenance of society by the gift of speech and through the intercourse of language, in fact as much as he is obliged to preserve himself.[22]

Now what sort of reason could Locke have had to move away from his theistic/Hobbesian-like views in the *Two Tracts* to, what has been called, "Christian/Aristotelian-like" views in the *Essays*? Richard Ashcraft concludes that:

> On the basis of a careful reading of all the manuscripts now available to us, however, an honest response must be that no obvious answer to this problem is contained in the documents themselves. Of course, several interpretations can be offered, with varying degrees of evidential support, but nowhere in the more than forty volumes of manuscripts does Locke tell us why he changed his mind about this or that issue, let alone why he reversed himself on the whole set of political propositions mentioned above. In the absence of such direct intentional statements to guide us, any interpretation must necessarily place a heavy reliance upon contextual evidence in its portrayal of the development of Locke's political thought.[23]

Although there isn't much evidence of why Locke changed his views between 1660 and 1664, there is, at least, one possible explanation. Locke, like many others who supported the return of Charles Stuart to the crown, became disillusioned by the centralization of the Crown. For example, Charles II, and then later, James II, carried on the traditions of James I and Charles I, both with respect to the consolidation of the Crown's power and the re-introduction of Catholicism into the Anglican Church and the government. For example, after only one year as King of England, Charles II enacted, among other things, the Corporation Act, the Militia Act, the Act of Uniformity, and the Act Against Tumultuous Petitioning. These Acts have been interpreted by many as a consolidation of Catholic and political ends,[24] and as a means to remove possible sources of opposition.[25] David Hume even remarks of Charles II that "as a sovereign, his character, though not altogether destitute of virtue, was in the main dangerous to his people, and dishonourable to himself."[26] In other words, there is a sense in which Locke may have changed his views in light of the growing centralization of the Crown.

Like the crisis before the Restoration, the political events happening around him may have had an important effect upon the security that he wanted to have for his life.

To sum up this section, I have given a description of the context and some reasons why the *Essays* was written. The key to understanding Locke's early work is to understand the sort of political crisis that surrounded him and which he attempted to avoid. What we see in Locke's early work is a subtle change in his views. For example, at the time of the Restoration, Locke, like many other Englishmen who were weary of the political instability of the late 1650s, supported the return of Charles Stuart:

> Only give me leave to say that the indelible memory of our late miseries, and the happy return of our ancient freedom and felicity, are proofs sufficient to convince us where the supreme power of these nations is most advantageously placed, without the assistance of any other arguments.[27]

However, by 1661 it became all too clear what Charles II's intentions were. Although Locke produced a work, which was orthodox as far as its content and structure were concerned, his views had subtly changed. Locke no longer held the authoritarian views that he held in the *Two Tracts*. This is not to say that Locke was not an absolutist, i.e., Locke still believed that there was an absolute right and wrong in moral matters. What he changed, however, was the location of the source of authority. In the *Two Tracts*, the source of authority of all moral and civil rules was in the crown. Ashcraft writes:

> Locke, in the early 1660s, that is, was willing to grant the civil magistrate absolute and arbitrary power over all action of individuals within society, he did not subscribe to a theory of natural rights; he was opposed to the toleration of religious dissent; he did not believe in parliamentary supremacy as an embodiment of the legislative power of society; there is no theory of property or of its importance to the origins of civil society in these writings; and he opposes the view that the people have a right to resist their rulers.[28]

But now, in the *Essays*, the source of authority is in the law of nature. In fact, Locke carefully adds that even the prince and senate are subject to this law as well (a claim he did not make in the *Two Tracts*). Given Locke's timidity, this view must have caused him a great deal of fear since opposing the Crown in those days meant, in many cases, putting your life in your own hands.

The Context of the *Essay*

Although the evidence for what prompted Locke to change his views from the *Two Tracts* to the *Essays* is limited, most contemporary scholars feel more confident about the context in which and the reasons why Locke wrote the *Essay*. For example, John W. Yolton confidently asserts:

> The *Essay* was primarily an examination into what has come to be called 'epistemology', the study of man's processes of gaining knowledge, the kinds and limits of this knowledge, and the distinction between knowledge and belief.[29]

The actual entire story (which is contained in the Epistle to the Reader) is a familiar one:

> *Were it fit to trouble thee with the History of this Essay, I should tell thee, that five or six Friends meeting at my Chamber, and discoursing on a Subject very remote from this, found themselves quickly at a stand, by the Difficulties that rose on every side. After we had a while puzzled our selves, without coming any nearer a Resolution of those Doubts which perplexed us, it came into my Thoughts, that we took a wrong course; and that, before we set our selves upon Enquiries of that Nature, it was necessary to examine our own Abilities, and see, what Objects our Understandings were, or were not fitted to deal with. This I proposed to the Company, who all readily assented; and thereupon it was agreed, that this should be our first Enquiry. Some hasty and undigested Thoughts, on a Subject I had never before considered, which I sit down against our next Meeting, gave the first entrance into this Discourse, which having been thus begun by Chance, was continued by Entreaty; written by incoherent parcels; and, after long intervals of neglect, resum'd again, as my Humour or Occasions permitted; and at last, in a retirement, where an Attendance on my Health gave me leisure, it was brought into that order, thou now seest it.*[30]

Alexander Campbell Fraser, in his own edition of Locke's *Essay* writes this about the above quotation:

According to his friend James Tyrrell, who was at the 'meeting', the 'difficulties' arose in discussing the 'principles of morality and revealed religion'. This is recorded in a manuscript note in his copy of the *Essay* now in the British Museum.[31]

Since many of the ideas which Locke penned in the *Essays* find a home in the *Essay*, e.g., Locke's view against innate ideas, and his view that morality, like mathematics, is capable of demonstration, it is generally thought that the discussion was about the law of nature as the basis of morality and its implications for natural as well as revealed religion:

Locke informs us that the topic discussed by the group at the outset was 'a subject very remote' from the special inquiries into the understanding which arose out of the discussions at a later stage and of which the *Essay* of 1690 was the final outcome. Tyrrell's comment on this point is more explicit. 'The discourse', he says, 'began about the principles of morality and reveal'd religion'. Now that we have come to know more about Locke's literary activities before 1671, Tyrrell's hint appears significant. I presume that the discussion among Locke's friends was at first about the law of nature as the basis of morality and its relation to natural and revealed religion. Locke's early thoughts on this topic served as a convenient starting-point; and some other member of the group, possibly Lord Ashley himself, may have contributed the short essay, originally among the Shaftesbury Papers, beginning: 'The Light of Nature is reason set up in the soul at first by God in man's Creation, second by Christ.' But then, as Locke tells us, difficulties arose in the course of the discussion, possibly concerning the question how natural law comes to be known. This question had played a prominent part in Locke's essays, but we can understand if his solution of it left room for doubts and puzzles. So it was decided to start afresh and to approach the subject-matter under discussion on a strictly epistemological basis, i.e., to inquire into the origin and extent of human knowledge.[32]

Perhaps a more laconic description of this story of the origin of the *Essay* grew out of a desire of these individuals, and in particular Locke himself, to formulate in greater detail the epistemological basis of the knowledge of the law of nature which Locke had begun in the *Essays*.[33] An implication of this view is the very thesis, which I am attacking in this discussion, viz., that the views of moral knowledge, which appear in both the *Essay* and the *Essays*, even though not clearly consistent, are, nonetheless, reconcilable.

In any case, whatever questions Locke may have had which led to his writing the *Essay*, internal examinations of the *Essays* and the *Essay* show Locke's task in the *Essay* to be broader and nowhere near as narrow as the (mere) effort to undergird the moral doctrines of the *Essays*. Indeed what is exhibited is the staying force of concerns Locke brought over from Boyle and the amount of intellectual energy Locke put into the effort to find a philosophy of knowledge on par with Boyle's views and themes. This effort led him in so many ways away from the *Essays* and the older Aristotelian view of the world; that is, it is highly unlikely that he remained at peace with a "Christian-Aristotelian" approach to metaphysics and knowledge in general (with its reliance on substantial forms or scholastic essences), and specifically to moral and religious knowledge.

Although I argue in chapter 4 of this book why I think that the *Essays* and the *Essay* are incompatible,[34] I will spend the rest of this chapter articulating an alternative explanation for why Locke volunteered to write the *Essay*.

I shall argue that the *Essay*, like the *Two Tracts*, was an attempt to respond to a crisis—not a political crisis as before—but an epistemological crisis created by the new views of the universe of Sir Robert Boyle (1627-1691).[35] That is, the *Essay* was an attempt to bridge the gap between Boyle's corpuscular views and traditional philosophy, or as Yolton writes: "Locke sought to elaborate an account of human understanding which would make sense of the new science of nature."[36]

What sort of crisis did the works of Boyle create? This can be explained by contrasting the views of Boyle with the views of the older science and its method. The older science and its method, although not Aristotelian or scholastic,[37] still shared an important assumption with Aristotle, viz., that scientific knowledge leads to certainty:

> What science is, is evident from the following, if we must speak exactly and not be guided by [mere] similarities. For we all suppose that what we know scientifically does not even admit of being otherwise; and whenever what admits of being otherwise escapes observation, we do not notice whether it is or is not, [and hence we do not know about it]. Hence what is known scientifically is by necessity. Hence it is everlasting; for the things that are by unqualified necessity are all everlasting, and everlasting things are ingenerable and indestructible.[38]

One such scientist, Francis Bacon (1561-1626),[39] shared this assumption with Aristotle. For example, Bacon believed that his inductive method would lead to certain knowledge by penetrating beneath the level of phenomena and perception to forms:

> [T]o generate and superinduce a new nature or new natures, upon a given body, is the labor and aim of human power: whilst to discover the form or true difference of a given nature, or source from which it emanates (for these terms approach nearest to an explanation of our meaning), is the labor and discovery of human knowledge. . . .[40]

Another individual who also shared the same assumption was Rene Descartes (1596-1650),[41] i.e., for Descartes, scientific knowledge[42] is certain knowledge:

> All knowledge is certain and evident cognition. Someone who has doubts about many things is no wiser than one who has never given them a thought; indeed, he appears less wise if he has formed a false opinion about any of them. Hence it is better never to study at all than to occupy ourselves with objects which are so difficult that we are unable to distinguish what is true from what is false, and are forced to take the doubtful as certain; for in such matters the risk of diminishing our knowledge is greater that our hope of increasing it. So, in accordance with the Rule, we reject all such merely probable cognition and resolve to believe only what is perfectly known and incapable of being doubted.[43]

Boyle presents a contrast to these two early scientists. Margaret J. Osler points out that as a practicing scientist, Boyle explicitly contradicted the traditional ideal for science. Instead of striving toward certain knowledge of substantial forms of material objects, he sought an ordering of phenomenal experience which would enable him to predict nature's course, regardless of whether substantial forms exist or can be known.[44] Peter Alexander also makes clear that Boyle aimed "to describe the mechanisms underlying observable events and . . . to avoid final causes and teleological explanations."[45] As evidence of this view, Osler[46] cites the following passage from Boyle's *Origin of Forms and Qualities*:

> The origin, Pyrophilus, and nature of the qualities of bodies is a subject that I have long looked upon as one of the most important and useful that the naturalist can pitch upon for his contemplation. For the knowledge we have of the bodies without us being, for the most part, fetched from the information the mind receives by the senses, we

scarce know anything else in bodies, upon whose account they can work upon our sense, save their qualities; for as to the substantial forms which some imagine to be in all natural bodies, it is not half so evident that there are such, as it is that the wisest of those that do admit them confess that they do not well know them. And as it is by their qualities that bodies act immediately upon our senses, so it is by virtue of those attributes likewise that they act upon other bodies, and by that action produce in them, and oftentimes in themselves, those changes that sometimes we call alterations, and sometimes generation or corruption. And it is chiefly by the knowledge, such as it is, that experience (not art) hath taught us of these differing qualities of bodies, that we are enabled, by a due application of agents to patients, to exercise the little empire that we have either acquired or regained over the creatures.[47]

And again:

And it is evident by the clear solutions (untouched by many vulgar philosophers) we meet with of many phenomena in the statics and other parts of the mechanics, and especially in the hydrostatics and pneumatics, how clearly many phenomena may be solved without employing a substantial form. And on the other side, I do not remember that either Aristotle himself (who perhaps scarce ever attempted it), or any of his followers, has given a solid and intelligible solution of any one phenomenon of nature by the help of substantial forms: which you need not think it strange I should say, since, the greatest patrons of forms acknowledging their nature to unknown to us, to explain any effect by a substantial form must be to declare (as they speak) *ignotum per ignotius*, or at least per *aeque ignotum*. And indeed, to explicate a phenomenon being to deduce it from something else in nature more known to us than the thing to be explained by it, how can the employing of incomprehensible (or at least uncomprehended) substantial forms help us to explain intelligibly this or that particular phenomenon?[48]

Osler also argues that Boyle recognized the uncertainty of scientific knowledge, and concluded from this that, it was no longer possible to assume that we can acquire knowledge of substantial forms of material substances.[49] In addition to this, Osler[50] makes clear that for Boyle, corpuscularism was all that was needed to describe the world:

I see no necessity of admitting in natural things any such substantial forms, matter and the accidents of matter being sufficient to explicate as much of the phenomena of nature as we either do or are like to understand.[51]

According to Osler, because scientists like Boyle outgrew the strictures of traditional philosophy of science and its idea of certain knowledge, she writes that "Their implicit rejection of the traditional theories of knowledge called for a new epistemology, more in line with the actual practice of contemporary science and better able to provide its conceptual foundation."[52] She concludes that Locke's *Essay* "can be seen as having taken a major step toward providing new epistemological underpinnings for empirical science. Locke's epistemology reflects the tensions in the changing assumptions about scientific method."[53]

This much is generally recognized: Boyle had a profound effect on Locke's thinking.[54] Aaron points out, for example, that Locke could have known Boyle as early as 1654 because Boyle was at Oxford from 1654 to 1668.[55] Additionally, he points out that there is evidence by 1665 Locke and Boyle had become close friends. In fact, Boyle included Locke in many of his experiments.[56] This may explain why Locke abandoned his study of the law of nature in 1664.[57] By 1666 Locke was engaged in his own experiments.[58] Eventually, Locke was elected a member to the Royal Society in 1668, which had been in existence since 1660.[59] As a result of Boyle's influence, as Rogers argues, "Their views run remarkably parallel on many issues crucial to the production of the *Essay*."[60]

The first similarity is based on the fact that both Boyle and Locke were not strict empiricists.[61] Because of this, both were inclined to accept the existence of entities that cannot be observed but only inferred. For example, Rogers argues that even though he is an empiricist of sorts, Locke is still "quite definitely committed to the existence of entities not empirically observable."[62] Thus, for example, in the *Essay*, Locke accepts the existence of unobservable entities called corpuscles.[63]

Regarding Boyle, Sargent makes a parallel observation:

[A]lthough Boyle spoke of an experiential grounding for the new philosophy, it should be clear from the above discussion that he did not advocate a simple empiricist epistemology. . . . Boyle saw experimentalism as an alternative to empiricism. Despite his use of the term 'probability', he did not believe that knowledge must be limited to the simple ordering of phenomenal appearances.[64]

In support of this, Sargent[65] refers to Boyle's *A Discourse Of Things Above Reason, Enquiring Whether A Philosopher Should Admit There Are Any Such*:

> [T]he other thing that I was to observe about the nature of the mind is that it is so constituted that its faculty of drawing consequences from known truths is of greater extent than its power of framing clear and distinct ideas of things: so that, by subtle or successive inferences, it may attain to a clear conviction that somethings are, of whose nature and properties (or at least of some of them) it can frame no clear and satisfactory conceptions. And that men should be better able to infer propositions about divers things, than to penetrate their nature, needs the less be wondered at, both because it is oftentimes sufficient for our uses to know that such things are, though that knowledge be not accompanied with a clear and distinct idea, and because often time the rules (such as, whatever is produced must have a cause, and from truth nothing rightly follows but truth) are clear and easy, that enable
> · the mind to infer conclusions about things whose nature is very dark and abstruse.[66]

Another important similarity is based on the fact that both Locke and Boyle believed in the possibility of the "demonstration" of moral truths.[67] For example, Rogers[68] points out that Boyle writes in his *Some Considerations about the Reconcileableness of Reason and Religion*:

> And lastly, there are moral demonstrations, such as those, where the conclusion is built, either upon some one such proof cogent in its kind, or some concurrence of probabilities, that it cannot be but allowed, supposing the truth of the most received rules of prudence and principles of practical philosophy. [A]nd this third kind of probation, though it comes behind the two others in certainty, yet it is the surest guide, which the actions of men, though not their contemplations, have regularly allowed them to follow. And the conclusions of a moral demonstration are the surest, that men aspire to. . . .[69]

Locke also argues for the possibility of moral demonstration, even more strongly than Boyle, in the following quotation taken from the *Essay*:

> [T]he *Idea* of a supreme Being, infinite in Power, Goodness, and Wisdom, whose Workmanship we are, and on whom we depend; and the *Idea* of our selves, as understanding, rational Beings, being such as are clear in us, would, I suppose, if duly considered, and pursued,

afford such Foundations of our Duty and Rules of Action, as might place Morality amongst the Sciences capable of Demonstration. . . .[70]

Still another similarity, which Rogers[71] points out between Boyle and Locke, is the distinction drawn by both between intuitive and deductive knowledge. For example, in *Advice in Judging of Things said to Transcend Reason*, Boyle writes:

> As the understanding is wont to be looked upon as the eye of the mind, so there is analogy between them, that there are some things, that the eye may discern (and does judge of) organically, if I may so speak, that is, by the help of instruments: as when it judges of a line to be straight, by the application of a ruler to it, or to be perpendicular, by the help of a plumb-line, or a circle to be perfect by the help of organs or instruments; as when by the bare evidence of the perception, it knows, that this colour is red, and that other blue. . . . For thus there are some things, that the intellect usually judges of in a kind of organical way, that is by the help of certain rules, or hypotheses, such as are a great part of the theorems and conclusions in philosophy and divinity. But there are others which it knows without the help of these rules, more immediately, and as it were intuitively, by evidence of perception; by which way we know many prime notions and effata, or axioms metaphysical, etc. as, that contradictory propositions cannot both be true; that from truth nothing but truth can legitimately be deduced. . . .[72]

Of intuitive knowledge, Locke writes in the *Essay*:

> For if we will reflect on our own ways of Thinking, we shall find, that sometime the Mind perceives the Agreement or Disagreement of two *Ideas* immediately by themselves, without the intervention of any other: And this, I think, we may call *intuitive Knowledge*. For in this, the Mind is at no pains of proving or examining, but perceives the Truth, as the Eye doth light, only by being directed toward it. Thus the Mind perceives, that *White* is not *Black*, That a *Circle* is not a *Triangle*, That *Three* are more than *Two*, and equal to *One* and *Two*. Such kind of Truths, the Mind perceives at the first sight of the *Ideas* together, by bare intuition, without the intervention of any other Idea; and this kind of Knowledge is the clearest, and the most certain, that humane Frailty is capable of.[73]

Of deductive knowledge, or what he calls demonstrative knowledge, Locke writes that it is knowledge brought about by intervening ideas where the perception of the ideas is not immediately known:

> [T]hose intervening *Ideas*, which serve to shew the Agreement of any two others, are called *Proofs*; and where the Agreement or Disagreement is by this means plainly and clearly perceived, it is called *Demonstration*, it being *shewn* to the Understanding, and the Mind made see that it is so.[74]

As Rogers points out, both Boyle and Locke reject the importance of substantial forms (a view which undergirds the *Essays*) on the grounds they are explanatorily irrelevant.[75] On explanatory irrelevance of substantial forms, Boyle writes in the *Origin of Forms and Qualities*:

> I know it is alleged as a main consideration on the behalf of substantial forms that, these being in natural bodies the true principles of their properties and consequently of their operations, their natural philosophy must needs be very imperfect and defective, who will not take in such forms; but, for my part, I confess that this very consideration does rather indispose than incline me to admit them. For if indeed there were in every natural body such a thing as a substantial form, from which all its properties and qualities immediately flow, since we see that the actions of bodies upon one another are for the most part (if not all) immediately performed by their qualities or accidents, it would scarce be possible to explicate very many of the explicable phenomena of nature with having recourse to them, and it would be strange if many of the abstruse phenomena were not explicable by them only: whereas indeed almost all the rational accounts to be met with of difficult phenomena are given by such as either do not acknowledge, or at least do not take notice of, substantial forms.[76]

Later, Locke writes in the *Essay*:

> [T]hose, therefore, who have been taught, that the several Species of Substances had their distinct internal substantial Forms; and that it was those Forms, which made the distinction of Substances into their true Species and Genera, were led yet farther out of their way, by having their Minds set upon fruitless Enquiries after substantial Forms, wholly unintelligible, and whereof we have scarce so much as any obscure or confused Conception in general.[77]

According to Stewart, another important contribution of Boyle's new theory of matter was his doctrine of qualities, especially the distinction between primary and secondary qualities. He points out that Boyle is not the first one to make use of this distinction:

> Indeed the language of 'primary' and 'secondary' (or 'first' and 'second') qualities, just as much as the language of 'matter' and 'form' (and 'substance' and 'essence'), is part of the scholastic inheritance that was redefined in the corpuscular theory of matter.[78]

In the "schools," primary qualities were qualities associated with the four elements, viz., hot, cold, wet, dry, and the secondary qualities are causal derivatives from these.[79] In Boyle, even though the secondary qualities are still thought of as causal derivatives or as he says "dependent upon" the primary qualities, primary qualities are not defined in terms of different elements. Instead, as Alexander points out, primary qualities are the properties that belong to minute corpuscles, e.g., shape, size and mobility.[80]

As to secondary qualities, much of Boyle's time in his, *Origin of Forms and Qualities*, is spent talking about the relationship between the primary qualities of bodies and our senses. Secondary qualities pose a most difficult question for his Corpuscular theory.[81] The difficulty for Boyle is due to the fact that whereas secondary qualities, e.g., colors, odors, etc., are thought of as being relative to our senses, it seems that they still have some sort of being independent of us:

> [B]ut here I foresee a difficulty, which being perhaps the chiefest that we shall meet with against the Corpuscular hypothesis, it will deserve to be, before we proceed any farther, taken notice of. And it is this, that whereas we explicate colours, odors, and the like sensible qualities, by a relation to our sense, it seems evident that they have an absolute being irrelative to us; for snow (for instance) would be white, and a glowing coal would be hot, though there were not man or any other animal in the world. And it is plain that bodies do not only by their qualities work upon our senses, but upon other, and those inanimate, bodies: as the coal will not only heat or burn a man's hand if he touch it, but would likewise heat wax (even some much as to melt it and make it flow), and thaw ice into water, though all the men and sensitive beings in the world were annihilated.[82]

Boyle's solution is to attribute to the primary qualities and the motions the power or disposition to cause sensations in our minds, the sensations we associate with secondary qualities:

if there were no sensitive beings, those bodies that are now the objects of our sense would be but dispositively, if I may so speak, endowed with colours, tastes, and the like, and actually but only with those more catholic affections of bodies—figure, motion, texture, &c.[83]

In a similar fashion, Locke writes:

[I] have in what just goes before, been engaged in Physical Enquiries a little farther than, perhaps, I intended. But it being necessary, to make the Nature of Sensation a little understood, and to make the *difference between the Qualities in Bodies, and the* Ideas *produced by them in the Mind*, to be distinctly conceived, without which it were impossible to discourse intelligibly of them; I hope, I shall be pardoned this little Excursion into Natural Philosophy, it being necessary in our present Enquiry, to distinguish the *primary*, and *real Qualities* of Bodies, which are always in them, (viz., Solidity, Extension, Figure, Number, and Motion, or Rest; and are sometimes perceived by us, viz. when the Bodies they are in, are big enough singly to be discerned) from those *secondary* and *imputed Qualities*, which are but the Powers of several Combinations of those primary ones, when they operate, without being distinctly discerned; whereby we also may come to know what *Ideas* are, and what are not Resemblances of something really existing in the Bodies, we denominate from them.[84]

Although there are many other important parallels to Boyle's theory, the last one that I will mention is the distinction between real and nominal essence. Both Rogers and Stewart point out that Locke borrowed this distinction directly from Boyle.[85] Boyle characterizes the scholastic version of a real essence in the following manner:

most of the writers of physics have been apt to think that, besides the common matter of all bodies, there is but one thing that discriminates it from other kinds and makes it what it is, and this for brevity's sake, they call a form: which, because all the qualities and other accidents of the body must depend on it, they also imagine to be a very substance, and indeed a kind of soul, which united to the gross matter, composes with it a natural body, and acts in it by the several qualities to be found therein, which men are wont to ascribe to the creature as composed.[86]

Ultimately, Boyle argues, such real essences or substantial forms are explanatorily irrelevant: the many different phenomena of nature that we seek to understand cannot be explained by appealing to the concept.[87] Instead, Boyle argues, talk of species and genus is a way for individuals to conveniently classify the conspicuous accidents that objects possess:

> We may now advance somewhat farther, and consider that, men having taken notice that certain conspicuous accidents were to be found associated in some bodies, and other conventions of accidents in other bodies, they did for convenience and for the more expeditious expression of their conceptions agree to distinguish them into several sorts, which they call gender or species. . . .[88]

Locke has a similar view of this matter:

> [T]hose therefore who have been taught, that the several *Species* of Substances had their distinct internal *substantial Forms*; and that it was those *Forms*, which made the distinction of Substances into their true *Species* and *Genera*, were led yet further out of the way, by having their Minds set upon fruitless Enquiries after *substantial* forms, wholly unintelligible, and whereof we have scarce so much as any obscure, or confused Conception in general.[89]

Indeed, ranking and denominating into genus and species does not even have anything to do with real essences (in what Locke took to be the proper sense of that term)[90]: "Nor indeed *can we* rank, and *sort Things*, and consequently (which is the end of sorting) denominate them *by their real Essences*; because we know them not."[91] Ranking and denominating substances into species involves reference only to the nominal essences[92] the mind makes:

> Our Faculties carry us no further towards the knowledge and distinction of Substances, than a Collection of those sensible *Ideas*, which observe in them; which however made with the greatest diligence and exactness, we are capable of, yet is more remote from the true internal Constitution, from which those Qualities flow, than, as I said, a Countryman's *Idea* is from the inward contrivance of that famous Clock at *Strasburg*, whereof he only sees the outward Figure and Motions.[93]

To sum this section, I have attempted to give an alternative description of the factors, which may have motivated Locke to write the *Essay*. According to Osler, the *Essay* was Locke's attempt to bridge the gap between Boyle's corpuscular views and traditional philosophy.[94]

This is a controversial point and my evidence for this point rests on the recognition of Boyle's influence on Locke plus the similarities of views of Boyle and Locke. If this is true, then the difficulties, as reported by Tyrrell, that arose in the group's discussion of the principles of morality and revealed religion appear to be aimed at Boyles' works and not at Locke's *Essays*.

Notes

1 von Leyden, introduction to the *Essays on the Law of Nature*, 60-82.
2 For a discussion of the Ancient Constitution, see Michael P. Zuckert, *Natural Rights and the New Republicanism* (Princeton: Princeton University Press, 1994), 51-56.
3 The roots of this conflict can be discovered as early as the rule of James I as the text of one of his speeches indicates:

And the like power have kings: they make and unmake their subjects; they have power of raising and casting down; of life and of death; judges over all their subjects, and in all causes, and yet accountable to none but God only. They have power like men at the chess—a pawn to take a bishop or a knight—and to cry up or down any of their subjects as they do their money. And to the kind is due both the affections of the soul and the service of the body of his subjects. (Ann Hughes, ed., *Seventeenth-Century England: A Changing Culture* [Englewood Cliffs, NJ: Barnes and Noble Books, 1980], 21)

4 Ibid.
5 According to Conrad Russell, Sir Edward Coke initially took this view. Coke argued that William the Conqueror and the Saxons had merely confirmed the Ancient Constitution and that Parliament could be traced back to the days of the Romans (Conrad Russell, *The Crisis of Parliament* [Oxford: Oxford University Press, 1971], 268). Christopher Hill writes that Coke's views were so influential that Charles I attempted to suppress his views by refusing to let some of his views to be published (Christopher Hill, *Puritanism and Revolution* [New York: Schocken Books, 1958], 66).
6 Zuckert, *Natural Rights and the New Republicanism*, 52.
7 One example is that in 1633 Charles I gave permission to William Laud, the Archbishop of Canterbury, to verbally and physically persecute certain members of Parliament.
8 However, there is good evidence to believe that because of the Crown's attempt to consolidate its power throughout the late sixteen hundreds, the crisis continued until the Catholic wing of the Stuart Crown was eventually overthrown again and replaced by the Protestant monarchs, William and Mary of Orange in 1688.
9 The actual date of this letter is uncertain. However, according to von Leyden, from internal evidence of the letter it must have been written in December 1659 (von Leyden, introduction to *Essays on the Law of Nature*, Fn. 1, 17).
10 The English and Latin text of both pamphlets, including a translation of the Latin text are in John Locke, *Two Tracts on Government*, ed. and trans. Philip Abrams (Cambridge: Cambridge University Press, 1967), hereafter *Two Tracts*.
11 Although I will discuss what I take to be the main reason why Locke wrote the *Essays*, there is also another reason that I should mention. At the time Locke wrote the *Essays*, he was Censor of Moral Philosophy at Oxford. Von

Leyden suggests that the *Essays* was probably written as a series of lectures while a teacher at Christ Church:

> When addressing the *Baccalaurei* in his Censor's speech, Locke himself refers to the 'wranglings' . . . of his students in which he had participated and by which he had greatly benefited during the year, and he expressly mentions the fact that the disputations were about the law of nature. There can be little doubt, therefore, that it was on this subject that Locke was lecturing in 1664 and that it was for this purpose that he had his early draft essays copied by an amanuensis in his notebook of 1663 (MS. B) and extensively revised them in his own hand. (von Leyden, introduction to the *Essays on the Law of Nature*, 12)

12 Ibid., 23.

13 In both tracts Locke defines what he means by the term "magistrate." His second definition is, perhaps, the most interesting:

> [B]y magistrate we here understand one who has responsibility for the care of the community, who holds a supreme power over all others and to whom, finally, is delegated the power of constituting and abrogating laws; for this is that essential right of command in which alone resides that power of the magistrate by which he rules and restrains other men and, at will and by any means, orders and disposes civil affairs to preserve the public good and keep the people in peace and concord. Nor is there any need to enumerate the particular tokens of sovereignty and the rights defined as regal, such as the final appeal, the right of life and death, of making war and peace, the authority to coin money, to raise revenue and taxes. . . . (Locke, *Two Tracts*, 212-213)

14 Locke understands 'indifferent things' in the second tract as a term referring to things that are "indifferent in respect of moral good and evil, so that all things which are morally neither good nor evil are called indifferent" (Ibid., 221).

15 Abrams, introduction to the *Two Tracts*, op. cit., 8.

16 Locke, *Two Tracts*, 159-60.

17 Abrams, introduction to the *Two Tracts*, 19-20.

18 In the *Two Tracts*, Locke does mention the law of nature, but compared to his use of the scriptures and revelation, it receives little attention. Locke writes in the *Two Tracts* that the two sources of authorization for laws are the Divine law and Human law (or Law of the Magistrate). Of the Divine law, Locke writes in the second of the *Two Tracts*:

> [T]he divine law is that which, having been delivered to men by God,

is a rule and pattern of living for them. And according as it either becomes known by the light of reason which is natural and implanted in men, or is made manifest in divine revelation, it is in turn divided into natural and positive law. And each of these I describe under the same head as 'moral' since each is exactly the same in its content and matter and they differ only in the manner of their promulgation and the clarity of their precepts. For this is that great rule of right and justice and the eternal foundation of all moral good and evil and which can be discovered even in things indifferent by the mediation of an inferior law. (224)

Of the Law of the Magistrate, Locke writes in the same tract:

However that may be, this much is certain, that, if the magistrate is born to command, and if he possesses the throne and sceptre by divine institution and by the distinction of his character and nature, then it is beyond dispute that he is the sole ruler of the land and its inhabitants without contract or condition and that he may do whatever is not forbidden by God, to whom alone he is subjected and from whom alone he received his title to live and to rule. Nor can anyone deny that all indifferent actions, of whatsoever sort they may be, lie under the power of him to whose discretion are delivered the liberty, fortunes and the life itself of every subject. But, if men enjoy a right to an equal liberty, being equal by virtue of their common birth, then it is clear that no union could occur among men, that no common way of life would be possible, no law, nor any constitution by which men could, as it were, unite themselves into a single body unless each one first divests himself of that native liberty—as they suppose it to be—and transfers it to some other, whether a prince or a senate (depending on the constitution on which they happen to agree) in whom a supreme power must necessarily reside. (230)

19 Locke, *Essays*, 197; f. 97 & 98.
20 Ibid., 195. f. 96.
21 Abrams, introduction to the *Two Tracts*, 24.
22 Locke, *Essays*, 157; f. 61.
23 Richard Ashcraft, *Revolutionary Politics and Locke's Two Treatises of Government* (Princeton: Princeton University Press, 1986), 76.
24 Ibid., 100.
25 Ibid., 118. The Act Against Tumultuous Petitioning in 1661 prevented an individual from submitting petitions, complaints, remonstrances, and declarations addressed to the King without the consent by three or more justices of their county or by the major part of the grand jury of the county. The Corporation Act sought to exclude dissenters from political power (Hughes, *Seventeenth-Century England*, 255). Charles did this by taking control over local governments and the appointment of magistrates (Ashcraft, *Revolutionary Politics and Locke's Two Treatises of Government*, 118). The text of the Act itself

reveals this and much more. Those affected by this Act included:

> mayors, aldermen, recorders, bailiffs, town clerks, common council-
> men and other persons then bearing any office or offices of magis-
> tracy or places of trusts or other employment relating to or concern-
> ing the government of the said respective cities, corporations and
> boroughs and cinque ports and their members, other port towns. . . .
> (Hughes, *Seventeenth-Century England*, 260)

Individuals filling these positions had to take the "Oaths of Allegiance and
Supremacy" to the King. The oaths included swearing allegiance to and recognizing the King's authority over political and moral matters as supreme.
    The Act of Uniformity is described by Ashcraft as an act which forced "a
great number of worthy, learned, pious and orthodox divines . . . to give up
their livings and to leave the Anglican church" (Ashcraft, *Revolutionary Politics and Locke's Two Treatises of Government*, 118). Hughes also writes:

> the Act of Uniformity led to some 1,000 non-conformist ministers
> losing their livings in 1662, in additions to those who had been forced
> out after 1660 by the return of ministers removed in the 1640's and
> 1650's. (Hughes, *Seventeenth-Century England*, 255)

Moreover, the text of the Act itself reveals that it was intended to reduce the
religious and political instability of England by drastic means. Peace was to be
brought about by enforcing the Catholic worship service. Members of the
clergy also had to take the similar oath of allegiance declaring and acknowledging that the King of England had supreme political and moral authority. Finally,
the Militia Act gave the Crown control over the militia and a standing army.
    26 David Hume, *The History of England* (Indianopolis: Liberty Classics,
Inc., 1983), 2: 447.
    27 Locke, *Two Tracts*, 125.
    28 Ashcraft, *Revolutionary Politics and Locke's Two Treatises of Gov-
ernment*, 76.
    29 John W. Yolton, *John Locke and the Way of Ideas* (Oxford: Oxford
University Press, 1957, viii.
    30 Locke, *Essay*, 7.
    31 Alexander Campbell Frazer, ed., *An Essay Concerning Human Under-
standing*, by John Locke (New York: Dover, 1959), Fn 2, 9.
    32 Von Leyden, introduction to the *Essays*, 61.
    33 In his introduction, von Leyden spends several pages in defense of the
claim "that Locke's early doctrine of natural law formed the starting-point for
the discussions that gave rise to the drafts of the *Essay* of 1671" (Ibid., 62).
However, after his discussion, von Leydon backs off a bit: "[W]e may conclude
then that *to a certain extent* Locke's drafts of the *Essay* of 1671 were quarried
out of his early essays on the law of nature" (Ibid., 65; emphasis added). More-

over, in an attempt to assure us of the tenability of his thesis, he restates his thesis briefly only to immediately undercut it again:

> It is true that the drafts were meant by him as epistemological inquir-ies into the extent and limitation of knowledge, containing a wealth of new discussion ranging from the principles of empiricism, the na-ture and origin of ideas, and the signification of words to inquiries into cause and effect, substance, space, time, number, and infinity. But though the drafts were thus professedly divorced by Locke from his previous interests in the principles of morality and religion, some of the inspiration and material of his speculations on natural law could conveniently be fitted into their scheme. (Ibid., 65-6)

34 I think that it would be beneficial to distinguish two theses in order to clarify the issue here. First, there is what I call the weak thesis of the relation-ship of the *Essays* and the *Essay*. This is the thesis that the views in the *Essays* served as the inspiration of the *Essay*. On this view, we may say that the issues raised in the *Essays* served as the starting-point for the discussions which even-tually lead Locke to write the *Essay*. I can also formulate a second more stronger and interesting thesis, viz., that the *Essay* is Locke's attempt to phi-losophically sustain his thoughts, which began in the *Essays*. It is this second, stronger thesis that is at stake in this chapter.

35 It could also be argued that the works of John Wilkins (1614-1672), John Ray (1627-1705), Christopher Wren (1632-1723), Robert Hooke (1635-1703), and (especially) Sir Isaac Newton (1642-1727) all contributed to the general epistemological crisis. But for the purposes of this chapter, I will only talk briefly about Boyle.

36 John Yolton, *Locke and the Compass of Human Understanding* (Cam-bridge: Cambridge University Press, 1970), 16. For the connection between Boyle and Locke see, e.g., G. A. J Rogers, "Boyle, Locke, and Reason," *Jour-nal of the History of Ideas* 27 (1967); Margaret Osler, "John Locke and the Changing Ideal of Scientific Knowledge," *Journal of the History of Ideas* 31 (1970); Richard I. Aaron, *John Locke* (Oxford: Clarendon Press, 1965); John W. Yolton, *Locke and the Compass of Human Understanding*; R. S. Wool-house, *Locke's Philosophy of Science and Knowledge* (New York: Barnes and Noble, 1971); James Gibson, *Locke's Theory of Knowledge and its Historical Relations* (Cambridge: Cambridge University Press, 1917); F. H. Anderson, "The Influence of Contemporary Science on Locke's Methods and Results," in *University of Toronto Studies, Philosophy*, vol. 2 (Toronto, 1925); Maurice Mandelbaum, *Philosophy, Science, and Sense Perception* (Baltimore: Johns Hopkins Press, 1964); Laurens Laudan, "The Nature and Sources of Locke's Views on Hypotheses," *Journal of the History of Ideas* 28, no. 2 (1967); See also Hans Aarsleff, who comments that "the *Essay* was, as it were, intended as a manual in the epistemology of the Royal Society" (Hans Aarsleff, "Leibniz on Locke on Language," *American Philosophical Quarterly* 1, no. 3 [1964]: 178) and "Posterity lost the key to its understanding [i.e., the *Essay*], but there can be no doubt that Locke's "half a dozen" friends did possess the key. Our

understanding of the *Essay* depends, in turn, on our success in regaining their knowledge, chiefly from Boyle" (Ibid., 183).

37 By the phrase 'the older science and its method' I mean primarily to refer to that period in time roughly from the early to middle fourteen hundreds characterized by the rise of Humanism and a renewed interest in empiricism, experimentation, and nature. To say that Bacon, and the other scientists of the this period, e.g., Leonardo da Vinci (1452-1519), William Gilbert (1544-1603), Kepler (1571-1630), Galileo (1564-1642), Rene Descartes (1596-1650), and Thomas Hobbes (1588-1679) were not Aristotelian or Scholastic means that many of these individuals believed that the views of Aristotle and the methods employed by the Scholastics had been shown to be false. For example, Rose-Mary Sargent writes that "Galileo's telescopic observations had significantly contributed to the successful overthrow of Aristotelian cosmology [and] [I]n opposition to the Aristotelian doctrine that different bodies fall at different rates because of an innate difference in their natures, Galileo showed that the resistance of the medium was responsible for the observed phenomena" (Rose-Mary Sargent, "Learning from Experience: Boyles's Construction of an Experimental Philosophy," in *Robert Boyle Reconsidered*, ed. Michael Hunter [Cambridge: Cambridge University Press, 1994], 59-60).

38 Aristotle, *Nicomachean Ethics*, ed. and trans. Terrance Irwin (Indianapolis: Hackett Publishers, Inc., 1999), 1139b 19-24.

39 This is not to imply that Boyle did not have many views in common with Bacon. Sargent points out several examples (Sargent, "Learning from Experience: Boyle's Construction of an Experimental Philosophy," 58-9). Perhaps the most important view they shared, as Sargent writes, is that:

> Boyle followed Bacon's new 'physical logic' that inverted the order of discovery and proof. Instead of beginning with speculations about the universal causes that may be operative in nature, philosophers should first compile a vast amount of information about natural effects in order to discover how things have been or are really produced. (Ibid., 58)

40 Francis Bacon, *Novum Organum* (Chicago: University of Chicago Press, 1952), 137.

41 Sargent also points out that Boyle followed:

> the Cartesian programme that advocated 'the application of geometrical theorums, for the explication of physical problems'. The 'experimental and mathematical way of enquiring into nature' was once again gaining ascendancy because of the work of these 'restorers of natural philosophy', and their direct influence upon Boyle's early objections to Aristotelianism is undeniable. Descartes' influence can be seen in Boyle's acceptance of the idea that explanations in terms of occult forms and qualities should be replaced by hypothesis concern-

ing the motions of the least parts of matter. (Sargent, "Learning from Experience: Boyle's Construction of an Experimental Philosophy," 58)

42 I do not mean to imply here that Descartes' view of science was a view like Bacon's. Bacon was an empiricist and Descartes was a rationalist. For example, the term 'knowledge' which occurs in the first sentence of the quotation is from the Latin *scientia*. This was Descartes' term for systematic knowledge based on indubitable foundations. This term goes back as far as Aristotle and is used by the Scholastics.

43 Rene Descartes, *Rules for the Direction of the Mind*, in *The Philosophical Writings of Descartes*, ed. and trans. John Cottingham, Robert Stoothoff, and Dugald Murdoch (Cambridge: Cambridge University Press, 1985), 10.

44 Margaret J. Osler, "John Locke and the Changing Ideal of Scientific Knowledge," *Journal of the History of Ideas* 31 (1970): 6.

45 Peter Alexander, *Ideas, Qualities and Corpuscles* (Oxford: Oxford University Press, 1985), 61.

46 Osler, "John Locke and the Changing Ideal of Scientific Knowledge," 7.

47 Robert Boyle, *The Origin of Forms and Qualities According to the Corpuscular Philosophy*, in *Selected Philosophical Papers of Robert Boyle*, ed. M. A. Stewart (Indianapolis: Hackett Publishing Company, 1991), 13.

48 Ibid., 67

49 Osler, "John Locke and the Changing Ideal of Scientific Knowledge," 8.

50 Ibid., 6-8.

51 Boyle, *The Origin of Forms and Qualities According to the Corpuscular Philosophy*, 54.

52 Osler, "John Locke and the Changing Ideal of Scientific Knowledge," 10.

53 Ibid., 16. Such a description of the *Essay* does not fit well with the *Essays*. This is so because such a commitment to the new way of doing science is nowhere to be found in the *Essays*. Instead, it remains committed to explaining the world in terms of substantial forms or essences.

54 For example, James Gibson writes: "Whilst it must remain a matter of uncertainty whether the scepticism of Glanville exerted any influence at all upon Locke, no such doubt can be felt in the case of Boyle. . . ." (James Gibson, *Locke's Theory of Knowledge and its Historical Relations* [Cambridge: Cambridge University Press, 1917], 260-1). Cranston also points out "There were two main currents which governed the development of Locke's mind. One was the unformulated ad hoc empiricism of Newton and Boyle and the other Royal Society virtuosi. The other was the systematic rationalism of Descartes" (Cranston, *John Locke: A Biography*, 265). Aaron writes "The really important influences on Locke from the empiricist side was the group that gathered around Sir Robert Boyle, and which ultimately founded the Royal Society. Indeed, the most important influence of all was Boyle himself" (Aaron, *John Locke*, 12).

55 Aaron, *John Locke*, 13.

56 Ibid.

57 von Leyden, introduction to the *Essays on the Law of Nature*, 20.

58 Lord King, introduction to the *Life and Letters of John Locke*, ed. Lord King (New York: Burt Franklin, 1972), 30.

59 Yolton, *Locke and the Compass of Human Understanding*, Fn. 1, 53.

60 Rogers, "Boyle, Locke, and Reason," 205.

61 By the term 'empiricism' I mean primarily what Bas C. van Fraassen writes, viz., "To be an empiricist is to withhold belief in anything that goes beyond the actual, observable phenomena, and to recognize no objective modality in nature. To develop an empiricist account of science is to depict it as involving a search for truth only about the empirical world, about what is actual and observable" (Bas C. van Fraassen, *The Scientific Image* [Oxford: Oxford University Press, 1980], 202-3).

62 Rogers, *Boyle, Locke, and Reason*, 208.

63 For evidence of this view, see the passage at IV. iii. 16 in the *Essay*. Here Locke mentions his dependence upon the Corpuscular view by name. What Corpuscularism is can be summarized, even as Boyle instructs us himself, into ten different points (Boyle, *The Origin of Forms and Qualities According to the Corpuscular Philosophy*, 50-3). 1. Matter of all natural bodies is the same. That is, it is a substance extended and impenetrable. 2. The differences that we ascribe to bodies does not arise from the matter of substances itself, but from the motion of the bodies. 3. Motion, as Boyle writes, "may be looked upon as the first and chief mood or affection of matter" (Ibid., 50). Elsewhere he writes that motion is "the grand agent of all that happens in nature" (Ibid., 19). 4. Matter, by means of motion, may be divided into insensible corpuscles or particles. 5. Each particle must have its own magnitude and shape. 6. The texture of a body is the result of the primary affections of the particles convening to form one body, and the affections that belong to a body are without relation to sensitive beings or other natural bodies. 7. Besides the primary affections of matter, we may also mention secondary qualities. Secondary qualities, which are dependent upon the simpler and more primitive affections of matter (Ibid., 32), work upon the senses and upon other bodies. Boyle also comments that secondary qualities are often thought of as having an "absolute being irrelative to us" (Ibid., 32). 8. An object is generated when men, by means of secondary qualities, perceive "a concurrence of all those qualities which men commonly agree to be necessary and sufficient to denominate the body" (Ibid., 52). 9. Objects are formed and discriminated by means of what Boyle calls "the convention of essential accidents" (Ibid.). By this, Boyle seems to mean that any body is the result of a peculiar state of matter, which makes it what it is at that time but was formed accidentally. However, since we discriminate bodies according to their present state, the properties, which we attribute to them are thought to be essential to them since if a body gains or loses a property, we will discriminate and denominate it in a different way. 10. An object is corrupted or destroyed when men, by means of secondary qualities,

perceive that it has lost its essential attributes and "is no more a body of that kind" (Ibid., 45).

In response to IV. iii. 16, Fraser writes: "It is to the 'corpuscularian hypothesis' that he appeals in the many passages in the *Essay* which deal with this favorite subject—the *ultimate physical cause* of the secondary qualities and other *powers* of material substances, and the relative subject of their nominal and real essences" (Fraser, *An Essay Concerning Human Understanding*, 2: Fn. 5, 205). Moreover, in the *Essay*, Locke argues for the existence of God: "[T]hus from the Considerations of our selves, and what we infallibly find in our own Constitutions, our Reason leads us to the Knowledge of the certain and evident Truth, That *there is an eternal, most powerful, and most knowing Being*; which whether any one will please to call God, it matters not" (Locke, *Essay*, IV. x).

64 Sargent, "Learning from Experience: Boyle's Construction of an Experimental Philosophy," 65.

65 Ibid.

66 Robert Boyle, *A Discourse Of Things Above Reason, Enquiring Whether A Philosopher Should Admit There Are Any Such*, in *Selected Philosophical Papers of Robert Boyle*, ed. M. A. Stewart (op. cit.), 234.

67 Sargent, "Learning from Experience: Boyle's Construction of an Experimental Philosophy," 212.

68 Rogers, "Boyle, Locke, and Reason," 212-13.

69 Robert Boyle, *Some Considerations about the Reconcileableness of Reason and Religion*, in *The Works of the Honourable Robert Boyle*, ed. Thomas Birch (London: 1772), 4: 182. The other two referred to here are metaphysical and physical demonstrations. Metaphysical demonstration is "where the conclusion is manifestly built on those general metaphysical axioms, that can never be other than true; such as *nihil potest simul esse and nonesse; non entis nullae sunt proprietates reales*, etc." (Ibid.). Physical demonstrations are those in which "the conclusion is evidently deduced from physical principles such as are *ex nihilo nihil fit; Nullo substantio in nihilum redigitur*, etc., which are not so absolutely certain as the former, because, if there be a God, he may (at least for ought we know) be able to create and annihilate substances" (Ibid.).

70 Locke, *Essay*, IV, iii, 18.

71 Rogers, "Boyle, Locke, and Reason," 214.

72 Robert Boyle, *Advice in Judging of Things said to Transcend Reason*, in *The Works of the Honourable Robert Boyle*, ed. Thomas Birch (London: 1772), 4: 460-1.

73 Locke, *Essay*, IV. ii. 1.

74 Ibid., IV. ii. 3.

75 Rogers, "Boyle, Locke, and Reason," 215.

76 Boyle, *The Origin of Forms and Qualities according to the Corpuscular Philosophy*, 67.

77 Locke, *Essay*, III. vi. 10.

78 M. A. Stewart, introduction to the *Selected Philosophical Papers of Robert Boyle*, ed. M. A. Stewart (Indianapolis & Cambridge: Hackett Publishing Company, 1991), xiv.

79 The schools that made use of the four elements were known as the Aristotelians or Peripatetics. Alexander writes: "[T]he Aristotelian elements, earth, water, air and fire were thus considered by the peripatetics to be unanalysable components, in various combination, of observable bodies and substances whose observable qualities could be explained in terms of properties attributed to these elements" (Alexander, *Ideas, Qualities and Corpuscules*, 19). There was another school called the Chymist or Spygrists. They were like the Peripatetics except that they held to three elements instead of four: salt, sulfur, and mercury. They were called the '*tria prima*'. Alexander adds: "They too were regarded as being responsible for the observable properties of observable substances and the basis of all explanation of chemical phenomena" (Ibid.).

80 Ibid., 70.

81 Boyle, *The Origin of Forms and Qualities according to the Corpuscular Philosophy*, 32.

82 Ibid.

83 Ibid., 34.

84 Locke, *Essay*, II. viii. 22. The discussion of primary and secondary qualities is entirely absent from the *Essays*. The closest Locke comes to articulating anything like this occurs on page 159 of the *Essays*. This does not automatically underscore the inconsistency of the *Essays* and the *Essay*. This is so because anyone like Locke who is committed to an Aristotelian view of the world in the *Essays* could articulate such a distinction. However, what makes these two views at odds is the way primary and secondary qualities become redefined in Boyle and for those like Locke who becomes committed to the new science. I shall make this point clearer later on.

85 Rogers, "Boyle, Locke, and Reason," 215; Stewart, introduction to the *Selected Philosophical Papers of Robert Boyle*, xv.

86 Boyle, *The Origin of Forms and Qualities according to the Corpuscular Philosophy*, 38.

87 Ibid., 67.

88 Ibid., 37.

89 Locke, *Essay*, III. vi. 10. Again, as I shall show later, such a negative attitude toward substantial forms is entirely missing in the *Essays*. Instead, Locke relies heavily on the existence of substantial forms including metaphysical explanations, which employ substantial forms.

90 Locke's understanding of essences is contained in the following quotation and is contrasted with the view of essence or substantial forms which he rejects:

[C]oncerning the real Essences of corporeal Substances (to mention these only) there are, if I mistake not, two Opinions. The one is of those, who using the Word *Essence*, for they know not what, suppose a certain number of those Essences, according to which, all natural things are made, and wherein they do exactly every one of them partake, and so become of this or that *Species*. The other, and more rational Opinion, is of those, who look on all natural Things to a real, but unknown Constitution of their insensible Parts, from which flow those sensible Qualities, which serve us to distinguish them one for another, according as we have Occasion to rank them into sorts, under common Denominations. The former of these Opinions, which supposes these *Essences*, as a certain number of Forms or Molds, wherein all natural Things, that exist, are cast, and do equally partake, has, I imagine, very much perplexed the Knowledge of natural things. (Locke, *Essay*, III. iii. 17)

91 Ibid., III. vi. 9.
92 By the term 'nominal essence,' Locke wants us to understand as an idea closely connected to meaning of real essence:

[T]is true, I have often mentioned a *real Essence*, distinct in Substances, from those abstract *Ideas* of them, which I call their *nominal Essence*. By this *real Essence*, I mean, that real constitution of any Thing, which is the foundation of all those Properties, that are combined in, and are constantly found to co-exist with the *nominal Essence*; that particular constitution, which every Thing has within itself, without any relation to any thing without it. (Locke, *Essay*, III. vi. 6)

Thus we see that a nominal essence is a list of abstract ideas of those properties found to co-exist together
93 Ibid., III. vi. 9.
94 Osler, "John Locke and the Changing Ideal of Scientific Knowledge," 10 and 16.

2
Essays On the Law of Nature

Introduction

The *Essays*, as I have argued so far, was partly written to show that Charles II and his supporters had no solid basis on which to claim that the Crown should have absolute and arbitrary political power. By demonstrating that the law of nature exists and that it is knowable by anyone who is normal and who will but take the time to discover it, Locke seems convinced that the existence of the law of nature would undercut any claim to arbitrary and absolute political power.[1] This is so because there would be a source of moral precepts independent of the beliefs of humans to which all people, including the prince or senate, are obligated to conform their lives. Moreover, whereas in the *Two Tracts* the prince or senate were only accountable to God for their actions and not to their subjects, there is now an important sense in which the law of nature makes the prince or senate accountable to the society that he organizes:

> In fact, what is to be the shape of a body politic, the constitution of a state, and the security of its interests, if that part of a community which has the power to do most harm may do everything as it pleases, if in the supreme authority there is the most unrestrained liberty? For since the rulers, in whose power it is to make or remake laws at their will and as the masters of others to do everything in favour of their own dominion, are not, and cannot be, bound either by their own or by other people's positive laws, supposing there is no other, superior, law of nature, i.e. one which they are bound to obey, in what condition, pray, would be men's interests, what would be the

privileges of society, if men united in a commonwealth only to become a more ready prey for the power of others?[2]

Locke attempts to do this by demonstrating that the universe is a
purposive system, which stipulates the end for all creatures, including
humans. The end set for humans is, however, different from the end set
for other animals because the animals have their own laws, which govern their birth and life, and which are suited to their own nature.[3] These
laws, and others like them, have a certain deterministic flavor to them.
This means that the animals must always obey these laws as long as
they remain alive.

On the other hand, the laws set out for humans are contained
within the Law of nature. It is a "law," according to Locke, because (i)
it is the "decree of the divine will,"[4] (ii) "discernible by the light of
nature," i.e., by reason and sensation, and (iii) "indicating what is and
what is not in conformity with rational nature."[5] It is "natural" because
its moral precepts are designed by God to promote the natural end of
humans, viz., their happiness or flourishing.

In the rest of this chapter I intend to lay out in more detail the purposive universe to which Locke appeals and how he fits into the Christian Natural Law Tradition. Locke's argument in the *Essays* involves
three important commitments to an Aristotelian essentialism, to a clas-
sical view of the nature of virtue and vice, and to moral absolutism.
These topics, which appear in the *Essays*, are especially important, not
only for what Locke is attempting to accomplish in the *Essays*, but also
for how he changes his mind by the time he publishes the *Essay*.

The Essentialism of the *Essays*

The first question of Locke's *Essays* is entitled, "Is There A Rule
of Morals, or Law of Nature Given to us? Yes."[6] Locke straightforwardly asserts that the five arguments persuade that the law of nature
exists.[7] The third argument, which is teleological in nature, is of special
importance for the present discussion[8]:

[T]he third argument is derived from the very constitution of this
world, wherein all things[9] observe a fixed law of their operations and
a manner of existence appropriate to their nature. For that which prescribes to every thing the form and manner and measure of working,
is just what law is. Aquinas says that all that happens in things created is the subject-matter of the eternal law, and, following Hippo-

crates, 'each thing both in small and in great fulfilleth the task which destiny hath set down', that is to say nothing deviates even by an inch from the independent of laws while everything else is bound. On the contrary, a manner of acting is prescribed to him that is suitable to his nature; for it does not seem to fit in with the wisdom of the Creator to form an animal that is most perfect and ever active, and to endow it abundantly above all others with mind, intellect, reason, and all the requisites for working, and yet not assign to it any work, or again to make man alone susceptible of law precisely in order that he may submit to none.[10]

From this argument for the existence of the law of nature, we see Locke's reliance upon an Aristotelian outlook of the world.[11] This position paints a picture of the universe, which is dominated by two concepts: final causality and order. There is a law of nature for man because "a manner of acting is prescribed to him that is suitable to his nature." In this passage, Locke gives two reasons for this. First, all things, including man, "observe a fixed law of their operations and a manner of existence appropriate to their nature." Second, it would "not seem to fit in with the wisdom of the Creator to form an animal that is most perfect and ever active, and to endow it abundantly above all others with mind, intellect, reason, and all the requisites for working, and yet not assign to it any work, or again to make man alone susceptible of law precisely in order that he may submit to none." I will discuss both reasons. Then I will discuss why it follows from the claim that man has a prescribed mode of action that the law of nature exists.

One reason why Locke believes that man has a law or a prescribed mode of action, which suits his nature is because "all things observe a fixed law of their operations and a manner of existence appropriate to their nature." That is, there are causal laws for the change and/or growth of inorganic bodies (e.g., rocks, planets, etc.), as well as causal laws for organic bodies (e.g., vegetation, acorns, etc.), and natural agents (e.g., animals).[12]

Moreover, these are laws because, as Locke explains, "For that which prescribes to every thing the form and manner and measure of working, is just what law is." Here Locke uses the traditional language of Aristotelian essentialism. For example, every particular thing, whether it is a physical object or some sort of living organism, has an essence or a form or a fixed nature. The essence of an object determines what kind of thing it is and its function within the universe, i.e., it determines, as Locke writes, its "form and manner and measure of working." It is that set of properties that an object has which if it lost, it would cease to be that kind of object.[13] For example, the essence of a person rests partly on the possession of the property of rationality. If an unfortunate person loses his rationality permanently, the person will no longer exist.

Moreover, the change and/or growth that take place, guided by the essence, can be interpreted in terms of Aristotle's distinction between actuality and potentiality. Consider, for example, the causal laws that govern the growth and change of an acorn. The acorn is actually an acorn, but it is potentially an oak tree in virtue of the potential for change, which it possesses internally in virtue of its essence. Therefore, once the right conditions obtain and nothing externally hinders it (and from our perspective if nothing internally hinders the genetic component either), the acorn will begin to pursue and strive for its full actualization, which is its final cause, or end, or that-for-the-sake-of-which it grows and changes.

Locke in the *Essays* does break, however, from traditional Aristotelian doctrine by adding an additional view, which is characteristic of the Christian Natural Law tradition, viz., "all that happens in things created is the subject-matter of the eternal law." That is, according to this tradition, the essence of a thing plus its function is due to God's creative act. This creative act is not an arbitrary act but an act, which is governed by an eternal law, i.e., a law, which is coextensive with God's own nature.[14]

Creation is, therefore, governed by various laws, which are all aspects of God's one eternal law. Immediately after this, Locke draws his conclusion, viz., "This being so, it does not seem that man alone is independent of laws while everything else is bound. On the contrary, a manner of acting is prescribed to him that is suitable to his nature." But as far as humans are concerned, Locke at this point is not just referring to the non-rational parts of the soul, which are unresponsive to reason and which control nutrition and growth. According to this view, the essence in humans guides this just as the essence in other animals guides their growth and nutrition. But there is an important difference between the essence of a normal human and an animal. The essence of a human, unlike the essence of an animal, guides it to become an animal with different kinds of capacities. Some of these capacities are mentioned in the second half of the quotation, i.e., "for it does not seem to fit in with the wisdom of the Creator to form an animal that is most perfect and ever active, and to endow it abundantly above all others with mind, intellect, reason, and all the requisites for working, and yet not assign to it any work, or again to make man alone susceptible of law precisely in order that he may submit to none."

This is Locke's additional reason for the claim that man also has a prescribed mode of action, which suits his nature. He reasons that it would be inconsistent with the wisdom of God if man did not have a proper function assigned to him. This is so because God made man with many properties that the other animals do not possess. For example, man is made "with mind, intellect, reason, and all the requisites for working." All of these capacities are necessary for man's activity, which means that there is a way for humans to act, which will contribute to happiness. But from Locke's Christian Natural Law view, this way to act has been assigned by God and is prescribed by the law of nature. Even though humans are subject to certain causal laws, which they cannot depart from, there are also other laws, which are not causal but are prescriptions for acting given only to man by God. That is, there are moral precepts that indicate what is and is not consonant with a rational nature and which man can choose to follow which are suited to his specific nature in virtue of his capacities, and which if followed will contribute toward his happiness.

In virtue of these two reasons, Locke concludes that man has a prescribed mode of action, which suits his nature. But now we have to ask Locke why it follows from the claim that man has a prescribed mode of action that the law of nature exists. I think finding out what the prescribed mode of action is can provide Locke's answer better. This is found in his first argument for the existence of the law of nature:

> [T]he first argument can be derived from a passage in Aristotle's Nicomachean Ethics, Book I, chapter 7, where he says that 'the special function of man is the active exercise of the mind's faculties in accordance with rational principle'. For since in the preceding passages he had shown by various examples that there is a special sort of work each thing is designed to perform, he tried to find out what this may be in the case of a human being also. Thus, having taken account of all the operations of the vegetal and sentient faculties which men have in common with animals and plants, in the end he rightly concludes that the proper function of man is acting in conformity with reason, so much so that man must of necessity perform what reason prescribes. Likewise in Book V, chapter 7, where he draws a distinction between legal justice and natural justice, Aristotle says 'A natural rule of justice is one which has the same validity everywhere'. Hence it is rightly concluded that there is law of nature, since there is a law which obtains everywhere.[15]

Locke's answer is taken directly from Aristotle, i.e., "the special function of man is the active exercise of the mind's faculties in accordance with rational principle."

Now, again, why does Locke believe that the law of nature exists by virtue of the existence of a proper function of man, which is activity of the soul according to reason? Locke's argument appears to be that if the law of nature were not to exist, then there would not be a proper function of man. That is, although this sounds circular, since there is evidence that there is a proper function of man, the best explanation for why this evidence exists is by virtue of the existence of the law of nature. However, this is so because, from a Christian Natural Law point of view, when God made the natural law (i.e., the very thing that Locke is attempting to show exists) for man, he placed in man the propensities or natural inclinations (i.e., the evidence which Locke thinks is explained by appealing to the existence of the law of nature) which correspond to the precepts of the law of nature. Evidence for this explanation is in both the *Essays* as well as in Aquinas. For example, concerning the place where these natural inclinations reside, Locke writes:

> It may be said, however, that the law of nature is to be inferred not from men's behavior but from their innermost ways of thinking—we must search not the lives of men but their souls—for it is there that the precepts of nature are imprinted and the rules of morality lie hidden together with those principles which men's manners cannot corrupt; and that, since these principles are the same in every one of us, they can have no other author than God and nature. And it is for this reason that the internal law, whose existence is often denied by vices, is acknowledged by men's conscience and the very men who act perversely feel rightly.[16]

Moreover, in Aquinas we read that some of our natural dispositions correspond to the precepts of the law of nature:

> [S]ince, however, good has the nature of an end, and evil, the nature of the contrary, hence it is that all those things to which man has a natural inclination are naturally apprehended by reason as being good, and consequently as objects of pursuit, and their contraries as evil, and objects of avoidance. Therefore, the order of the precepts of the natural law is according to the order of natural inclinations. For there is in man, first of all, an inclination to good in accordance with the nature which he has in common with all substances inasmuch, namely, as every substance seeks the preservation of its own being, according to its nature; and by reason of this inclination, whatever is

a means of preserving human life, and of warding off its obstacles, belongs to the natural law. Secondly, there is in man an inclination to things that pertain to him more specially, according to that nature which he has in common with other animals; and in virtue of this inclination, those things are said to belong to the natural law which nature has taught to all animals, such as sexual intercourse, the education of offspring and so forth. Thirdly, there is in man an inclination to good according to the nature of his reason, which nature is proper to him. Thus man has a natural inclination to know the truth about God, and to live in society; and in this respect, whatever pertains to this inclination belongs to the natural law: e.g., to shun ignorance, to avoid offending those among whom one has to live and other such things regarding the above inclination.[17]

Finally, in Locke we read something closely related to what Aquinas said about the relationship between our natural propensities and the precepts of the law of nature:

Further, he feels himself not only to be impelled by life's experience and pressing needs to procure and preserve a life in society with other men, but also to be urged to enter into society by a certain propensity of nature, and to be prepared for the maintenance of society by the gift of speech and through the intercourse of language, in fact as much as he is obliged to preserve himself. But since man is very much urged on to this part of his duty by an inward instinct, and nobody can be found who does not care for himself or who disowns himself, and all direct perhaps more attention to this point than is necessary, there is no need for me here to admonish. But there will be room perhaps elsewhere to discuss one by one these three subjects which embrace all that men owe to God, their neighbour, and themselves.[18]

I am now going to leave this discussion, and instead, move on to discuss the nature of virtue and vice. It is sufficient for my purposes in this section to bring out the relationship between the essence of man and the existence of the law of nature.

The Nature of Virtue and Vice

There is also another discussion, which underlies Locke's arguments for the existence of the law of nature:

[T]he fifth argument is that without natural law there would be neither virtue nor vice, neither the reward of goodness nor the punishment of evil: there is no fault, no guilt, where there is no law. Everything would have to depend on human will, and, since there would be nothing to demand dutiful action, it seems that man would not be bound to do anything but what utility or pleasure might recommend, or what a blind and lawless impulse might happen perchance to fasten on. The terms 'upright' and 'virtuous' would disappear as meaningless or be nothing at all but empty names. Man would not be able to act wrongfully, since there was no law issuing commands or prohibitions, and he would be the completely free and sovereign arbiter of his actions. Granted that, undisciplined as he would then be, he would seem, perhaps, to have taken but little thought for his life and health, yet he seems in no way to have disregarded honour and duty, since whatever honour or baseness our virtues and vices possess they owe it all to his law of nature; for the nature of good and evil is eternal and certain, and their value cannot be determined either by the public ordinances of men or by any private opinion.[19]

The main point here is, of course, that the existence of virtue and vice is evidence for the existence of the law of nature. What does Locke means by the terms virtue and vice? Unfortunately, Locke says very little about what he takes virtue and vice to be. Therefore, in order to bring to light what Locke means, I will appeal to the discussions of virtue and vice by Aquinas and Aristotle, because much of what they say appears to be consistent with what Locke says above.

Aquinas defines virtue as "a good quality of the mind, by which we live righteously, of which no one can make bad use, which God works in us without us."[20] Aquinas adds: "This definition comprises perfectly the whole essential notion of virtue."[21]

How are we to understand the phrase "good quality"? Aquinas suggests that by the term "quality" he means "habit": "To be sure, the definition would be more suitable if for *quality* we substitute *habit*, which is the proximate genus."[22] With regard to the latter term, Aquinas follows Aristotle by defining habit as a disposition.[23]

A habit is therefore a certain kind of disposition in which there is a prior arrangement or positioning of something toward something else. And what is being disposed is one of the three conditions of the soul: feelings (*pathe*), capacities (*dunameis*), or states of the mind (*hekseis*). However, a virtue is not just an indifferent sort of habit, but, as the phrase point out, it is a *good* habit. Here Aquinas explicates the term "good" in two different ways. On the one hand, virtue is called a good habit because by it something is made good. On the other hand, Aquinas uses the term "good" in the phrase "good quality" to refer to that thing which is fixed or dictated by reason.[24]

As to the former use, to praise something as virtuous is to point out a condition of that thing which makes it good. For example, the virtue of a knife is a condition of the knife that makes the knife a good knife, e.g., the knife's ability to cut well, and perhaps the durability of the blade's sharpness, etc. Likewise, the virtue of a person is also a condition that makes the person a good person.

Where persons are concerned, though, it is important to distinguish between being good at something from being a good person. For example, if someone has the virtue of knife-making, then he will possess a condition which makes him a good knife-maker. Presumably, this condition will be the knife-maker's craft-knowledge of knife-making. But this sort of reasoning will not apply to being a good person because in Aquinas, as well as in Aristotle, the virtues of character are not craft-knowledge. Instead, the virtuous man is a good person in virtue of possessing the condition of aiming at actions, which are right. This condition, as Aristotle explains, "makes a human being good and makes him perform his function well."[25]

As to the latter use, according to Aquinas, some of the good qualities or habits are things that exist according to nature and not according to convention. This means that some of the virtues are good habits, which exist independently of a person's beliefs in virtue of being infused in man by God.[26] Thus, reason does not create some virtues as much as it approves or directs the agent to act rationally.

Next, virtue is a good quality "of the mind." Aquinas explains that this prepositional phrase is not to be interpreted as the matter out of which virtue is formed. On the contrary, the phrase indicates "the matter *about which* it is concerned, and the matter *in which* it exists."[27] In both cases, then, the matter about which virtue is concerned is its object, viz., the mind. This means, then, that virtue is an arrangement or positioning of the states of mind, and not feelings or capacities.[28]

Third, we learn that virtue is a good quality "by which we live righteously, of which no one can make bad use."[29] Here, Aquinas points out that a habit is an action, which is directed toward some end:

> But it must be observed that some operative habits are always referred to evil, as are vicious habits. Others are sometimes referred to good, sometimes to evil. For instance, opinion is referred both to the true and to the untrue.[30]

However, Aquinas writes that a virtue is a habit which is referred to good and is to be distinguished from those habits which are referred to evil, and so, a virtue is the means "by which we live righteously."[31] Aquinas adds, though, that virtue is something "of which no one can make bad use."[32] According to Aquinas, this means that virtue is *always* referred to good and is to be distinguished from those habits, which, as the quotation above points out, are sometimes referred to good and sometimes referred to evil, and those habits, which are vicious.

Finally, Aquinas points out that virtue is a good quality, "which God works in us without us."[33] Here Aquinas describes God as the efficient cause of infused virtue. This is a distinction he later develops in Q. 94. Art. 3, viz., that the term "virtue" can refer to the "virtues" which have been infused into the nature of man according to which man is naturally inclined to perform. But "virtue" can also refer to the way that something was done to which nature does not primarily incline, and yet, the action still contributes toward a good life: "For many things are done virtuously, to which nature does not primarily incline, but which, through the inquiry of reason, have been found by men to be conducive to well-living."[34]

Against the background of this sort of account of virtue, why does Locke take the existence of virtue and vice to be evidence for the law of nature? Locke's main reason is contained in the following sentence: "without natural law there would be neither virtue or vice, neither the reward of goodness nor the punishment of evil: there is no fault, no guilt, where there is no law."[35] The argument here, of course, presupposes that there is a real distinction between virtue and vice, something, which Locke simply takes for granted throughout the *Essays*. Locke believes, along with Aquinas, that the three or four precepts of the law of nature, which are infused by God into the nature of man. They act like propensities and dispositions, and men are considered virtuous when they act on these dispositions and vicious when they do not.[36] More importantly we have only to look inward to take the sense of our being so disposed, and in this sense we have the clearest evidence of there being a real distinction between virtue and vice.[37]

But if we can assume for the sake of argument a real distinction between virtue and vice, why does Locke believe that if the law of nature did not exist, then there would be no virtue or vice? Locke hints at the answer when he writes, "there is no fault, no guilt, where there is no law."[38] His reason appears to be that it is a necessary condition of any wrong-doing and guilt based on wrong-doing that some sort of law be in place. For without some sort of law, whether the natural law or some sort of conventionally based law:

> Everything would have to depend on human will, and, since there would be nothing to demand dutiful action, it seems that man would not be bound to do anything but what utility or pleasure might recommend, or what a blind and lawless impulse might happen perchance to fasten on. The terms 'upright' and 'virtuous' would disappear as meaningless or be nothing at all but empty names. Man would not be able to act wrongfully, since there was no law issuing commands or prohibitions, and he would be the completely free and sovereign arbiter of his actions.[39]

However, in the case of natural law, if it were not in place, then there would be no natural inclinations in place either, and without the natural inclinations there would be no virtue since, according to Aquinas, "all the acts of the virtues are prescribed by the natural law."[40] Moreover, since each person's reason dictates to him to act virtuously in light of these natural inclinations, without these natural inclinations, reason would only have the will of man to refer to and to whatever interest or pleasure urged upon the will at that time (or some conventionally based law).

Finally, Locke writes: "whatever honour or baseness our virtues and vices possess they owe it all to this law of nature; for the nature of good and evil is eternal and certain, and their value cannot be determined either by the public ordinances of man or by any private opinion."[41] Two points are important. First, Locke writes that the source of goodness for virtue is to be explained in terms of the law of nature, as opposed to convention, because the nature of virtue is such that it is fixed and eternal. This is a point that Locke makes later by explaining that since God made man and fixed his good according to man's essence, virtue and man's good will never change as long as God does not change human nature.

Second, in the last part of the quotation above, Locke makes a distinction between the sorts of value it is possible to ascribe to virtue and vice. Is virtue to be valued because its nature is fixed and eternal, or is it to be valued because it is something valued by the public decrees of men or some private opinion? If it is the latter, Locke appears to reason earlier in the quotation, that man would be the measure of all things. However, Locke denies such a position. Virtue and its relationship to the good for man is something clearly objective in Locke's writings in the *Essays*.

The Moral Absolutism of the *Essays*

The final topic to discuss is the moral absolutism of the *Essays*. Moral absolutism is the view that there is a single, ultimate, moral standard, which is binding for all people at all times. In the *Essays*, this single, ultimate, moral standard is the law of nature.

The plausibility of this view depends upon several conditions being in place. First, the law of nature has to exist. I have already discussed two of these arguments. Second, the law of nature has to be a moral standard for all people at all times. This claim is discussed and defended in Question 7 of the *Essays*: "Is The Binding Force of the Law of Nature Perpetual and Universal? Yes." And third, the law of nature has to be a moral standard, which is binding for those for whom it was designed. This is discussed and defended in Question 6: "Are Men Bound by the Law of Nature? Yes." In the rest of this chapter, I will discuss each condition. First, I will discuss Locke's arguments for the existence of the law of nature, including some objections that have been raised against them. Second, I will discuss Locke's reasoning for why he believes that the law of nature is binding on all men. Finally, I will discuss Locke's arguments for why he believes that the law of nature is perpetual and universal.

Five Arguments for the Existence of the Law of Nature

The first question of the *Essays* is dedicated to demonstrating that the law of nature exists. As evidence for this view, Locke generates five different arguments, which allegedly demonstrate this point. This is, however, a controversial point. There are some scholars who believe that these arguments do not establish it. This is so because later on in the *Essays*, Locke rejects each argument in Question 1 by allegedly rejecting every reason that he gives to justify each of the five arguments. Later, after my reconstruction and assessment of these 5 arguments, I will examine this objection and argue that Locke does not reject these arguments.

Locke straightforwardly asserts that the five arguments persuade that the law of nature exists.[42] John Colman, however, argues that these arguments will not work because these arguments assume what they purport to prove.[43] As a result, the value of Locke's arguments is only that they throw light on his conception of the law of nature.[44] Colman is right that these arguments will not work. But it is not because Locke assumes what he purports to prove. They will not work because each argument contains a false premise. Locke's arguments can be reconstructed to avoid Colman's criticism.

In the first argument, Locke argues that there exists a law of nature because "there is a law which obtains everywhere."[45] Locke derives this assertion in two different ways from Aristotle. First, Locke derives it from Aristotle's famous argument for the function of man:

> [T]he first argument can be derived from a passage in Aristotle's *Nicomachean Ethics*, Book 1, chapter 7, where he says that 'the special function of man is the active exercise of the mind's faculties in accordance with rational principle'. For since in the preceding passages he had shown by various examples that there is a special sort of work each thing is designed to perform, he tried to find out what this may be in the case of a human being also. Thus, having taken account of all the operations of the vegetal and sentient faculties which men have in common with animals and plants, in the end he right concludes that the proper function of man is acting in conformity with reason, so much so that man must of necessity perform what reason prescribes.[46]

Locke evidently means that if man must perform those actions, which are according to reason, then there exists some law, which obtains everywhere.

Next, Locke advances another argument from Aristotle: "Likewise in Book V, chapter 7, where he draws a distinction between legal justice and natural justice, Aristotle says 'A natural rule of justice is one which has the same validity everywhere.'"[47]

Later, Locke considers two objections to the first argument.[48] The first objection states that the law of nature is nowhere to be found:

> [S]ome people here raise an objection against the law of nature, namely that there is no such law in existence at all, since it can nowhere be found, for most people live as though there were no rational ground in life at all nor any law of such a kind that all men recognize it.[49]

Locke argues that this objection is unsound because it is possible to have a law of conduct, which obtains everywhere, which is not recognized by many people. Its precepts, for example, could be neglected because of idleness, or because of bad habits, or because of mental defects.[50]

The second objection argues that there is no agreement about what the edicts of the law of nature are even among those who are of the sounder part of mankind. Locke's reply is as follows:

> [S]econdly, I answer that, although even the more rational of men do not absolutely agree among themselves as to what the law of nature is and what its true and known precepts are, it does not follow from this that there is no law of nature at all.[51]

Moreover, Locke argues that the sounder part of mankind does believe in the same natural laws, but differs in how they are to be interpreted.[52]

Zuckert also points out an important objection concerning this first argument:

> The first argument appeals to a combination of Aristotelian points, one to the effect that "the function of man is activity according to reason," from which Aristotle, or Locke, concludes that "man must necessarily perform those actions which are dictated by reason" (fol. 13). But Locke has on the preceding page explicitly rejected the idea of law of nature as "dictate of reason," and therefore it does not appear that the "law of nature" Locke attributes to Aristotle can be the same as the law Locke seems to accept.[53]

Zuckert appears to be right as Locke writes about his own view of the law of nature:

> It appears to me less correctly termed by some people the dictate of reason, since reason does not so much establish and pronounce this law of nature as search for it and discover it as a law enacted by a superior power and implanted in our hearts."[54]

One way to respond to Zuckert's objection is to point out that the phrase, "dictate of reason," is used equivocally. For example, as the editors of the *Questions* point out,[55] Locke is referring to Hugo Grotius' view of the law of nature:

> Natural law is a dictate of right reason, which indicates the presence of either moral turpitude or moral necessity in a given act by reason or its agreement or disagreement with our rational nature itself and which indicates, as a consequence, that such an act is either forbidden or commanded by God, the author of nature.[56]

However, it is not entirely clear that Locke means the same thing on the following page. This is due to the fact that Locke's use of the phrase, "dictate by reason," appears to mean the same thing as Aristotle's phrase, "according to reason." If this is true, then, Locke must mean that man must perform those actions, which reason, after it has found what is consistent with man's function, prescribes with authority to the desires that this is the right thing to do. This latter interpretation is consistent with Locke's view of the law of nature because it is a law that is consonant with a rational nature or man's function.

I shall turn now to a critical examination of the remaining four arguments, and then discuss an objection by Robert Horwitz who attempts to demonstrate that Locke rejects all of the arguments for the existence of the law of nature in Question 1. The structure Locke uses for these last four arguments is what contemporary philosophers, such as Gilbert Harman, call "the inference to the best explanation." Reasoning of this kind infers from the fact that a certain hypothesis would explain the evidence, to the truth of that hypothesis.[57] Generally, this inference can be made as long as it is possible to reject all other competing hypotheses. This gives us the confidence, then, to say that one hypothesis is better than all the rest.

Given this approach, Locke argues in the second argument that the law of nature exists because this is the best explanation for the existence of men's consciences. Locke believes that each person pronounces upon himself some sort of judgment when he has performed some sort of moral action. For example, Locke explains quoting Juvenal, "no one who commits a wicked action is acquitted in his own judgement."[58] In other words, according to Locke, no one can escape the judgment of his own conscience even though he may escape the censure of the legal or moral community.

Again Zuckert points out that the kind of law implicit in this argument also seems not to satisfy Locke's definition of the law of nature. This is so because it does not satisfy the requirement that the law be knowable by the light of nature, where the term "light of nature" appears to be reason understood as that faculty of the intellect by which it articulates and deduces arguments.[59] However, this argument is in no way inconsistent with his definition of the law of nature. That is, Locke is not using the existence of men's conscience as a means to the knowledge of the law of nature. Instead Locke argues that there are many explanations, which we can give for the fact that all men have some sort of conscience. This use of conscience does not imply that all men judge themselves in the same way concerning actions. It only implies that they judge themselves. Locke reasons that the existence of the law of nature is not only one of these explanations but it is also the best explanation. By describing Locke's argument this way, the law of nature in the second argument and the law of nature described in his definition of the law of nature remain identical.

The third argument by Locke is teleological: Locke argues that everything including man observes a fixed law, which is suited to its own nature. Although man is not without laws that he shares with all animals, nevertheless, there are also additional laws man is subject to that nonhuman animals are not required to perform. Locke writes that man also has "a manner of acting [that] is prescribed to him that is suitable to his nature."[60] To make sense of this distinction, the term "prescribed" is typically contrasted with the term "fixed." The term "fixed" brings with it the notion of causality. Locke implies this distinction in the text by indicating that there are laws that nothing deviates from even by an inch. The term "prescribed," however, brings with it a much different notion. This term indicates that there is a set of laws or rules, which instructs, recommends, or advises a certain kind of life. This means that man is designed in such a way that if he follows the prescription of these rules, it will lead to human happiness.

However, having made this distinction, a number of objections immediately arise. First, Horwitz argues that Locke confounds the notions of eternal and natural law here; whereas, the distinction is kept quite separate in the mind of Aquinas.[61] The distinction is confounded because he does not clearly distinguish the law which no thing can depart from as much as a nail's breadth and the natural law suited to man's own nature. Second, Zuckert again complains that "Locke's third argument fails to embody the final clause of his own definition of the nature law."[62] Finally, from my point of view, Locke does not explicitly state what the existence of the law of nature best explains. He seems to be saying that the existence of the law of nature is the best explanation for the existence of a set of rules, which prescribes a certain kind of life for humans. However, this set of rules is presumably just the law of nature. If this is the case, then Colman's criticism mentioned earlier might be true, i.e., Locke's third argument assumes the truth of the existence of the law of nature in order to prove that it exists.

Horwitz's worry appears to be grounded within the text of the *Essays*. This is due to the fact that Locke appears to use the terms, "fixed" and "prescribed" interchangeably. For example, Locke writes, "[T]he third argument is derived from the very constitution of this world, wherein all things observe a fixed law of their operations and a manner of existence appropriate to their nature. For that which prescribes to every thing the form and manner and measure of working, is just what law is."[63] However, even though Locke does not clearly delineate these terms in the passage above, the meaning is delineated in an additional sentence taken from the same passage:

> This being so, it does not seem that man alone is independent of laws while everything else is bound. On the contrary, a manner of acting is prescribed to him that is suitable to his nature; for it does not seem to fit in with the wisdom of the Creator to form animal that is most perfect and ever active, and to endow it abundantly above all others with mind, intellect, reason, and all the requisites for working, and yet not assign to it any work, or again to make man alone susceptible of law precisely in order that he may submit to none.[64]

This additional passage does capture the sense of the law of nature that is prescriptive and not causal.

Zuckert's objection appears to rest partly on Horwitz's objection. That is, if it is true that he does not keep the two terms in question conceptually distinct, then Locke has failed to keep the notion of law of nature implied in this passage consistent with his definition of the law of nature. However, even though Locke failed to keep the terms conceptually distinct in one part of the passage, he does recover later in the same passage and he appears to use the term "prescribed" in a non-causal sense. Therefore, Zuckert has failed to establish that the notions of the law of nature in the third argument are inconsistent.

Finally, concerning the last objection, there is a way to understand this third argument that avoids Colman's criticism and, at the same time, remains true to the text. The law of nature best explains the existence of a proper function of man. Thus, Locke is also committed to the view that there is a proper function of man, i.e., a function, which leads to human happiness or flourishing. By making this distinction, Locke avoids Colman's criticism.

The fourth argument states that the existence of a law of nature is the best explanation for the continuing existence of societies. Again, it seems as if Locke is positing some sort of causal relationship between the existence of the law of nature and the existence of societies. In fact, Zuckert points out the same thing about this and the fifth argument that "Locke's final two arguments in favor of the existence of the law of nature do not so much say what the law is as describe what it does."[65] The law of nature, then, creates societies in some sense. However, what Locke means can be made clear in this way: Since most normal people have both a disposition to live with others like themselves implanted in them by God and some sense of what the law of nature prescribes in virtue of this disposition, they prescribe laws for themselves to ensure that their own societies remain intact. For example, Locke mentions the act of covenant keeping. He explains that this is one of the foundations on which human society seems to rest.[66] Since most people understand that keeping promises is important and that moral and legal censures are needed to correct those who refuse to keep their covenants, many societies are organized partly around this foundation. Locke adds: "Every community among men falls to the ground if these are abolished, just as they themselves fall to the ground if the law of nature is annulled."[67]

Finally, the fifth argument states that "without natural law there would be neither virtue nor vice, neither the reward of goodness nor the punishment of evil: there is no fault, no guilt, where there is no law."[68] Here he means that the law of nature is the best explanation for both the existence of virtue and vice, and the existence of praise for praiseworthy actions and punishment for untoward actions. That is, most normal individuals have some sense of right and wrong because of the existence of some of the precepts of the law of nature within their minds. It is partly because of this sense of right and wrong that individuals create moral systems for themselves and society in general in order to give to themselves some indication of moral order. Without the existence of the law of nature and the corresponding dispositions, Locke argues that man would only have himself to determine what his duty is. This would mean that man's will would be subject only to what either interest or pleasure urged upon him. He would be "the completely free and sovereign arbiter of his actions."[69]

With a better view of the arguments Locke used to justify the existence of the law of nature, I am in a position to explain why these arguments will not work. Horwitz argues that the second argument fails because appeal to conscience does not demonstrate that it is anything other than an "opinion."[70] This means that since it is only our opinions that condemn or praise us, they cannot serve as a proof of the existence of the law of nature. Horwitz's objection is right on the mark. In other words, Locke's second argument, as well as the others, will not work because in every case it is possible to think of an equally plausible hypothesis that also explains the evidence in question. For example, in Locke's second argument, the fact that people condemn themselves or praise themselves can be explained by the fact that most, if not all, people are taught, when they are very young, to believe what is right and what is wrong. Locke employs this type of counter-explanation in the *Essays* against those who believe in innate ideas. Ideas which men take to be innate are merely ideas which:

> are inculated by our parents or teachers or others with whom we live. For since these believe that such opinions are conducive to well ordering of life, and perhaps have also themselves been brought up in them in the same manner, they are inclined to inure the still fresh minds of the young to opinions of this kind, which they regard as indispensable for a good and happy life.[71]

Because many people are trained so early about what is right and wrong, they forget where the knowledge of right and wrong came from, and as a result we think that such information comes from the law of nature.

The third argument is not so easily confounded. What other explanation could we give to explain why there is, from Locke's point of view, a proper function for man? We could, however, appeal to the genetic code of humans, and argue that it determines the kind of capacities we have and the limits with which we can actualize these capacities. Thus, for example, we could argue that the genetic code explains why it is suited to our nature to propagate our own kind.

Locke's fourth argument rests on the claim that without the law of nature there can be no association or union of men among themselves. Here we may respond to Locke's view with an appeal to Hobbes. Hobbes argues that men incline to peace and the formation of civil societies because of "fear of death, desire of such things as are necessary to commodious living; and a hope by their industry to obtain them."[72] Although these may not be sufficient to explain why humans form societies, these things, nevertheless, seem to be legitimate counter-explanations to the law of nature and partly explain why societies form.[73] Whatever that list may be, it seems as though we do not need the notion of a law of nature as part of that explanation. Thus, for example, Horwitz argues that agreements based on calculations of utility would perhaps be just as good and underwrite at least minimally tolerable societies and reasonably stable states.[74]

Finally, the counter-explanation to the fifth argument is like the second. That is, we can explain why there is virtue and vice by explaining how most people are taught about morality, viz., from their parents, teachers, etc. Moreover, the fears that Hobbes points out, may motivate enough people to invent rules in order to censure those who become a threat to the peace of the community and a threat to private property.

There are, then, a variety of counter-explanations that seem to undercut the explanations that Locke gives. There is one final view concerning the *Essays* that we need to consider, viz., Horwitz writes: "The *Questions* abound with manifest and massive contradictions."[75] More specifically, Horwitz claims that Locke argues for the existence of the law of nature in Question 1, but later on he denies a premise in each argument. Horwitz explains that Locke does this intentionally, and that this is just the style of writing that he used:

> Initially he strongly states a position, and thereby gives it an authoritative cast, but then he gradually raises doubts about it, or even flatly contradicts it. For this reason, it is wise for the reader to regard every assertion in the *Questions* as provisional in character, rather than as a pronouncement by Locke of a definitive doctrine.[76]

The text of his excellent commentary, however, reflects only one example of where he takes Locke to deny one of the premises of the arguments for the existence of the law of nature. According to Horwitz, the alleged contradiction occurs between passages found in Essay 1 of the *Essays* and passages found in Essay 5 and Essay 7.[77] Horwitz briefly explains:

> For example, he [i.e., Locke] flatly contradicts here his earlier contention that the workings of conscience established the existence of the law of nature. Near the very beginning of the *Questions* he asserted that "men's consciences" prove 'that a law of nature exists; . . . that is, from the fact that 'no one who is guilty wins acquittal when he himself is judge.'[78]

To see if this is really a contradiction, I will attempt to compare the passages in Essays 5 and 7 that allegedly contradict Locke's view of the conscience in Essay 1.

Horwitz claims that Locke contradicts in Essay 5 the earlier view that men pass judgment on themselves in the absence of any kind of civil authority or religious authority. For example, he argues that Locke denies this claim in Question 5 because, as the following passage indicates, conscience becomes for Locke nothing more than a reflection of dominate opinion[79]:

> For while men, led by the prevailing opinion, have performed this or that according to the moral practice of their country (though perhaps, and not without reason, it appeared to others wrong and wicked) they

did not think they had transgressed the law of nature but rather had observed it; they felt no pangs of conscience nor that inward mental scourge which usually punishes and torments the guilty, for they believed that their action, whatever it may have been, was not only lawful but laudable.[80]

But is this what Locke means? I do not think this is the correct interpretation. To explain why I think it is wrong, I must first expound upon the context of this passage. Here Locke has been arguing against consensus as a means of knowledge of the law of nature. He distinguishes two varieties, viz., positive and natural consensus. Positive consensus is an agreement, which issues from either a tacit or expressed contract.[81] Locke argues: "Neither form of general consent, since both wholly depend on a contract and are not derived from any natural principle, proves at all a law of nature."[82] Natural consent is "one to which men are led by a certain natural instinct without the intervention of some compact."[83] Locke reasons that if this is true, then knowledge of the law of nature would be brought about by a kind of natural instinct either in the consensus of conduct or actions, opinions, or principles. He denies all three of these natural instincts.

The passage above is discussed in the second part of this argument under the natural instinct in the consensus of opinions. Specifically, Locke is discussing why there exists among men no consensus of opinions concerning right conduct. He argues first that one has only to consult the histories of the world to see that there is no such consensus. In fact, as Locke writes: "But if we would review each class of virtues and vices—and nobody doubts that this classification is the actual law of nature—it will easily appear that there is none of them of which men do not form different opinions buttressed by public authority and custom."[84]

Next he argues: "if the general consent of men is to be regarded as the rule of morality, there will either be no law of nature at all or it will vary from place to place."[85] Locke adds, however, that this is something that "no one will maintain" because each culture, i.e., a culture with some sort of view about the law of nature, believes that they are acting in accordance with the law of nature.[86] They believe this for two reasons (and understanding these reasons is the key to understanding why Horwitz and Zuckert's interpretation is mistaken). First, they believe this because while men "led by the prevailing opinion, have performed this or that according to the moral practice of their country (though perhaps, and not without reason, it appeared to others wrong and wicked) they did not think they had transgressed the law of nature but rather had observed it."[87] That is, even though they think that they are obeying the law of nature, they have been guided instead by the mistaken view of the dominant opinion of the culture. Second, they believe this because "they felt no pangs of conscience nor that inward mental scourge which usually punishes and torments the guilty, for they believed that their action, whatever it may have been, was not only lawful but laudable."[88] That is, each individual believes his view of the law of nature is correct because each can generate evidence for his own view of the law of nature. He does this by appealing to his own psychological experience of not feeling guilt when he performs and action approved by his own culture.

After making explicit my alternative interpretation of this passage, I see nothing that contradicts the earlier view that men pass judgment on themselves in the absence of any kind of civil authority or religious authority. For example, this claim says that people judge themselves even when there is no dominate religious or civil opinion in place. This does not mean that they judge themselves according to the specific laws of nature, only that they judge themselves. The passage in Essay 5 says that individuals often defend their own views of the law of nature by appealing to the fact that what they are doing is confirmed by their own consciences. In fact, as Locke makes clear, they do this even if views of the law of nature are mistaken. This is, then, not a denial of Locke's earlier claim, but a support for it because the conscience is doing what it was designed to do, viz., praise and blame.

The other passage is in Essay 7. It is a difficult passage to understand:

> [T]he only thing, perhaps, about which all mortals think alike is that men's opinion about the law of nature and the ground of their duty are diverse and manifold—a fact which, even if tongues were silent, moral behaviour, which differs so widely, would show pretty well. Men are everywhere met with, not only a select few and those in a private station, but whole nations, in whom no sense of law, no moral rectitude, can be observed. There are also other nations, and they are many, *which with no guilty feeling disregard some at least of the precepts of natural law* and consider it to be not only customary but also praiseworthy to commit, and to approve of, such crimes as are utterly loathsome to those who think rightly and live according to nature. Hence, among these nations, thefts are lawful and commendable, and the greedy hands of robbers are *not debarred from violence and injury by any shackles of conscience.* For others there is no disgrace in debauchery; and while in one place there are no temples or altars of the gods, in another they are found spattered with human blood.[89]

Here Horwitz points out that Locke contradicts himself by pointing out that there are people who do bad things without any conscience of wrong and are not restrained by any fetters of conscience. This shows, according to Horwitz, that conscience is nothing more than a reflection of the dominant opinion.[90]

Does the above quotation bear any evidence of contradicting Locke's earlier view? I think the answer is no for two reasons. First, regardless of what Locke means in this passage, he states that from these considerations "it seems necessary to conclude, either that there is no law of nature in some places, or that some nations at least are not bound by it, so that the binding force of natural law is not universal."[91] This indicates that the above quotation is not Locke's view at all, but an objection that he is considering. Unfortunately, Locke never addresses these objections fully except to assert flatly, in a sort of head-to-head fashion, that regardless of what anyone says no one is above the law of nature and everyone has other duties depending upon his relationship with other people: "[I]n spite of these objections, we maintain that the binding force of the law of nature is perpetual and universal."[92]

Second, let us suppose that the passage in question is Locke's view. Does Locke say any thing at all that contradicts his earlier view? No, because Locke never states that men do not pass judgment on themselves in the absence of any kind of civil authority or religious doctrine. In fact, what he says in this passage is exactly what he says in the passage in Question 5, viz., that, in the light of the dominant opinion, their consciences approve and sanction crimes, which are often the proper objects of the greatest detestation to other people. Therefore, regardless of what someone's conscience approves or disapproves, his conscience is still doing what it was designed to do.

There are apparently other texts in which Locke allegedly contradicts himself. Zuckert also points out a number of these in his excellent book.[93] I have only looked at a few of these. However, in my mind, most of these can be resolved by considering the context in which the claims occur. I have not, however, completely cleared Locke of these serious charges. I have only attempted to build a case for the view that Locke believed that the first five arguments in Essay 1 were sound. Finally, as I mentioned at the beginning of this section, describing Locke as a moral absolutist in the *Essays* depends upon whether or not we can find within the text some kind of dedication to a single, ultimate, moral standard. Such a commitment typically implies that law of nature has to exist as a source of moral knowledge independently of what humans believe about it. This condition is satisfied because of the five arguments he gives in Essay 1. In the next section, I will consider whether or not Locke is loyal to a moral absolutism in virtue of whether or not he committed to the view that the law of nature is a moral standard binding for those it was designed for. This is in fact the view Locke discusses in Essay 6.

The Obligation of the Law of Nature is Binding on All Men

In Essay 6, Locke gives us five different arguments to establish the following claim: "the law of nature is binding on all men primarily and of itself and by its intrinsic force."[94] Before I discuss those arguments, it might be helpful to ask what Locke means by this. According to Locke, to say that the law of nature is binding on all men is to say that all men have some sort of obligation or duty to discharge. The question now is to whom the obligation is due and what sort of obligation or duty it is. According to Locke, we are obligated to obey the law of nature because it is the declaration of a superior will, viz., God[95]:

> Hence it is pretty clear that all the requisites of a law are found in natural law. For, in the first place, it is the decree of a superior will, wherein the formal cause of a law appears to consist.[96]

Consider now the five arguments he uses to establish the claim set forth in Essay 6. Locke's first argument appears to be based upon his view of the formal definition of law:

> [B]ecause this law contains all that is necessary to make a law binding. For God, the author of this law, has willed it to be the rule of our moral life, and He has made it sufficiently known, so that anyone can understand it who is willing to apply diligent study and to direct his mind to the knowledge of it. The result is that, since nothing else is required to impose an obligation but the authority and rightful power of the one who commands and the disclosure of His will, no one can doubt that the law of nature is binding on men.[97]

Earlier Locke gave us the general requirements for law: "For, in the first place, it is the decree of a superior will. . . . Secondly, it lays down what is and what is not to be done. . . . Thirdly, it binds men. . . ."[98] As Locke points out the law of nature satisfies the first requirement because it is the declaration of God's will. It also satisfies the second condition because the law of nature prescribes what is to be done. Finally, Locke writes that it satisfies the third condition because God published it sufficiently so that men can perceive it.[99]

Locke reasons in the second argument that the law of nature is binding upon men:

> For, in the first place, since God is supreme over everything and has such authority and power over us as we cannot exercise over ourselves, and since we owe our body, soul, and life—whatever we are, whatever we have, and whatever we can be—to Him and to Him alone, it is proper that we should live according to the precept of His will. God has created us out of nothing and, if He pleases, will reduce us again to nothing: we are, therefore, subject to Him in perfect justice and by utmost necessity.[100]

This argument turns upon his evoking what is typically called the sovereignty of God. The "sovereignty of God" in theological circles refers to the representation of God as the Creator and to His will as the cause of all things. It is invoked by theologians to point out that we are obligated to live the way God wants us to since these characteristics amount to the fact that God owns us. For example, in line with this, Louis Berkhoff, an early twentieth century Calvinist theologian, writes that:

> In virtue of His creative work heaven and earth and all that they contain belong to Him. He is clothed with absolute authority over the host of heaven and the inhabitants of the earth. He upholds all things with His almighty power, and determines the ends which they are destined to serve. He rules as King in the most absolute sense of the word, and all things are dependent on Him and subservient to Him.[101]

Locke argues in much the same way in the quotation above.

Locke's third argument for the bindingness of the law of nature turns upon the claim that it is knowable to all: "this law is the will of this omnipotent lawmaker, known to us by the light and principles of nature; the knowledge of it can be concealed from no one unless he loves blindness and darkness and casts off nature in order that he may avoid his duty."[102] This quotation contains in it a brief synopsis of Locke's reasoning in Essay 2, i.e., "Can The Law of Nature Be Known By The Light of Nature? Yes."[103] Previously, in the second essay, Locke makes it clear that the phrase that he uses above, viz., that law of nature becomes known by means of the light and principle of nature, is not to be taken as an appeal to the innate notion of knowledge about the existence of the law of nature:

> But while we assert that the light of nature points to this law, we should not wish this to be understood in the sense that some inward light is by nature implanted in man, which perpetually reminds him of his duty and leads him straight and without fail whither he has to go. We do not maintain that this law, written as it were on tablets, lies open in our hearts, and that, as soon as some inward light comes near it. . . . Rather, by saying that something can be known by the light of nature, we mean nothing else but that there is some sort of truth to the knowledge of which a man can attain by himself and without the help of another, if he makes proper use of the faculties he is endowed with by nature.[104]

The law of nature is binding upon men because its precepts are sufficiently known. That is, its existence is readily available by the right use of those faculties, viz., sensation and reason (as Locke explains in Essay 4 later on).

Locke's fourth argument proceeds by *modus tollens*:

> [I]f natural law is not binding on men, neither can positive divine law be binding, and that no one has maintained. In fact, the basis of obligation is in both cases the same, i. e. the will of a supreme Godhead. The two laws differ only in method of promulgation and in the way in which we know them: the former we know with certainty by the light of nature and from natural principles, the latter we apprehend by faith.[105]

Locke reasons that since the foundation of obligation is the same for both the law of nature and the Divine Law, then if one is binding then the other is binding. This is so because, according to Locke, God is the efficient cause of both. The only difference between these two laws is the way that they have been promulgated. For example, while the law of nature is known by sensation and reason, the divine law is apprehended by faith.

Locke ends Essay 6 with the fifth argument:

> [I]f natural law is not binding on men, neither can any human positive law be binding. For the laws of the civil magistrate derive so far as the majority of men is concerned. In fact, since the definite knowledge of a divine revelation has not reached them, they have no other law, both divine and binding by its very nature, than natural law; so

that, if you abolish the law of nature among them, you banish from among mankind at the same time the whole body politic, all authority, order, and fellowship among them. For we should not obey a king just out of fear, because, being more powerful, he can constrain (this in fact would be to establish firmly the authority of tyrants, robbers, and pirates), but for conscience' sake, because a king has command over us by right; that is to say, because the law of nature decrees that princes and a law-maker, or a superior by whatever name you call him, should be obeyed. Hence the binding force of civil law is dependent on natural law; and we are not so much coerced into rendering obedience to the magistrate by the power of the civil law as bound to obedience by natural right.[106]

Again, the argument proceeds by *modus tollens*: Locke argues that if the law of nature is not binding on men because human positive law is not binding, but since human positive law is binding, then the law of nature is also binding on men. Although the text does not indicate this, the reason that Locke believes the former premise is true, i.e., that human positive law is binding, is taken from the New Testament: "Let every soul be subject to the governing authorities. For there is no authority except from God, and the authorities that exist are appointed by God."[107] Locke's reason for why the latter premise is true is that the efficient cause is God. Locke had made a similar remark in Essay 1, viz., that if without the law of nature, human society would not exist.[108] He also makes the additional point (which he indirectly mentioned only briefly in Question 6) that, in the consideration of why and whom we should obey, the source of their authority is important to keep in mind. We are bound to obey the king and magistrate not out of fear, because he is more powerful and can compel us, but (again) we obey because their authority is derived from the law of nature. That is, fear alone is neither a sufficient nor a necessary condition of obedience.

The Obligation of the Law of Nature is Perpetual and Universal

Locke breaks Essay 7 into three parts. First, he briefly sketches an argument, which he takes to be contrary to his own position. Next, with this argument in mind, he argues that the obligation of the law of nature is perpetual and that it is universal. I will begin with the argument that Locke takes to be contrary to his own.

This argument occurs in the quotation that is reproduced on page 55 of this chapter. After that quotation, Locke draws the following conclusion:

> Since such is the case, it may be justly doubted whether the law of nature is binding on all mankind, unsettled and uncertain as men are, accustomed to the most diverse institutions, and driven by impulses in quite opposite directions. . . .[109]

Locke initially responds to this conclusion with a denial and a concession. First, "for that the decrees of nature are so obscure that they are hidden from whole nations is hard to believe."[110] However, "That some men are born defective in mind as well as in eyesight, and are in need of a guide and do not know whither they ought to go, can readily be admitted."[111]

After this, however, Locke returns to his initial denial and supports it more firmly:

> But who will say that entire nations are born blind, or that a thing is according to nature, of which whole nations and a multitude of men are absolutely ignorant, or that the light infused into human hearts either differs not at all from darkness or like an *ignis fatuus* leads into error by its uncertain gleam?[112]

But, Locke argues that, if any would still want to maintain this outlook, he would insult nature and:

> Hence it seems necessary to conclude, either that there is no law of nature in some places, or that some nations at least are not bound by it, so that the binding force of natural law is not universal.[113]

Locke begins his attack of these considerations in the following way. In this passage, Locke dismisses both objections contained in the disjunction above, viz., either there is no law of nature anywhere or that some peoples are not bound by this law and thus that the obligation of the law of nature is not universal. First, Locke explicitly dismisses the right disjunct by pointing out that this has already been refuted. Locke is right about this because it was discussed in Essay 6. Second, he dismisses the left disjunct if only implicitly. The reason was discussed in Essay 1, where he argues for the existence of the law of nature.

Locke turns the discussion to the topic of the perpetual character of the obligation or what he calls the *extent* of the obligation of the law of nature. He makes two basic points. First, Locke writes:

> We say then that in the first place the binding force of the law of nature is permanent, that is to say, there is no time when it would be lawful for a man to act against the precepts of this law; no interregnum is provided here, in this realm there are no Saturnalian holidays given to either freedom or licence. The bonds of this law are perpetual and coeval with the human race, beginning with it and perishing with it at the same time.[114]

Second, right after this, Locke qualifies his view in the light of some sort of counter-example. He writes that even though there are no times of license this does not mean that we can conclude that "men would be bound at all times to perform everything that the law of nature commands."[115] This appears to be some sort of response to a *reductio ad impossible* because, as someone might argue, if it is true that there is no time in which a man would be permitted to violate the precepts of this law, then there is a possible situation at which it is true that men are obligated to perform inconsistent actions at the same time.[116] Locke responds by writing:

> This would be simply impossible, since one man is not capable of performing different actions at the same time, and he can no more observe several duties at once than a body can be in several places.[117]

To make things clearer and avoid the *reductio*, Locke attempts to spell out his notion of the perpetual character of the obligation of the law of nature by writing:

> Still, we say that the binding force of nature is perpetual in the sense that there neither is, nor can be, a time when the law of nature orders men, or any man, to do something and he is not obliged to show himself obedient; so that the binding force is continuous though it is not necessary that the action be so. The binding force of the law never changes, though often there is a change in both the times and circumstance of actions, whereby our obedience is defined. We can sometimes stop acting according to the law, but act against the law we cannot. In this life's journey rest is sometimes allowed, but straying at no time.[118]

But, now, given this further explication of what he means by the term "perpetual," how does this avoid the reductio just mentioned?

The key to understanding how Locke's use of the term "perpetual" avoids the *reductio* is contained in the quotation above. Unfortunately, Locke never describes in any detail just what he means. This makes what Locke says here, although tantalizing, insufficient for our purposes. There is, however, one way to understand this. For example, there is a passage in Aquinas, which bears striking similarities to this passage and to the problem at hand.

Aquinas addresses a similar kind of problem. He asks whether the natural law can be changed? He writes:

> a change in the natural law may be understood by way of subtraction, so that what previously was according to the natural law, ceases to be so. In this sense, the natural law is altogether unchangeable in its first principles. But in its secondary principles, which, as we have said, are certain detailed proximate conclusions drawn from the first principles, the natural law is not changed so that what it prescribes be not right in most cases. But it may be changed in some particular cases of rare occurrence, through some special causes hindering the observance of such precepts, as was stated above.[119]

In this passage, Aquinas indicates that although no change in the natural law can take place with regard to its first principles (a claim certainly consistent with Locke's views), a change can take place with regard to its secondary principles. At least in Aquinas, to make this distinction is to see a difference between the unchanging nature of the first principles of the law of nature and the way we apply them to the dynamic circumstances in which we find ourselves. For example, the law of nature requires that we preserves ourselves since, according to Aquinas, "there is in man . . . an inclination to good in accordance with the nature which he has in common with all substances, inasmuch, namely, as every substance seeks the preservation of its own being, according to its nature."[120] This is one of the first principles that Aquinas speaks of. Moreover, we occasionally find ourselves in different types of circumstances in which the issue of our own preservation may be at stake. When these circumstances arise, we may find it necessary to apply the first principle to a particular circumstance in order to maintain our own life. To do this, we may need to create a principle, which combines elements from the circumstance and the first principle. For example, I conclude that I ought to avoid circumstance C because I perceive that it threatens my life. Moreover, I reason by generalizing this situation into the following conditional, viz., that if circumstance C (or any circumstance like it) threatens my life, then it (and every circumstance like it) ought to be avoided.

In this practical syllogism, the conditional, *if circumstance C (or any circumstance like it) threatens my life, it ought to be avoided*, is often called the Principle of Evaluation since it indicates that there is some sort of relationship between ethical statements and factual statements.[121] In my understanding of Aquinas, this principle approximates what he calls a secondary principle. Moreover, this is the same sort of thing that I think Locke is referring to when he says that the obligation of this law never changes, although the times and circumstances of the actions by which our obedience is defined might change.

Perhaps I can further illustrate this. Suppose we live in a society in which part of our obedience to preserve ourselves is defined by acting a certain way, e.g., showing respect to our leader by bowing down in front of him at the appropriate circumstances. Moreover, it is argued in this society by moral scholars that this is part of what the law of nature requires. Now suppose we leave this society to live in another society (for whatever reason). However, we learn that in this society if you bow down to the leader in any kind of circumstance it is interpreted as a sign of weakness and you are immediately put to death. In this different circumstance someone might conclude that in order to preserve himself he would be required to bow and not bow down. Since this would be impossible to do, the foreigner would probably be left in a state of perplexity.

Locke and Aquinas might respond to this situation by reasoning that the individual who concludes this is confusing what one of the first principles of the law of nature requires with what the secondary principles require. For example, the first principle requires the duty of self-preservation. Moreover, even though humans live in circumstances, which can often change, the circumstances that we find ourselves living in are still required for us to define or instantiate what our duty is. In the first case, then, since the circumstances required bowing down to the leader upon threat of death, the duty to self-preservation was defined or instantiated in terms of these circumstances. However, in the second case, the way our duty is defined is changed with the circumstance. This appears to be what Locke had in mind with the first claim of the above quotation. However, Locke continues that whereas we can occasionally cease acting in conformity with this law, we cannot act against the law. How do we make sense that sentence?

One way of understanding this is to make the same distinction as Aquinas made above. That is, we can cease acting in conformity with the law of nature when our circumstances change. This is due to the fact that the circumstance serves, in a sense, to instantiate or to define what our duty is. If we are required to perform an action in a circumstance, then it does not automatically mean that the action will be required in all circumstances (even though the first principle is required in all circumstances). If the circumstances change, then it is possible that the way we define our duty will also change. The change in circumstances will require us to cease acting in conformity with the law of nature as it was defined in one situation and act consistently with the first principle as it is instantiated or defined for a different circumstance. By explicating Locke in this way and by making these kinds of distinctions, he avoids the counterexample by showing that there is an interpretation under which the claim that there is a possible situation at which it is true that men are obligated to perform different actions at the same time, is false.[122]

After this discussion, Locke moves on to a debate of the universal character of the law of nature. This new topic is also directed at the objections he mentioned in the first two paragraphs of this question. Against the objections, Locke argues that the law of nature holds universally in the sense that "the binding force of the law of nature holds its power undiminished and unchanged both throughout all ages and over the whole world."[123] Unlike the first reason about the perpetual character, which amounts to just essentially denying that the objections are true, Locke gives two reasons why the law of nature is universally applicable and binding.

First, Locke writes, summing up what he has argued thus far:

> Because if this law is not binding on all men the reason is either that it has never been given at all to any part of mankind, or that it has been repealed. Neither of these two things, however, can be maintained.[124]

Finally, Locke argues that the law of nature is universally binding because:

> [I]n the second place, this natural duty will never be abolished; for human beings cannot alter this law, because they are subject to it, and it is not the business of subjects to abrogate laws at their liking, and because God certainly would not wish to do so. For since, according to His infinite and eternal wisdom, He has made man such that these

duties of his necessarily follow from his very nature, He surely will not alter what has been made and create a new race of men, who would have another law and moral rule, seeing that natural law stands and falls together with the nature of man as it is at present.[125]

Two points should be made about this passage. First, the reason that he gives for why the natural law will never be abrogated appears to be true just by definition because if something is true independently of what humans believe, then it stands to reason that (in most cases) it is not something that humans can change. Second, Locke adds in the last sentence of this quotation that the natural law will never be abrogated because God would not abrogate the law of nature himself since he has made man in such a way that his duties would necessarily follow from his very nature.

There appears to be (at least) two ways to interpret the last sentence. The first interpretation emphasizes that the relationship between the duties of man and man's nature is a essential relationship. This means that once we understand what the very nature of humans is, we will be able to understand what duties necessarily follow, i.e., we will be able to deduce from the nature of man what his duties are. The second interpretation emphasizes that the relationship is a causal relationship. This means that God has created man in such a way that he naturally does what is required of him, i.e., God has placed into men several dispositions, which contribute causally to their behavior but do not completely determine what they do.

Although there is evidence for both views in the *Essays*, neither one of these views is the correct interpretation of what Locke means. For example, it is not the causal view because, as we have already seen, this position turns upon the view that there are dispositions in man placed there by God which only *contribute* toward certain acts, e.g., acts like self-preservation, propagation, the creation of societies, and the worship of God. But those who habituate themselves in different ways defeat these dispositions easily. This is a common view among natural law theorists. Is the essential view, then, the correct view? There appears to be evidence for the other view contained in the following quotation. Locke writes:

In fact it seems to me to follow just as necessarily from the nature of man that, if he is a man, he is bound to love and worship God and also to fulfil other things appropriate to the rational nature, i.e. to observe the law of nature, as it follows from the nature of a triangle that, if it is a triangle, its three angles are equal to two right angles, although perhaps very many men are so lazy and so thoughtless that for want of attention they are ignorant of both these truths, which are so manifest and certain that nothing can be plainer.[126]

It is very tempting to believe, based on this passage that the phrase, "necessarily follows," points primarily to the essential relationship. However, Locke is not advocating the view that we can discover what man's duties are just by deducing them from what we take human nature to be as we can with the properties of triangle. This is due to the fact that if Locke advocates such a view, then there should be some sort of textual evidence for them. However, in Essay 4, Locke writes that the deductions of man's duties are revealed from the nature of God and the nature of man.[127] This leads, then, to the question of just what the analogy is. What sort of view is he advocating here?

Locke is advocating the view that the kind of duties man is obligated to obey have arisen out of necessity. That is, man's obligation to observe the law of nature is unavoidably determined by prior conditions or circumstances, i.e., it is inevitable. Therefore, since it is inevitable, it is so certain that it is like the certainty often associated with the properties of a triangle correctly being deduced from the notion of a triangle. There is complete certainty associated with this property and so, in the same way, man, "if he is a man, he is bound to love and worship God and also to fulfil other things appropriate to the rational nature." This, then, is the interpretation that I give to Locke's view that man's duties necessarily follow from his nature.

Finally, Locke qualifies his view about the universal character of the law of nature in the same way that he qualified the perpetual character of the law of nature. He appears to have in mind a similar counterexample when he writes:

> Next we say that the binding force of natural law is universal, but not because any and every law of nature is binding on any and every man, since this impossible. For most precepts of this law have regard to the various relations between men and are founded on these. Princes have many privileges which are not granted to the common people, and subjects, in their capacity as subjects, have many duties which cannot be appropriate to a king. While it is a general's duty to assign soldiers their posts, it is the soldier's duty to hold them; and it would not become a parent to salute his children ceremoniously and humbly.[128]

Locke is confident that by arguing for the claims that the obligation to the law of nature is both perpetual and universal it will defeat the objections, which are contrary to his view. The objections in his mind supported the premise that either there is no law of nature anywhere or that this law does not bind some people. I argued that the left disjunct has to be modified to read that there is no obedience to the law of nature anywhere. By wording it this way, it appears to be more consistent with the context and with what Locke is arguing against, viz., that the law of nature is not universal. Locke's attack of the objections, at least in my mind, amount to saying that (1) regardless of the various and manifold opinions men have concerning the law of nature, (2) regardless of whether or not there are people in whom there can be observed no sense of law, or no rectitude of conduct, and (3) regardless of whether there are those who without any conscience of wrong pay no heed to at least some of the precepts of the law of nature, the obligation to the law of nature is perpetual, i.e., there is no time in which a man would be permitted to violate the precepts of this law. Finally, the obligation to the law of nature is universal, i.e., the obligation of the law of nature holds its force undiminished and unshaken throughout all ages and over the entire globe.

After finishing the *Essays*, as far as we know, Locke did not write much more on nature law nor, as Laslett points out, was he ever to get much further as a natural law theorist.[129] The *Treatises* might be thought of as an exception to these claims; however, it remains an unsettled issue whether or not the views of the law of nature in the *Essays* and the *Treatises* are compatible. To settle such an issue it would be necessary to see whether or not the same sort of Aristotelian, purposive universe underlies his views in the *Treatises*. It is my view that there does not seem to be any kind of devotion by Locke to such a universe.[130]

Although Locke did not write much more on natural law, there is evidence that he was still interested in the questions surrounding the possibility of moral and religious knowledge. However, as I attempted to make clear in Chapter One, the answers to the questions of moral and religious knowledge were not sought in a universe that he described in the *Essays*. Instead, as Yolton writes, "Locke sought to elaborate an account of human understanding which would make sense of the new science of nature."[131] That is, Locke had given up his early teleological view of the universe for a view of the universe dominated by Corpuscular Philosophy. The question of the possibility of moral and religious knowledge therefore had to be readdressed, because neither the concept of a purposive or ordered universe nor an essentialist view of human nature found in the *Essays* can be used in Corpuscular Philosophy to justify moral and religious doctrines.

In 1689, Locke's views about moral and religious doctrines emerge again with the publication of the *Essay*. In fact, we see some of his views of the *Essays* brought forward into the *Essay*, e.g., his view concerning the existence of innate ideas.[132] The *Essay*, however, is largely dominated by the attempts to describe the understanding of humans. Locke's thoughts on moral knowledge are left shrouded and cloaked. In the next two chapters, however, I attempt to uncover some of these views by underscoring Locke's view of the nature of good and evil and his view of the nature of moral goodness.

Notes

1 Zuckert argues that Locke was interested to find a view of the law of nature, which would also undercut the theological politics of the various parties in post-Reformation Europe (Zuckert, *Natural Rights and the New Republicanism*, 189). Colman argues something very similar to this in chapter two of his book (Colman, *John Locke's Moral Philosophy*, 21-50).

2 Locke, *Essays*, 119; f. 19.

3 Ibid., 109; f. 9 and f. 10.

4 Michael Zuckert points out that here we have evidence of a break with the tradition of natural law associated with Grotius (Zuckert, *Natural Rights and the New Republicanism*, 188). This, I might add, is also a break from the Cambridge Platonist, specifically, Ralph Cudworth, *A Treatise Concerning the Eternal and Immutable Morality*, in *British Moralists, 1650-1800*, 2 vols. ed. D. D. Raphael (Oxford: Oxford University Press, 1969), 1:105-119; and Samuel Clark, *A Discourse Concerning the Unchangeable Obligations of Natural Religion, and the Truth and Certainty of the Christian Revelation*, in *British Moralists, 1650-1800*, 1:191-225. The reason is that both Grotius and the Cambridge Platonists argued that the law of nature would exist even if God did not exist; whereas, as Zuckert explains, "Locke insists that God is simply indispensable for the law of nature" (Zuckert, *Natural Rights and the New Republicanism*, 188). Zuckert's book contains, among other things, an invaluable discussion of the differences and similarities between Locke's and Grotius' views on natural law.

5 Locke, *Essays*, 111; f. 11 and f. 12.

6 Ibid., 109-121; f. 9-f. 21.

7 Ibid., 113; f. 13.

8 I discuss the first argument in this section as well. However, I discuss the fifth argument in the next section. Finally, I discuss the remaining arguments plus the third and fifth again in the last section of this chapter.

9 The editors of the *Questions* add the phrase "other than man" to the text right after "wherein all things" (Locke, *Questions*, 113). Apparently, it is necessary to fix the text in order to keep Locke from including man within the set of all things, which observe a fixed law, a view which he clarifies a few sentences later. But the editors fail to understand that from an Aristotelian point of view there are aspects of the operations of humans, which observe fixed laws like other animals. These aspects are part of the non-rational part of the soul, which are unresponsive to reason and are the cause of growth and nutrition. For example, Aristotle writes:

> Consider the nonrational [part]. One [part] of it, i.e., the cause of nutrition and growth, would seem to be plantlike and shared [with all living things]; for we can ascribe this capacity of the soul to everything that is nourished, including embryos, and the same capacity to full-grown living things, since this is more reasonable than to ascribe another capacity to them. [H]ence the virtue of this capacity is apparently shared, not [specifically] human. (Aristotle, *Nicomachean Ethics*, 1102a 34-1102b 4)

10 Locke, *Essays*, 117; f. 18.

11 Even though it is true that the *Essays* is essentially a document within the Christian Natural Law tradition, the reader must not assume that just because Locke has two Aristotelian-like arguments at the beginning of his discussion that this automatically puts the *Essays* within this tradition. As we shall see, however, there is much evidence within the work itself that Locke relies upon an Aristotelian outlook of the world.

12 Within the Christian Natural Law tradition it was also customary to talk of the law, which angels have. It was called the Celestial Law. Richard Hooker, e.g., points out "that which Angels do clearly behold and without any swerving observe is a law Celestial and heavenly" (Richard Hooker, *Of the Laws of Ecclesiastical Polity*, eds. A. S. McGrade and Brian Vickers [New York: St. Martin's Press, 1975], 113). Horwitz also points out that:

In view of the subsequent discussion of Locke's understanding of natural law, it is essential to emphasize that the Christian teaching, as expounded by Culverwel and others, holds that the natural law cannot be transgressed by either the highest beings, viz., obedient angels, or by the lowest beings, "the very dregs of entity." It is the humans alone who, having the God-given capacity for moral choice, may and do commit transgressions against this law. (Horwitz, introduction to the *Questions*, 14)

Unfortunately, Horwitz's discussion betrays an equivocation on the term natural law. The reason why I say this is that within this tradition there is usually a clear distinction of the kinds of laws different to which entities are subject. For example, Hooker writes:

Now that law which, as it is laid up in the bosom of God, they call Eternal, receiveth according unto the different kinds of things which are subject unto it different and sundry kinds of names. That part of it which ordereth natural agents we call usually Nature's law; that which Angels do clearly behold and without any swerving observe is law Celestial and heavenly; the law of Reason, that which bindeth creatures reasonable in this world, and with which by reason they may most plainly perceive themselves bound. . . . (Hooker, *Of the Laws of Ecclesiastical Polity*, 113)

13 For an excellent discussion of Aristotle's essentialism see, Baruch A. Brody, *Identity and Essence* (Princeton: Princeton University Press, 1980).

14 As Zuckert points out and the text of the *Essays* indicates, Locke owes this point to Aquinas (Zuckert, *Natural Rights and the New Republicanism*, 200). Locke confirms the importance of the law of nature by implying that it is derived from the Eternal Law of God. This means that since the Eternal Law is the exemplar of the Divine Intellect, and as a consequence, each thing within the Divine Intellect has truth in virtue of and in so far as it is like the Divine

Intellect, the law of nature has truth on the basis of two considerations. First, on the grounds of being derived from the supreme exemplar and on the grounds of being like the supreme exemplar since it denotes a plan directing acts toward an end. For an interesting discussion and elaboration of this point, see Thomas Aquinas, *Introduction to Thomas Aquinas*, ed. Anton C. Pegis (New York: Random House, Inc., 1945), Q. 93. Art. 1 and 3.

15 Locke, *Essays*, 113; f. 13.

16 Ibid., 167; f. 67.

17 Aquinas, *Introduction to Thomas Aquinas*, Q. 94, Art. 2.

18 See a similar discussion in Aristotle, *Politics*, ed. W. D. Ross (Oxford: Oxford University Press, 1957), I. 2 and III. 6.

19 Locke, *Essays*, 119-120; f. 20-f. 21.

20 Aquinas, *Introduction to Thomas Aquinas*, Q. 55, Art. 4.

21 Ibid., Compare this definition to Aristotle's definition:

[V]irtue, then, is a state that decides, consisting in a mean, the mean relative to us, which is defined by reference to reason, that is to say, to the reason by reference to which the prudent person would define it. It is a mean between two vices, one of excess and one of deficiency. (Aristotle, *Nicomachean Ethics*, 1107a 1-4)

There are certainly both similarities and differences. The similarity is that both Aquinas and Aristotle recognize virtue to be some sort of state (*heksis*). The differences, however, are more important. Whereas Aristotle has no concept of God as part of the efficient cause of virtue, Aquinas includes it. Because of this difference, I used Aquinas' definition since it is bears a closer resemblance to Locke's overall outlook of the universe, including the part God plays in this universe. In fact, Simmons also points out: "Locke's theory of natural law can be positioned at least largely within the Thomist tradition" (Simmons, *The Lockean Theory of Rights*, FN. 3, p. 16). Another important difference is Aristotle's emphasis on the kind of state a virtue is, viz., virtue "is a state that decides, consisting in a mean." This is not to say that Aquinas does not discuss this aspect of virtue. For example, in Q. 64, Art. 1 and 2, Aquinas discusses "On the Mean of Virtue." In this question, Aquinas brings out this aspect of the definition of virtue. However, it is unclear why this aspect is not included in the original definition Aquinas puts forth.

22 Aquinas, *Introduction to Thomas Aquinas*, Q. 55, Art. 4.

23 In the Greek, the word for disposition is *diathesis*. It is translated: a disposing in order, arrangement.

24 Aquinas, *Introduction to Thomas Aquinas*, Q. 55, Art. 4.

25 Aristotle, *Nicomachean Ethics*, 1106a 23-24.

26 This claim would appear to be in direct opposition to much of what Aristotle writes about habits. His view is that habituation is a necessary condition of both the virtue of thought as well as virtue of character. However, Aristotle carefully distinguishes habituation from something, which is brought about by a process of nature. For example, Aristotle writes:

if something arises in us by nature, we first have the capacity for it, and later perform the activity. This is clear in the case of the senses; for we did not acquire them by frequent seeing or hearing, but we already had them when we exercised them, and did not get them by exercising them. (Ibid., 1103a 27-31)

However, in contrast to this, virtues are acquired in much the same way products are produced by a craft:

Virtues, by contrast, we acquire, just as we acquire crafts, by having first activated them. For we learn a craft by producing the same product that we must produce when we have learned it; we become builders, for instance, by building, and we become harpists by playing the harp. Similarly, then, we become just by doing just actions, temperate by doing temperate actions, brave by doing brave actions. (Ibid., 1103a 32-1103b 2)

However, Aquinas' view can be reconciled with Aristotle's view by pointing out that Aquinas' view of those habits which are infused by God are not like those things that Aristotle describes as arising by nature. Although they are there by nature, they are only conditions, which make man disposed to do something. They do not cause individuals to do something in the strongest sense of cause.

27 Aquinas, *Introduction to Thomas Aquinas*, Q. 55, Art. 4.

28 This is also the same thing that Aristotle finally concludes. Virtue is not a feeling because, among other reasons, we are not, as Aristotle writes, "praised nor blamed insofar as we have feelings" (Aristotle, *Nicomachean Ethics*, 1105b 31-33). Instead, Aristotle adds: "We are praised or blamed, however, insofar as we have virtues or vices" (Ibid., 1106a 2-3). Moreover, the same sort of reason applies to capacities, viz., "For these reasons the virtues are not capacities either; for we are neither called good nor called bad, nor are we praised or blamed, insofar as we are simple capable of feelings" (Ibid., 1106a 8-10).

29 Aquinas, *Introduction to Thomas Aquinas*, Q. 55, Art. 4.

30 Ibid.

31 Ibid.

32 Ibid.

33 Ibid.

34 There is still one further point, which is important to consider, i.e., the relationship between virtue and states of pleasure and pain. This point, which is explicit in Aristotle, is not discussed at all in either Aquinas (at least with reference to virtue or natural law) or in the *Essays*. But this is still a point to consider since Locke later on devotes an extensive discussion to the topic of the relationship between what we call good and evil and pleasure and pain. Aristotle makes a number of points about the relationship between virtue and pleasure and pain. First, Aristotle expounds that we can tell whether or not someone is in a virtuous state by the way he reacts to pleasure or pain. For example,

Aristotle writes:

> But we must take someone's pleasure or pain following on his actions to be a sign of his state. For if someone who abstains from bodily pleasures enjoys the abstinence itself, he is temperate; if he is grieved by it, he is intemperate. Again, if he stands firm against terrifying situations and enjoys it, or at least does not find it painful, he is brave, if he finds it painful, he is cowardly. (Aristotle, *Nicomachean Ethics*, 1104b 5-10)

Moreover, Aristotle also makes plain other reasons why virtue is concerned with pleasure and pain. First, it is concerned with pleasure and pain because "pleasure causes us to do base actions, and pain causes us to abstain from fine ones" (Ibid., 1104b 10-11). Second because "every feeling and every action implies pleasure or pain" (Ibid., 1104b 14-15). Third, corrective treatment for vicious actions "uses pleasure and pain" (Ibid., 1104b 16-17). Finally, although this does not exhaust Aristotle's reasons, virtue is concerned with pleasure and pain because we estimate actions as well as feelings by pleasure and pain since "pleasure grows up with all of us from infancy on. That is why it is hard to rub out this feeling that is dyed into our lives" (Ibid., 1105a 3-4). These reasons point to a specific view, viz., that virtue is a state, which seeks to bring pleasure and pain into a right relationship with itself.

35 Locke, *Essays*, 119; f. 20.

36 Ibid., 157-8; f. 61.

37 Although both Aquinas and Locke argue that man perceives that he is inclined and ready to perform the works of God as part of the natural law in virtue of these dispositions, both have different accounts of the means to the knowledge of the law of nature. For example, as Zuckert points out, Aquinas believes that the natural inclinations are the means to the knowledge of the law of nature because the natural inclinations point to the proper ends of action (Zuckert, *Natural Rights and the New Republicanism*, 200-1). In contrast to this, as von Leyden points out, at the end of Question 4, Locke added the title of another question, which he never finished, viz., "Can the Law of Nature be Known from Man's Natural Inclination? No" (von Leyden, *Essays on the Law of Nature*, 158, Fn. 3). It is unclear why Locke did not finish this question. Perhaps he thought that the discussion would have been redundant. The reason is that this question would be just a variation of the inscription thesis he rejected in Question 3: "Is The Law of Nature Inscribed n the Minds of Men? No." For example, Locke might reason that without some sense of who God is, there is no way of discriminating between the inclinations which push us to do our duty and those which push us away from our duty.

38 Locke, *Essays*, 119, f. 20.

39 Ibid., 119-120; f. 20-21.

40 Aquinas, *Introduction to Thomas Aquinas*, Q. 94, Art. 3. Aquinas carefully qualifies this statement by adding that when we speak of the class of virtuous acts, i.e., in their proper species, not all virtuous acts are prescribed by

the law of nature. The reason he gives is that "for many things are done virtuously, to which nature does not primarily incline, but which, through the inquiry of reason, have been found by men to be conducive to well-living"
(Ibid.).

41 Locke, *Essays*, 121; f. 21.

42 Ibid., 113, f. 13; 115, f. 16; and 137, f. 37.

43 Colman, *John Locke's Moral Philosophy*, 30.

44 Ibid.

45 Locke, *Essays*, 113, f. 15.

46 Ibid., 113; f. 13. Aristotle's function argument is at 1097b 35-1098a 1-
5.

47 The editors of the *Questions* point out that in this additional argument
Locke misinterprets Aristotle at 1134b19. Apparently, Locke mis-read or did
not correctly remember the Greek text that he quotes (Locke, *Questions*, 103
and 105, Fn. 14).

48 I should add that in between the first argument and these two objections, the editors of the *Questions* include three additional pages, viz., 105, 107,
and 109, which appear to be some of Locke's elaborations of his thoughts about
positive and natural law. However, as the same editors point out, Locke deleted
these pages in the manuscript, viz., MS B (Locke, *Questions*, Fn. 15). Von
Leyden also points out that these pages were also deleted and reprints them at
the back of his own translation (Locke, *Essays*, 282, Note B). The deletion
probably represents some sort of evolution in Locke's own thought as he wrote
the *Essays*.

49 Locke, *Essays*, 113; f. 15.

50 Ibid., 113 & 115; f. 16.

51 Ibid., 115; f. 17.

52 Ibid.

53 Zuckert, *Natural Rights and the New Republicanism*, 193. Zuckert's
discussion of Locke's *Essays* relies upon Diskin Clay's translation of the *Essays*. The first translation of "dictate of reason" in Clay's edition is based on
the Latin, *dictatum rationis* (Locke, *Questions*, 100-1). The second occurrence
of "dictate of reason" is based on the Latin, *dictat ratio* (Ibid., 102-3). Von
Leyden's translation is slightly different. In his edition, he translates the first
occurrence in the same way as Clay (Locke, *Essays*, 110-1). However, he translates *dictat ratio* slightly different: "reason prescribes" (Ibid., 112-3).

54 Locke, *Essays*, 111; f. 12.

55 See Locke, *Questions*, 101, Fn. 9; See also Zuckert, *Natural Rights and
the New Republicanism*, 190.

56 Hugo Grotius, *De Jure Belli ac Pacis* (Paris, 1625), I. i. sec. 10.1.

57 Gilbert Harman, "The Inference to the best Explanation," *Philosophical Review* 74 (1965): 89.

58 Locke, *Essays*, 117; f. 17. Juvenal, *Satires* (LL 1607 [1590]), xiii, 2-3.

59 Zuckert, *Natural Rights and the New Republicanism*, 194.

60 Locke, *Essays*, 117, f. 18.

61 Robert Horwitz, "John Locke's Questions Concerning the Law of Nature: A Commentary," *Interpretation* 19, no. 3 (Spring 1992): 257-8.

62 Zuckert, *Natural Rights and the New Republicanism*, 194.

63 Locke, *Essays*, 117, f. 18. I am indebted to Michael Zuckert for bringing this point to my attention.

64 Ibid.

65 Zuckert, *Natural Rights and the New Republicanism*, 194.

66 Locke, *Essays*, 119; f. 18 and f. 19.

67 Ibid., 119; f. 19.

68 Ibid., 119; f. 20.

69 Ibid., 121; f. 20.

70 Horwitz, "John Locke's Questions Concerning the Law of Nature: A Commentary," 257.

71 Locke, *Essays*, 141-142; f. 43.

72 Thomas Hobbes, *Leviathan*, ed. Edwin Curley (Indianapolis and London: Hackett Publishing Co., 1994), 102.

73 Horwitz, "John Locke's *Questions Concerning the Law of Nature*: A Commentary," 259. That is, a law of nature conceived by Locke and Aquinas as a body of moral knowledge which exists independently of the subjective beliefs of humans.

74 Ibid. Additionally, we may argue that, from a sociobiological point of view, humans have evolved so as to be disposed to sociality. Darwin (1871/1952) argues along these lines in *The Descent of Man.* I am indebted to Fred D. Miller, Jr. for bringing my attention to this point.

75 Horwitz, "John Locke's *Questions Concerning the Law of Nature*: A Commentary," 252. The following discussion is more fully developed in Samuel Zinaich, Jr., "The Internal Coherency of Locke's Moral Views in the *Questions Concerning the Law of Nature*," *Interpretation: A Journal of Political Philosophy* 29, no. 1 (Fall 2001): 55-73. Notre Dame scholar, Michael Zuckert, has published a response to my essay. See Michael P. Zuckert, "On the Lockean Project of a Natural Law Theory: Reply to Zinaich," *Intrepretation: A Journal of Political Philosophy* 29, no. 1 (Fall 2001): 75-89.

76 Horwitz, "John Locke's *Questions Concerning the Law of Nature*: A Commentary," 253.

77 Essay 5 and Essay 7 of von Leyden's edition of the *Essays* corresponds to Essay 7 and Essay 10 respectively of the Horwitz, et. al., edition of the *Questions*.

78 Horwitz, "John Locke's *Questions Concerning the Law of Nature*: A Commentary," 283.

79 Ibid.

80 Locke, *Essays on the Law of Nature*, 169; f. 70. Zuckert also argues the same point and adds that from this passage we see Locke now arguing that "Human beings feel the 'lashes of conscience' not when they violate the law of nature but when they violate the standards set by 'dominant opinion'" (Zuckert, *Natural Rights and the New Republicanism*, 200).

81 Locke, *Essays on the Law of Nature*, 161; f. 63.

82 Ibid., 163; f. 63.
83 Ibid., 165; f. 65.
84 Ibid., 167 and 169; f. 69.
85 Ibid., 169; f. 69 and f. 70.
86 Ibid., f. 70.
87 Ibid.
88 Ibid.
89 Ibid., 191; f. 91. Italics are mine.
90 Horwitz, "John Locke's *Questions Concerning the Law of Nature*: A Commentary," 283.
91 Locke, *Essays on the Law of Nature*, 193; f. 93.
92 Ibid.
93 Zuckert, *Natural Rights and the New Republicanism*, 188-215.
94 Locke, *Essays on the Law of Nature*, 187; f. 88. As far as I can tell, the main reason Locke gives this topic a separate discussion is that without it certain kinds of objections could be raised against the relevance of the law of nature for our lives. That is, even though it would seem to be enough just to argue that the law of nature exists and that it is perpetual and universal, someone could legitimately object that there is no real obligation to obey the law of nature. This objection demonstrates that without some discussion as to the bindingness or validity of the law of nature, the law of nature has no real authority over the lives of men. In such a case, it becomes, as Zuckert points out, mere advice or inauthoritative commendation (Zuckert, *Natural Rights and New Republicanism*, 189). Locke appears to be dissatisfied with such a view. Zuckert argues that this view was held by Grotius, and that "Thomas Hobbes, Samuel Pufendorf, and Nathaniel Culverwell also refused to follow Grotius on this issue" (Ibid., 191).
95 The claim that Locke held that man is obligated to obey the law of nature because the law of nature is a declaration of his will is, however, is a topic, which is disputed by W. von Leyden. Von Leyden maintains that in Question 10 we see a shift in Locke's thinking. The shift is one from (what has been called) a theistic voluntarism concerning obligation to an (what has also been called) intellectualism concerning obligation. Theistic voluntarism concerning obligation, as Colman explains, is a view, which can be expressed in three different but related theses. First, the precepts, which make up morality, have their source in God's unconditioned will. "Thus the only possible answer to the question why, say, murder is wrong is that it is so because God forbids murder" (Colman, *John Locke's Moral Philosophy*, 33). Second, God is above all moral norms. Thus, "What God Himself does, or what He commands particular men to do, is in no way conditioned by moral norms, but is simply the expression of His supreme power" (Ibid.). Finally, theistic voluntarism can be expressed by the view that God's will is conditioned by reasons which "are —at least very often—inscrutable from man's point of view" (Ibid.). Colman rightly concludes that the second position described above is roughly Locke's position (Ibid., 38). For a further discussion of the controversy surrounding these theses, see Appendix 1 at the end of this chapter.

96 Locke, *Essays on the Law of Nature*, 111 and 113; f. 12.

97 Ibid., 187; f. 88.

98 Ibid., 111 and 113; f. 12.

99 Ibid.

100 Ibid., 187; f. 88.

101 Louis Berkhoff, *Systematic Theology* (Grand Rapids, MI: Wm. B. Eerdmans Publishing Co., 1939), 76.

102 Locke, *Essays on the Law of Nature*, 187 and 189; f. 89.

103 Ibid., 123-135.

104 Ibid., 123; f. 22 and 23.

105 Ibid., 189; f. 89.

106 Ibid., 189; f. 89 and 90.

107 Romans 13:1 (New International Version)

108 Locke, *Essays on the Law of Nature*, 119; f. 18 and 19.

109 Ibid., 191; f. 92.

110 Ibid., 191; f. 92.

111 Ibid.

112 Ibid.

113 Ibid., 193; f. 93.

114 Ibid.

115 Ibid., 193; f. 94.

116 Although I do not fully understand why he thinks that his view is open to this *reductio*, we can imagine a world in which (under a strict interpretation of the terms of his claim) I am obligated not to deprive a person of his property by fraud nor to murder another. But at this world I am holding the rifle of an individual who, one day, demands it from me in order to kill another person. In order to protect the other person from being murdered and to protect myself from being implicated in the murder, I lie to him by saying that I sold it to someone else. But since I am obligated not to lie, even though I save a life, I am still morally culpable for lying. This may be the kind of situation Locke may have wanted to avoid.

117 Ibid.

118 Ibid.

119 Aquinas, *Introduction to St. Thomas Aquinas*, Q. 94, Art. 5.

120 Ibid., Q. 94, Art. 2.

121 This relationship is normally one of material implication, although for first principles the relationship is stronger, e.g., entailment, analyticity, or identity. See, e.g., Robert B. Scott, "Five Types of Ethical Naturalism," *American Philosophical Quarterly* 17 (1980): 261ff.

122 Actually, what Locke has done is that he has shown that under a different interpretation of the terms of the first claim, viz., *there is no time in which a man would be permitted to violate the precepts of this law*, the conjuncts of the counterexample, i.e., *there is a possible situation at which it is true that men are obligated to perform incompatible actions at the same time*, are incompatible.

123 Locke, *Essays on the Law of Nature*, 197; f. 98.

124 Ibid., 197; f. 99.

125 Ibid., 201; f. 101.

126 Ibid., 199 and 201; f. 101.

127 For Additional information concerning the deduction Question 4, see Appendix B.

128 Locke, *Essays on the Law of Naure*, 197; f. 97.

129 Laslett, introduction to the Treatises, 34.

130 Laslett also underscores this view when he points out that the expression 'law of nature' in the *Treatises* is never analyzed (Laslett, introduction to the *Treatises*, 97).

131 Yolton, *Locke and the Compass of Human Understanding*, 16.

132 For further discussion of Locke's argument against innate ideas as they appear in the *Essays*, see Appendix C.

3
An Essay Concerning Human Understanding

Introduction

The purpose of this chapter is to present three doctrines of the *Essay*, which correspond to the three doctrines of the *Essays*. These are Locke's view of essences, his account of the nature of good and evil, and finally his explanation of moral goodness and evil. I will begin with Locke's view of innate ideas and relations, because much of what Locke has to say about the nature of goodness and moral goodness turns upon his view of innate ideas and relations. My primary purpose in chapter 3 will be only to present these doctrines; I will not compare them to the corresponding doctrines in the *Essays*. That will be the task for the fourth chapter.

Innate Ideas

Understanding why Locke begins the *Essay* with a polemic against innate ideas is crucial to understanding the *Essay* itself. Locke writes that the *Essay* is an "enquiry into the *Original* of those *Ideas*, Notions, or whatever else you please to call them [and an] endeavour to shew, what *Knowledge* the Understanding hath by those *Ideas*."[1] It is a document, then, that is (roughly) in two parts. First, we discover where our ideas come from. Second, given that we have accomplished the first part, we discuss what kind of knowledge can be based upon those ideas.

Accomplishing the first part is, of course, a complex issue. This was obvious to Locke as each edition of the *Essay* grew in length. The issues were, perhaps, more complex than Locke had anticipated. However, as Locke understood this first part, not only was it important to discuss his own views of the origin of ideas, but he was also, in some sense, obligated to discuss and argue against the current view of origin of ideas that his colleagues held. The current view was, of course, innate ideas.

Yolton outlines this view in a great deal of detail.[2] For example, most, if not all the criticism that Locke initially received from the *Essay* concerned his view of innate ideas. The reason is that the views which he specifically attacks, which are describe as the naive form of innate ideas, viz., that God wrote into or impressed upon the soul or mind at birth certain ideas and precepts for the guidance of life and the foundation of morality, were held by Richard Carpenter, Edward Stillingfleet, and Robert South. Such an attack was interpreted by them and others as a direct attack at the existing values of the society, and an attack against the belief in the existence of God.[3] Another, little known, attack came from Thomas Burnett roughly between 1697 and 1699.[4] Like Colman and others, Burnett accuses Locke of creating a straw man with reference to innate ideas.[5] Moreover, he explains that this principle of discerning good and evil without ratiocination is an ability humans have, and it is analogous to the ability we have to distinguish colors before reflection or ratiocination.[6]

Locke's discussion of innate ideas in the *Essay* is the object of mixed evaluation by contemporary writers. For example, Peter A. Schouls writes that Locke's attack against innate ideas made the *Essay* such a revolutionary document.[7] J. B. Schneewind confirms such a view when he writes:

> [I]n these few pages Locke attacked a widely held view about the source of moral knowledge and set up some tests that any satisfactory replacement of that view must pass. The attack was deeply offensive to received opinion not only because it ran counter to entrenched philosophical commonplaces but also because it was meant as a polemical interpretation of the biblical support for those commonplaces, Saint Paul's central dictum in Romans 2.14-15: For when the Gentiles, which have not the law, do by nature the things contained in the law, these, having not the law, are a law unto themselves: Which shew the work of the law written in their hearts, their consciences also bearing witness. . . .[8]

Yolton also points out that Locke's polemic against innate ideas was even "thought to be against a straw man."[9] However, Yolton has shown that Locke's attacks were directed at views, which were actually held in the seventeenth century.[10] Other scholars, e.g., J. L. Mackie,[11] follow Yolton in this regard. R. I. Aaron, however, writes that the first book of the *Essay* is "badly written [and] it emphasizes the relatively unimportant and neglects the important."[12] Moreover, John Colman, although convinced that Locke's polemic against innate ideas is "not a belaboring of the empty air;" nevertheless, it is "difficult to find a suitable target for the polemic."[13] John Marshall points out that "[T]he source of Locke's rejection of innatism is unclear."[14] Although this claim does not sit well with Locke's own quote above (nor even for that matter what Locke wrote in the *Essays*), Marshall does, however, make a connection not mentioned by many scholars, viz., Boyle's influence on Locke in this area of his thinking:

> [T]he source of Locke's rejection of innatism is unclear. It probably was influenced by a growing interest in scientific investigation in collaboration with Boyle and others in Oxford who argued that hypotheses should be generated by the thrust of empirical evidence; participation in experiments moved Boyle from scholasticism to empiricism. One of the major claims of those who argued for the existence of innate moral principles was that there were also innate speculative principles, and that these were largely principles of science.[15]

In the *Essay*, Locke's arguments against the existence of innate ideas and principles are in two parts (with a third part addressing some theistic considerations which I will not address). The first part concerns the existence of innate speculative principles. The second part concerns the existence of innate practical principles.

In his attack against innate speculative principles, Locke first states the position he will contend with and then he puts forth two different objections against it:

> [T]here is nothing more commonly taken for granted, than that there are certain Principles both *Speculative* and *Practical* (for they speak of both) universally agreed upon by all Mankind: which therefore they argue, must needs be the constant Impressions, which the Souls of Men receive in their first Beings, and which they bring into the World with them, as necessarily and really as they do any of their inherent Faculties.[16]

Locke begins his attack by denying that there are any speculative principles, e.g., "*Whatsoever is, is*; and '*Tis impossible for the same thing to be, and not to be*" that are universally assented to.[17] But Locke's attack shifts from one of denying that there are speculative principles universally assented to, to an attack that assumes that even if there are speculative principles universally assented to, this does not prove them innate.[18] The method Locke uses to expound his point is that there are other explanations, which do not employ innate ideas, and which show why men may come to a universal agreement to the things they assent to.[19]

Chapter 3 of the first Book of the *Essay* contains Locke's defense of the claim that there are no innate practical principles. Locke's basic reason for this claim is that, like speculative principles, there is no universal assent to practical principles. In fact, Locke writes that this is clearer in the case of practical principles than speculative principles:

> [I]f those speculative Maxims, whereof we discoursed in the foregoing Chapter, have not an actual universal assent from all Mankind, as we there proved, it is much more visible concerning *practical Principles*, that they *come short of an universal Reception*: and I think it will be hard to instance any one moral Rule, which can pretend to so general and ready an assent as, *What is, is*, or to be so manifest as Truth as this, *That it is impossible for the same thing to be and not to be*.[20]

Since this is the case about practical principles, Locke adds (in the same section) that "they are further removed from a title to be innate; and the doubt of their being native Impressions on the Mind, is stronger against those moral Principles than the other." This is, of course, as Locke assures us, not be taken to mean that they are not equally true. The truth-value of practical principles is determined in much the same way as speculative principles, viz., from a perception that arises from an understanding of the meanings of the subject and predicate. The difference between the two is that practical principles require reasoning and discourse:

> Not that it brings their Truth at all in question. They are equally true, though not equally evident. Those speculative Maxims carry their own Evidence with them: But moral Principles require Reasoning and Discourse, and some Exercise of the Mind, to discover the certainty of their Truth. They lie not open as natural Characters ingrave on the Mind; which if any such were, they must needs be visible by

themselves, and by their own light be certain and known to every Body.[21]

However, whereas Locke proposes some of the same reasons why practical principles are not innate as he does with speculative, Locke adds a new reason to the discussion against the existence of practical innate ideas:

> [A]nother Reason that makes me doubt of any innate practical Principles, is, That I think, *there cannot any one moral Rule be propos'd, whereof a Man may not justly demand a Reason*: which would be perfectly ridiculous and absurd, if they were innate, or so much as self-evident; which every innate Principle must needs be, and not need any Proof to ascertain its Truth, nor want any Reason to gain it Approbation.[22]

Locke's reasoning, at bottom, is that practical principles cannot be innate because there is no practical principle or moral rule, which is self-evidently true. As evidence of this, Locke writes that no matter which moral rule you propose, even the Christian Golden Rule, viz., That one should do as he would be done unto (and even where the meaning of the terms of the Golden Rule are made clear) someone can still without any absurdity ask a reason why this claim is true.[23] The reason is that, unlike (non-innate) speculative principles, "the truth of all these moral Rules, plainly depends upon some other antecedent to them, and from which they must be deduced, which could not be, if either they were innate, or so much as self-evident."[24]

The rest of this chapter in the *Essay* is spent looking at various objections to the two arguments he gives above. For example, concerning universal assent, Locke writes that there is often among various societies a general approbation of the same law. Locke writes that this is because God has "joined *Virtue* and publick Happiness together."[25] Because of this, then, "it is no wonder, that every one should, not only allow, but recommend, and magnifie those Rules to others, from whose observance of them, he is sure to reap Advantage to himself."[26] But this is no proof that such rules are innate. The reason is that self-interest and conveniences of life often make men applaud these rules.

Nevertheless, Locke adds, one may still reject such a line of reasoning when we consider the commitment men have to the Christian Golden Rule. For example, as I read Locke, one might ask whose conscience can advocate and who can sincerely teach to others that it is not a rule nor obligatory? Locke responds that such things "would be considered Madness, and contrary to that Interest Men sacrifice to, when they break it themselves."[27] Therefore, Locke remarks "Perhaps *Conscience* will be urged as checking us for such Breaches, and so the internal Obligation and Establishment of the Rule be preserved."[28] Locke, however, points out that there are other better explanations of why men may "come to assent to several Moral Rules, and be convinced of their Obligation"[29]:

> Others also may come to be of the same Mind, from their Education, Company, and Customs of their Country; which, *Persuasion however got, will serve to set conscience on work,* which is nothing else, but our own Opinion or Judgment of the Moral Rectitude or Pravity of our own Actions."[30]

Moreover, against the view of the general approbation many men give to those laws thought to be innate, Locke argues that if they really were innate and stamped on their minds, "I cannot see how any *Men*, should ever *transgress* those *Moral Rules, with Confidence,* and *Serenity. . . .*"[31] But, Locke adds, perhaps having seen such a sight himself during the civil war, "View but an Army at the sacking of a Town, and see what Observation, or Sense of Moral Principles, or what touch of Conscience, for all the Outrages they do. *Robberies, Murders, Rapes,* are the Sports of Men set at Liberty from Punishment and Censure."[32] Against this additional objection, however, Locke remarks that someone might argue that "it is no Argument, that the *Rule* is *not known, because* it is *broken.*"[33] Immediately after this, Locke admits that this objection would be "good, where Men, though they transgress, yet disown not the Law; where fear of Shame, Censure, or Punishment, carries the Mark of some awe it has upon them." However, this objection will not work because "the *generally allowed breach of it* [i.e., a rule] *any where,* I say, *is a proof, that it is not innate.*"[34] As evidence of this (and in the same passage), Locke asks us to consider the general prescription, "*Parents, preserve and cherish your Children.*" The reason is that it is the "most obvious deduction of Humane Reason, and conformable to the natural Inclinations of the greatest part of Men, fewest people have had the Impudence to deny, or Inconsideration to doubt of." Locke argues that if the above prescription is innate in virtue of these reasons, then this means that "Either, that it is an innate Principle; which upon all Occasions, excites and directs the Actions of all Men: Or else, that it is a Truth, which all Men have imprinted on their Minds, and which therefore they know, and assent to." However, in neither sense can we say that the above prescription is innate. First, it is not a principle, which influences all men's actions as evidence of those cultures that "neglect, abuse, nay and destroy their Children."[35] Second, that all know it to be false. The reason is that if this is a duty, it cannot be understand as a law without:

> a Law-maker, or without Reward and Punishment: So that it is impossible, that this, or any other practical Principle should be innate; *i.e.* be imprinted on the Mind as a Duty, without supposing the *Ideas* of God, of Law, of Obligation, of Punishment, of a life after this, innate. For that Punishment follows not, in this Life, the breach of this Rule; and consequently, that it has not the Force of a Law in Countries, where the generally allow'd Practice runs counter to it, is in itself evident.[36]

Although Locke considers a few more objections against innate ideas, including his protests against Lord Herbert of Cherbury (1581-1648), the ones I have presented will serve as a representative of the types of arguments Locke brought forward from the *Essays* and the kinds of arguments that Locke added to his arsenal against innate ideas. This discussion is important to keep in mind not only because this is part of what Locke discusses in the *Essay*, but, as we shall see in a later chapter, also because of the way it contributes to the formulation of his account of moral knowledge in the *Essay*.

The Nature of Essences

Locke's discussion of essences occurs throughout all four books of the *Essay*. However, the most concrete discussion of the nature of essences occurs in book 3 of the *Essay*, and in particular in chapter 3 of that book. There Locke not only discusses what he means by the term essence, but he also discusses two competing views of essences, viz., essences according to the Scholastics and, a view which he accepts, i.e., essences according to Corpuscularism, and he gives several arguments against the Scholastic view. Additionally, in this chapter and the chapters that follow in book 3, Locke appears to assume that both views are exclusive and exhaustive so that a disjunctive syllogism is forthcoming for the rejection of the Scholastic view. This view is confirmed because whereas he gives numerous reasons for rejecting the scholastic view of essences, he spends little or no time in defense of the Corpuscularian view of essences.

Locke's discussion of the nature of essences occurs within his inquiry of the nature of language. In chapter 3 of book 3, Locke asks why, if we assume that all things that exist are particular, we come to use general terms.[37] For Locke such a question is important because he wants to show that the Scholastic's insistence that if there are no universals (i.e., properties, relations or kinds), there would be no corresponding general terms. His argumentation encompasses three points. First, in chapter 3, since all things that exist are particulars it is reasonable to assume that the terms in our language should be particular too. But this is not the case. The far greatest numbers of words are general terms:

> ALL Things that exist, being Particulars, it may perhaps be thought reasonable, that Words, which ought to be conformed to Things, should be so too, I mean in their Signification: but yet we find quite the contrary. The far *greatest part of Words*, that make all Languages, *are general Terms*. . . .[38]

Additionally, general terms have come about not by neglect or chance but by reason and necessity. There are three reasons why this is so:

> [F]irst, *It is impossible, that every particular Thing should have a distinct peculiar Name.* . . . *[S]econdly*, If it were possible, *it would yet be useless*; because it would not serve to the chief end of language. . . .[39] *[T]hirdly*, But yet granting this also feasible; (which I think is not,) yet *a distinct Name for every particular Thing, would not be of any great use for the improvement of Knowledge* which though founded in particular Things, enlarges itself by general Views.[40]

Locke's second point attempts to answer the question of how general words and ideas come to be made:

> [T]he next thing to be considered is, *how general Words come to be made.* For since all things that exist are only particulars, how come we by general Terms, or where find we those general Natures they are supposed to stand for? Words become general, by being made the signs of general *Ideas*: and *Ideas* become general, by separating from them the circumstance of Time, and Place, and any other *Ideas*, that may determine them to this or that particular Existence. By this way of abstraction they are made capable of representing more Individuals than one; each of which, having in it a conformity to that abstract *Idea*, is (as we call it) of that sort.[41]

This passage suggests that Locke thinks there are two competing views of how general words come about. The first, which Locke only briefly alludes to, is that we have general ideas because there are universals or what he calls *general natures*. The view that Locke sets in opposition to the realist position can be characterized as "definition by abstraction."[42] This means that people enlarge their ideas by learning to recognize common elements that are associated with different things. People begin, as children, with a sense of particulars:

> There is nothing more evident, than that the *Ideas* of the Persons Children converse with, (to instance in them alone) are like the Persons themselves, only particular. The *Ideas* of the Nurse, and the Mother are well framed in their minds; and, like Pictures of them there, represent only those Individuals. The Names they first gave to them, are confined to these Individuals; and the names of *Nurse* and *Mamma*, the Child uses, determine themselves to those Persons.[43]

With the acquaintance of others and the enlargement of our experience, however, we begin to see that the terms we used to refer to only one individual have other referents:

> Afterwards, when time and a larger Acquaintance have made them observe, that there are a great many other Things in the world, that in some common agreements of Shape, and several other Qualities, resemble their Father and Mother, and those Persons they have been used to, they frame an *Idea*, which they find those many Particular do partake in; and to that they give, with others, the name *Man*, for Example. And *thus they come to have a general Name*, and a general *Idea*. Wherein they make nothing new, but only leave out of the complex *Idea* they had of *Peter* and *James*, *Mary* and *Jane*, that which is peculiar to each, and retain only what is common to them all.[44]

Locke's attack on the competing "realist" view is directed at its metaphysical presupposition:

> To return to general Words, it is plain, by what has been said, That *General and Universal*, belong not to the real existence of things; but *are the Inventions and Creatures of the Understanding*, made by it for its own use, *and concern only Signs*, whether Words, or *Ideas*. Words are general, as has been said, when used, for Signs of general *Ideas*, and so are applicable indifferently to many particular Things; and Ideas are general when they are set up, as the Representatives of many particular Things: but universality belongs not to things them-

selves, which are all of them particular in their Existence, even those Words, and *Ideas*, which in their signification, are general. When therefore we quit Particulars, the Generals that rest, are only Creatures of our own making, their general Nature being nothing but the Capacity they are put into by the Understanding, of signifying or representing many particulars. For the signification they have, is nothing but a relation, that by the mind of Man is added to them.[45]

This passage suggests that the appeal to some sort of metaphysical status for universals presupposes that such an assumption is an essential part of our explanation of our having "general" ideas. But for Locke, at least, we do not need to posit the metaphysical existence of general natures. The best explanation for the existence of these impressions of complex ideas is not the existence of general natures "but in the leaving out something, that is peculiar to each Individual; and retaining so much of those particular complex *Ideas*, of several particular Existences, as they are found to agree in?"[46] General or universal natures, then, belong not to the real existence of things.

Locke's third point continues his discussion of the origin of general words; however, it is also coupled with an attack against Scholastic essences. His discussion directs us toward the question, *"What kind of signification it is that general Words have"*:

That then which general Words signify, is a sort of Things; and each of them does that, by being a sign of an abstract *Idea* in the mind, to which *Idea*, as Things existing are found to agree, so they come to be ranked under that name; or, which is all one, be of that sort.[47]

First, general words signify sorts. Here Locke becomes a little more specific about the relationship between our words and the abstract ideas they are signs of. Earlier, Locke expounded, in answer to the question of how general words come to be made, that general words are the signs or marks of general ideas, which he also explained that both are the inventions and creatures of the understanding. But now Locke modifies his view of what general words signify. What he now says is this: the ideas that general words are the signs of are not just the marks or signs of general ideas, but they signify general ideas that are sets or classes.

Second, Locke remarks that these sorts or classes are used to rank or classify an object or thing. An object becomes classified just in case the object has a property or properties to gain class membership. Locke states that if it gains membership, then it will be ranked under the general word that signifies the sort or class. In fact, Locke says that the object, in virtue of gaining class membership of the general idea or class, earns the *right* to be ranked under the general word that is a sign or the general idea.

One implication for Scholastic essences emerges in his next remark: "Whereby it is evident, that the *Essences of* the *sorts, or* (if the Latin word pleases better) *Species* of Things, are nothing else but these abstract *Ideas*."[48] Here Locke argues that from the discussion above, it follows (somehow) that the essences of sort or species are identical to the general ideas or classes that general words signify. Locke reasons that this is so because:

> For the having the Essence of any Species, being that which makes anything to be of that Species, and the conformity to the *Idea*, to which the name is annexed, being that which gives a right to that name, the having the Essence, and the having that Conformity, must needs be the same thing: Since to be of any Species, and to have a right to the name of that Species, is all one.[49]

Although it is not clear why Locke wants to argue that the essences of species are identical to (his view of) abstract ideas, such a claim appears to be necessary to draw the following conclusions:

> From whence it is easy to observe, that the essences of the sorts of things, and consequently, the sorting of Things, is the Workmanship of the Understanding, since it is the Understanding that abstracts and makes those general *Ideas*.[50]

On the Scholastic view, claims, which express essences or species in a judgment of a subject and predicate form, e.g., man is a rational animal, the predicate (i.e., is a rational animal), which expresses the genus and difference of the subject,[51] corresponds to a universal or general nature. Locke attempts to counter this by arguing that since all general abstract ideas are created by us, and since the essences of sorts or species are qualitatively identical to general abstract ideas,[52] then both the essences of the sorts and the sorting of things are the workmanship of the understanding, i.e., inventions and creatures of the understanding. On Locke's account, then, universals do not exist in nature. Rather, they refer only to abstract ideas in the mind.

R. H. Woolhouse underscores the same point. He discusses many of Locke's arguments against the Scholastic's explanation of the classification of things. He calls them anti-essentialist arguments.[53] In place of essentialism, Woolhouse argues that Locke defends a relativism with reference to the classification of things. By this he means that Locke defends the view that "there are no kinds . . . . [Moreover] independently of human classifications there is no such thing as the way things really are."[54] Concerning the passage above, Woolhouse writes:

> [A]s against this, Locke puts the relativist argument that whether a certain property is essential to a particular thing does not depend on its being a fact about the world that the thing belongs to a certain lowest kind and manifests a certain Essence. It depends, first, on how we decide to classify it, and, second, on what we have decided the essential properties of that class to be.[55]

Locke ends this discussion by drawing a further conclusion that since our abstract ideas of names are identical to essences of these names, as he attempted to show with the word man, it follows that since we are the creators of our abstract terms we are also the creators of those essences, which we use to classify and sort things. This point drives home Locke's insistence that Scholastic essences do not exist and are not needed to explain why we classify things the way we do.

Although Locke denies the existence of Scholastic essences, he does not deny that essences of some sort do exist:

> I would not here be thought to forget, much less to deny, that Nature, in the Production of Things, makes several of them alike: there is nothing more obvious, especially in the Races of Animals, and all Things propagated by Seed. But yet, I think, we may say, the *sorting* of them under Names, *is the Workmanship of the Understanding, taking occasion from the similitude* it observes amongst them, to make abstract general *Ideas*, and set them up in the mind, with Names annexed to them, as Patterns, or Forms, (for in that sense the word Form has a very proper signification,) to which, as particular Things existing are found to agree, so they come to be of that Species, have that Denomination, or are put into that *Classis*.[56]

Here Locke follows Boyle closely. Boyle writes:

> And so, though I shall for brevity's sake retain the word form, yet I would be understood to mean by it not a real substance distinct from matter, but only the matter itself of a natural body, considered with its peculiar manner of existence, which I think may not inconveniently be called either its specific or its denominating state, or its essential modification - or, if you would have me express it in one word, its

stamp. For such a convention of accidents is sufficient to perform the offices that are necessarily required in what men call a form, since it makes the body such as it is, making it appertain to this or that determinate species of bodies, and discriminating it from all other species of bodies whatsoever. . . .[57]

In the rest of this chapter Locke does basically two things. He continues his attack against the Scholastic view of essences, and he offers an account of the signification of the term essence.

The first comment against the Scholastic outlook is worded in such a way that it is not certain what the conclusion is:

[N]or will any one wonder, that I say these *Essences*, or abstract *Ideas*, (which are the measures of Names, and the boundaries of Species) are *the Workmanship of the Understanding*, who considers, that at least the complex ones are often, in several Men, different Collections of simple *Ideas*. . . .[58]

I think Locke is arguing, as he does so earlier, that given the alternatives for the best explanation of why we have abstract ideas, i.e., either Scholastic essences or essences created by the understanding, the latter appears to be the best explanation.

As reasons for his conclusion, Locke gives two examples in the same section of the last quotation. The first example concerns the abstract idea of covetousness. The species of covetousness is determined by the understanding because whoever "considers that at least the complex ones are often, in several Men, different Collections of simple *Ideas*: and therefore what is Covetousness to one Man, which is not so to another." The point is that the best explanation for the determination of the abstract idea of covetousness is the fact that men create it themselves because if it were determined in some way by a Scholastic essence, then there would only be one concept which most if not all men would ascribe to.[59]

Locke's second example concerns the abstract idea of man:

Nay, even in Substances, where their abstract *Ideas* seem to be taken from the Things themselves, they are not constantly the same; no not in that Species, which is most familiar to us, and with which we have the most intimate acquaintance: It having been more than once doubted, whether the Foetus[60] born of a Woman were a *Man*, even so far, as that it hath been debated, whether it were, or were not to be nourished and baptized: which could not be, if the abstract *Idea* or Essence, to which the Name Man belonged, were of Nature's making; and were not the uncertain and various Collection of simple *Ideas*, which the Understanding puts together, and then abstracting it, affixed a name to it.

Again, Locke reasons that the best explanation for the determination of our idea of man is not because there actually exists a Scholastic form or essence for man, but it is the creation of our understanding.[61] Therefore, like the word "covetousness," what the term "man" means to one person may not mean the same thing to another. This view appears, though, to have the implication that just as each particular object, which is the result of its specific or its denominating state, has its own particular essence, ideas, which are distinct, are also distinct essences. Locke wraps this argument up with such a thought:

> So that in truth *every distinct abstract* Idea, *is a distinct Essence*: and the names that stand for such distinct *Ideas*, are the names of Things essentially different. Thus a Circle is as essentially different from an Oval, as a Sheep from a Goat: and Rain is as essentially different from Snow, as Water from Earth; that abstract *Idea* which is the Essence of one, being impossible to be communicated to the other. And thus any two abstract *Ideas*, that in any part vary one from another, with two distinct names annexed to them, constitute two distinct sorts, or, if you please, *Species*, as essentially different, as any two of the most remote, or opposite in the World.[62]

Locke's discussion moves from this first argument to a discussion of what he takes to be the proper meaning of the term "essence." It is here also that Locke makes use of the distinction between real and nominal essence.

Of the term "essence" in general, Locke writes:

> [*F*]*irst, Essence* may be taken for the very being of anything, whereby it is, what it is. And thus the real internal, but generally in Substances, unknown Constitution of Things, whereon their discoverable Qualities depend, may be called their *Essence*. This is the proper original signification of the Word, as is evident from the formation of it."[63]

Here, although Locke adds more to what he means by the term "essence," he still leaves us with precious little to go on. First, he reiterates what we were already told earlier, viz., that the term "essence," even in its non-Scholastic form, refers to "the very being of anything, whereby it is, what it is." This is nothing new. However, he does add two other things. First, the individual essence of each external object is unknown.[64] Second, the qualities that we use to create species are qualities that depend, in some sense, upon the unknown constitution of things.

Thus having made a distinction between the qualities that essences have which are unknown and those qualities, which are used to categorize things, which are dependent upon the unknown qualities, Locke now makes his famous distinction between real and nominal essences at the end of the passage quoted above. However, just in case we have not made the connection ourselves, immediately following III. iii. 15 in the *Essay*, Locke makes clear the connection between what we use to categorize and classify (sort) things and the general name we give to what we categorize:

> [B]*etween the Nominal Essence, and the Name,* there is so *near* a *Connexion,* that the Name of any sort of Things cannot be attributed to any particular Being, but what has this *Essence,* whereby it answers that abstract *Idea,* whereof that Name is the Sign.[65]

This is the very same point that Locke made earlier, only the terms have been changed. He argued that if something satisfies the criteria of the Class, then it has a right to be called by the name of the class. Now, in this passage, the criterion by which we categorize things is called the nominal essence. Locke, therefore, reiterates the connection between the name of the nominal essence and the nominal essence, i.e., nothing can be called by the name of a nominal essence unless it satisfies the criteria of the nominal essence.

Having made the distinction between nominal and real essence, and having made explicit the connection between classes (sorts) and the term nominal essence, Locke finally gives us the clearest statement in the *Essay* of what he takes Corpuscularian essences to be:

> [C]oncerning the real Essences of corporeal Substances, (to mention those only,) there are, if I mistake not, two Opinions. The one is of those, who using the word *Essence,* for they know not what, suppose a certain number of those Essences, according to which, all natural things are made, and wherein they do exactly every one of them partake, and so become of this or that *Species.* The other, and more rational Opinion, is of those, who look on all natural Things to have a real, but unknown Constitution of their insensible Parts, from which flow those sensible Qualities, which serve us to distinguish them one from another, according as we have Occasion to rank them into sorts, under common Denominations. The former of these Opinions, which

supposes these *Essences*, as a certain number of Forms or Molds, wherein all natural Things, that exist, are cast, and do equally partake, has, I imagine, very much perplexed the Knowledge of natural Things.[66]

First, Locke tells us what essences are not. Essences are not the sort of things that there are just a certain number of. This refers to the Scholastic doctrine that there are only a finite number of essences that exist which account for all the different species that exist. In fact, the ones that do exist act like molds.

Locke also adds that such a view has very much perplexed the knowledge of natural things. Although he does not say how this has perplexed the knowledge of natural things, Boyle discusses this doctrine at length and arrives at the same conclusion. The controversy, as Boyle describes it, concerns "whether or no the forms of natural things . . . be in generation *educed*, as they speak [i.e., the views of the Scholastics], out of the power of the matter."[67] Boyle responds with three different arguments one of which is particularly interesting:

> For if the form produced in generation be, as they would have it, a substance that was not before to be found anywhere out of that portion of matter wherewith it constitutes the generated body, I say that either it must be produced by refining or subtiliating some parts of the matter into form, or else it must be produced out of nothing—that is, created (for I see no third way how a substance can be produced *de novo*).[68]

Boyle denies both disjuncts. He denies the former disjunct first by pointing out that if it is true, then "the form [will] be indeed a substance . . . since matter however subtiliated is matter still. . . ."[69] But, as Boyle immediately points out, the Scholastics cannot accept this because they also "teach that the form is not made of anything of the matter."

Boyle turns next to the latter disjunct mentioned above:

> But if they will not allow, as indeed they do not, that the substantial form is made of anything that is material, they must give me leave to believe that it is produced out of nothing, till they show me how a substance can be produced otherwise, that existed nowhere before.[70]

He denies this disjunct by pointing out that since no one believes, i.e., neither he himself nor the Scholastics, that a natural agent has the power to create matter, why, then, would we believe that they could create something like a form out of nothing:

> And since it is confessed on all sides that no natural agent can produce the least atom of matter, it is strange they should in generation allow every physical agent the power of producing a form—which, according to them, is not only a substance but a far nobler one than matter—and thereby attribute to the meanest creatures that power of creating substances which the ancient naturalists thought too great to be ascribed to God himself, and which indeed is too great to be ascribed to any other than him; and therefore some schoolmen and philosophers have derived forms immediately from God, but this is not only to desert Aristotle and the Peripatetic philosophy they would seem to maintain, but to put Omnipotence upon working I know not how many thousand miracles every hour, to perform that (I mean the generation of bodies of new denominations) in a supernatural way which seems the most familiar effect of nature in her ordinary course.[71]

In the end, Boyle writes that such doctrines are so inexplicable that it is no wonder so many men have worked on such problems:

> [T]he manner how forms are educed out of the power of the matter, according to that part of the doctrine of forms wherein the Schools generally enough agree, is a thing so inexplicable that I wonder not it hath put acute men upon several hypotheses to make it out.[72]

After Locke tells us what essences are not in III. iii. 17 of the *Essay*, he states what they are. First, all natural things have a real constitution of their parts. By using the term "real," Locke appears to be setting his view apart from those who might teach that being or existence is somehow dependent upon knowing it. Of course, this applies directly to the human consciousness, but for Locke it may even apply to God. In fact, Boyle writes that God created matter and put it into motion.[73] Locke also mentions that these real things, whatever they are, are made up of parts. This refers to the Corpuscularian doctrine that everything can be reduced to matter in motion. In fact, as Boyle teaches, "the matter of all natural bodies is the same, namely, a substance extended and impenetrable."[74]

In this same passage, Locke adds that these parts are unknown and insensible. Here we must not take Locke to mean that the terms "unknown" and "insensible" are two separate predicates modifying the term "parts." Instead, Locke is arguing that the corpuscles are unknown in the sense of being directly imperceivable. But this does not mean that Boyle and Locke were not convinced that there was no evidence at all for the existence of corpuscles. The reason is that both Locke and Boyle believed that corpuscles were needed to explain why objects interact with our senses the way they do, i.e., corpuscles causally contribute to those things, which causally interact with our senses.[75]

Locke's example of this sort of reasoning is mentioned in this passage. The corpuscles of which each object is made up are the best explanation for why we can empirically perceive the sensible qualities which he says "flow from" the corpuscles. These sensible qualities, as Locke relates, are what "serve us to distinguish them [i.e., each object] one from another, according as we have Occasion to rank them into sorts, under common Denominations."[76]

Although Boyle talks in these terms, he also describes many interesting experiments and makes clear that the results of the experiment are best explicated in terms of corpuscles and not substantial forms. One such experiment, perhaps the easiest to understand, involves turpentine:

> But among all my trials about the reintegration of bodies, that which seemed to succeed best was made upon turpentine: for having taken some ounces of this, very pure and good, and put it into a glass retort,[77] I distilled so long with a very gentle fire, till I had separated it into a good quantity of very clear liquor and a caput mortuum very dry and brittle; then breaking the retort, I powdered the caput mortuum, which when it was taken out was exceeding sleek and transparent enough and very red, but being powdered appeared of a pure yellow colour. This powder I carefully mixed with the liquor that had been distilled from it, which immediately dissolved part of it into a deep red; but by further digestion, in a large glass exquisitely stopped, that colour began to grow fainter, though the remaining part of the powder (except a very little, proportionable to so much of the liquor as may be supposed to have been wasted by evaporation and transfusion out of one vessel into another) be perfectly dissolved, and so well reunited to the more fugitive parts of the concrete, that there is scarce any that by the smell, or tasted, or consistence, would take it for other than good and laudable turpentine.[78]

What this experiment is supposed to show is described earlier by Boyle:

> if we could reproduce a body which has been deprived of its substantial form, you would, I suppose, think it highly probable, if not more

than probable, that . . . that which is commonly called the form of a
concrete, which gives it its being and denomination and form whence
all its qualities are, in the vulgar philosophy, by I know not what inexplicable ways, supposed to flow, may be in some bodies but a
characterization or modification of the matter they consist of, whose
parts, by being so and so disposed in relation to each other, constitute
other bodies of very differing natures from that of the concrete whose
parts they formerly were, and which may again result or be produced
after its dissipation and seeming destruction, by the reunion of the
same component particles, associated according to their former disposition.[79]

This is a good example because turpentine, also called oil of turpentine, or spirit of turpentine, is a substance which naturally occurs in
certain trees.[80] Boyle attempts to show that if we assume that turpentine
is a substance which occurs naturally and has its own substantial form,
which gives it its being and denomination and from where all its qualities are supposed to flow, then if we could reproduce the turpentine
which has been deprived of its substantial form, this would show that
turpentine exists by a modification of the matter it consists of, and not
by a substantial form. And indeed, as Boyle's experiment seems to
show, after it is broken down into its parts, it can be recreated into the
very substance from the parts it had been broken down into. In fact,
Boyle reports that the turpentine was "so well reunited to the more fu-
gitive parts of the concrete, that there is scarce any that by the smell, or
tasted, or consistence, would take it for other than good and laudable
turpentine."[81]

The final description of his view of essences that Locke gives is
that from the matter which constitutes the essence of things "flow those
sensible Qualities, which serve us to distinguish them one from another, according as we have Occasion to rank them into sorts, under
common Denominations."[82] Even though this is perhaps the most interesting part about this doctrine, neither Locke nor Boyle, spend much
time explicating this view. Of course, of the two, Locke spends the
most time at least making clear the distinctions between the primary
and secondary qualities of objects. But apart from making these distinctions, what Locke says about the relationship between these two qualities is precious little. For example, in one place, Locke briefly describes
this relationship as one of dependence:

[T]he First of these, as has been said, I think, may be properly called
real Original, or *primary Qualities*; because they are in the things

themselves, whether they are perceived or not: and upon their different Modifications it is, that the secondary Qualities depend.[83]

In the context in which this passage occurs, Locke proceeds as if we are supposed to know what he means. Fortunately, in an early passage, we find the following expansion of his thought:

> [I] have, in what just goes before, been engaged in Physical Enquiries a little further than, perhaps, I intended. But, it being necessary, to make the Nature of Sensation a little understood, and to make the *difference between the Qualities in bodies, and the* Ideas *produced by them in the Mind*, to be distinctly conceived, without which it were impossible to discourse intelligibly of them; I hope, I shall be pardoned this little Excursion into Natural Philosophy, it being necessary in our present Enquiry, to distinguish the *primary*, and *real Qualities* of Bodies, which are always in them (viz. Solidity, Extension, Figure, Number, and Motion, or Rest; and are sometimes perceived by us, viz. when the Bodies they are in, are big enough singly to be discerned) from those *secondary* and *imputed Qualities*, which are but the Powers of several Combinations of those primary ones, when they operate, without being distinctly discerned; whereby we may also come to know what *Ideas* are, and what are not Resemblances of something really existing in the Bodies, we denominate from them.[84]

What Locke seems to mean by the claim that secondary qualities are dependent upon the primary qualities has something to do with the notion of power. That is, Locke explicates secondary qualities in terms of "the Powers of several Combinations of those primary ones, when they operate, without being distinctly discerned." What this appears to mean is that when corpuscles or matter join in a certain way, the combination of the corpuscles and their primary qualities have a power to produce certain kinds of ideas in beings with senses sensitive enough to pick up the secondary qualities.[85]

After this, Locke's gives us two final arguments against the existence of Scholastic essences:

> The frequent Productions of Monsters, in all the Species of Animals, and of Changelings, and other strange Issues of humane Birth, carry with them difficulties, not possible to consist with this *Hypothesis*: Since it is as impossible, that two Things, partaking exactly of the same real *Essence*, should have different Properties, as that two Figures partaking of the same real *Essence* of a Circle, should have different Properties. But were there no other reason against it, yet the *supposition of Essences, that cannot be known*; and the making of

them nevertheless to be that, which distinguishes the Species of Things, *is* so *wholly useless,* and unserviceable to any part of our Knowledge, that alone were sufficient, to make us lay it by; and content our selves with such *Essences* of the Sorts or Species of Things, as come within the reach of our Knowledge: which, when seriously considered, will be found, as I have said, to be nothing else, but those abstract complex *Ideas,* to which we have annexed distinct general Names.[86]

First, then, Scholastic essences do not exist because their existence is incompatible with the observed incidence of "changelings" and the like. The second reason he gives is that the existence of Scholastic essences is explanatorily irrelevant. They are *"wholly useless,* and unserviceable to any part of our Knowledge" because they are unknown or imperceivable.[87]

Locke's final argument against the existence of Scholastic essences is directed at their view that essences or forms are all ingenerable and incorruptible.[88] The Scholastics take this view from Aristotle, who taught the same in *Metaphysics.*[89] However, following Aristotle in the *Metaphysics,*[90] the Scholastics have two different views of essences or forms.[91] First, Aristotle uses the term "form" in the sense of the inner nature of a thing, which is expressed in its definition or the plan of its structure.[92] The term "form" in this sense, is better expressed as "essence." The term "form" is also used to refer to the final cause in nature, i.e., to the common structure or universal formula of a species. Ross points out, it is to this universal formula that "individual members of the species strive without conscious purpose to give a fresh individual embodiment."[93] The latter sense of "form" is also known as the universal kind, which I will discuss in more detail in the next chapter. However, the terms "ingenerable and incorruptible" only apply to the latter. In other words, it was recognized by Aristotle that a form in the former sense, i.e., the essence, could perish, although he thought that the form of a species, i.e., the universal kind, was eternal.

Locke's attack appears to be directed at the form or essence of the species, i.e., the universal kind. This is so because he makes this explicit a few sentences later:

For, whatever becomes of *Alexander* and *Bucephalus,* the *Ideas* to which *Man* and *Horse* are annexed, are supposed nevertheless to remain the same; and so the *Essences* of those Species are preserved whole and undestroy'd, whatever Changes happen to any, or all of the Individuals of those *Species.* By this means the *Essence* of a *Spe-*

cies rests safe and entire, without the existence of so much as one Individual of that kind.[94]

He simply argues that the Scholastic view cannot be true because essences begin and perish when an object begins or perishes. That is, Locke seems to argue that from experience, the best explanation for the existence of matter and the changes it can go through is the real constitution of things, i.e., the corpuscularian essences described by Boyle, which begin when matter and motion combine to form an object. Contrary to the Scholastic view, when an object is destroyed in a Boyleian universe, the real constitution of the object, which is at the basis of the object, is also destroyed. Locke adds that even though an object may perish, its elements, viz., the corpuscles, will be combined with other things. What we call grass and the corpuscles which it is made up of will be destroyed, i.e., broken down, and recombined to make up the flesh of a sheep after it is eaten by the sheep, and so on.

After setting his own view of essences apart from the Scholastic essences, in the same passage, Locke discusses briefly a sense in which essences can be said incorruptible: "But *Essences* being taken for *Ideas*, established in the Mind, with Names annexed to them, they are supposed to remain steadily the same, whatever mutations the particular Substances are liable to." The key to understanding this sentence is to see that Locke is talking about nominal essences, i.e., those abstract ideas that we create to classify substances. The abstract idea, i.e., the nominal essence, then, which we form from primary and secondary qualities of the object, is that essence, which is supposed to remain steady whatever happens to the particular. But how can it remain steady even though the object is destroyed? The answer is that it will remain steady in our minds as long as we need to use the nominal essence to refer either to this particular object or to a set of which this object is a member.

This discussion leads us to another important point. In some cases, the real and the nominal essence are the same. However, Locke makes clear that this applies only to simple ideas and modes and not to substances:

> [*E*]*ssences* being thus distinguished into *Nominal and Real*, we may further observe, that *in* the Species of *simple* Ideas *and Modes*, they *are always the same*: But *in substances, always quite different*. Thus, a Figure including a Space between three Lines, is the real, as well as nominal *Essence* of a Triangle; it being not only the abstract *Idea* to which the general Name is annexed, but the very *Essentia*, or Being,

of the thing it self, that Foundation from which all its Properties flow, and to which they are all inseparably annexed.[95]

The point here is clearer with respect to modes than to simple ideas.[96] Locke's point about simple ideas is less clear than his point about modes. In the passage above (and what follows it), Locke only deals with modes.

Modes (whether simple or mixed) are made up of simple ideas joined together arbitrarily to form some sort of concept, or complex idea:

> we are now in the next place to consider those we call *Mixed Modes*, such are the Complex *Ideas*, we mark by the names *Obligation*, *Drunkenness*, a *Lye*, etc. which consisting of several Combinations of simple *Ideas* of different kinds, I have called *Mixed Modes*, to distinguish them from the more simple Modes, which consist only of simple *Ideas* of the same kind. These mixed Modes being also such Combinations of simple *Ideas*, as are not looked upon to be characteristical Marks of any real Beings that have a steady existence, but scattered and independent *Ideas*, put together by the Mind, are thereby distinguished from the complex *Ideas* of Substances.[97]

But how are we to understand Locke's point that the nominal and real essence of a mixed mode are the same? Moreover, why does he consider mixed modes to be essences at all? Locke answers both questions in III. iii. 18 of the *Essay*. First of all, a mixed mode is an essence in the sense that, like a real essence, the ideas, which form it are "that Foundation from which all its Properties flow, and to which they are all inseparably annexed." Second, the real and the nominal essence of a mixed mode are the same in the sense that the ideas used to form the idea are simple ideas which are taken arbitrarily from different sources, and as such, the concept does not have any firm foundation in reality except for its own logical consistency.

So, take, e.g., Locke's own example of a triangle. A triangle is formed, according to Locke, from the simple ideas gained from both sensation and reflection.[98] For example, from sensation and reflection we get the simple ideas of space and lines (a "line," I imagine, can be derived somehow from the simple idea of extension). From these basic ideas we can create the following complex idea of triangle. This is done when we arrange only three lines on three distinct noncollinear points. The union of the segments created by the points is called a triangle. Now from this point, or as Locke writes, its foundation, we can derive

all of the properties of a triangle. For example, it is a property of trian-
gles that the sum of two of its angles is less than 180°. This property
like many more can be demonstrated assuming a Euclidean geometry, a
geometry Locke seemed to be familiar with. In fact, Locke believes this
sort of demonstration is available for all mixed modes, including our
complex ideas of morality. However, this sort of demonstration or deduction is not available to complex ideas of substances.

Why are substances different? That is, why isn't the real and
nominal essence the same in substance? Again, part of the answer is
that the real essence is unknowable in substances. Locke makes this
point immediately after his description of the triangle:

> But it is far otherwise concerning that parcel of Matter, which makes
> the Ring on my Finger, wherein these two Essences are apparently
> different. For, it is the real Constitution of its insensible Parts, on
> which depend all those properties of Colour, Weight, Fusibility,
> Fixedness, *etc.* which are to be found in it. Which Constitution we
> know not; and so having no particular *Idea* of, having no Name that
> is the Sign of it. But yet it is its Colour, Weight, Fusibility, Fixed-
> ness, etc. which make it to be *Gold*, or gives it a right to that Name,
> which is therefore its nominal *Essence*. Since nothing can be call'd
> *Gold*, but what has a Conformity of Qualities to that abstract complex
> *Idea*, to which that Name is annexed.[99]

However, later on in the *Essay*, Locke adds that because of the unknowability of essences, there is no way to tell which secondary qualities, i.e., those qualities which become simple ideas if sensible, have a
necessary union or inconsistency with one another:

> [T]he *Ideas*, that our complex ones of Substances are made up of, and
> about which our Knowledge, concerning Substances, is most em-
> ploy'd, are those of their *secondary Qualities*; which depending all
> (as has been shewn) upon the primary Qualities of their minute and
> insensible parts; or if not upon them, upon something yet more re-
> mote from our Comprehension, 'tis impossible we should know,
> which have a necessary union or inconsistency one with another:
> For, not knowing the Root they spring from, not knowing what size,
> figure, and texture of Parts they are, on which depend and from
> which result those Qualities which make our complex *Idea* of Gold,
> 'tis impossible we should know what other Qualities result from, or
> are incompatible with, the same Constitution of the insensible parts
> of *Gold*; and so consequently must always *co-exist* with that complex
> *Idea* we have of it, or else are *inconsistent* with it.[100]

To sum up this section, Locke writes that the whole business of the Scholastic emphasis on genera and species and their essences amounts to no more than this: "That men making abstract *Ideas*, and settling them in their Minds, with names annexed to them, do thereby enable themselves to consider Things, and discourse of them, as it were in bundles, for the easier and readier improvement, and communication of their Knowledge, which would advance but slowly, were their Words and Thoughts confined only to Particulars."[101] Locke's comes to this conclusion in basically two ways. First, he attacks Scholastic essences by generating arguments against the existence of Scholastic essences. Second, he attacks the Scholastic view of essences by arguing that even if we assume for the sake of argument that they exist, Scholastic essences are still explanatorily irrelevant.

From these arguments we see Locke's thoughts emerge about what appears to be the proper Boylean view of essences: real essences do exist, i.e., everything that exists can be reduced to clusters of corpuscles moving in a certain way. However, these essences do not form species. Instead, given the way that God constructs our senses, we form species based on the secondary qualities, which are themselves dependent upon the primary qualities of the corpuscles.

The Nature of Relations

Before I move to discuss Locke's views of the nature of good and evil and, eventually, his view of the nature of moral goodness and evil, I must discuss his view of the nature of relations. For both discussions presuppose Locke's view of relations. In fact, as I will show in the following sections, Locke characterizes both nonmoral goodness and evil, and moral goodness and evil, as relations. To understand what he means and the important implications that this discussion has for the nature of goodness and evil, we need to first consider what Locke has to say about relations in general.

According to Locke, a relation is this: "[T]he nature therefore of Relation, consists in the referring, or comparing two things, on to another; from which comparison, one or both comes to be denominated."[102] This comparison may be expressed whenever the mind perceives that an object has some kind of characteristic, which leads the mind to another object distinct from the first one. Locke gives the following example of what he means:

Thus when the mind considers *Cajus*, as such a positive Being, it takes nothing into that *Idea*, but what really exists in Cajus; v.g. when I consider him, as a Man, I have nothing in my Mind, but the complex *Idea* of the Species, Man. So likewise, when I say Cajus is a white Man, I have nothing but the bare consideration of a Man, who hath that white Colour. But when I give Cajus the name *Husband*, I intimate some other Person: and when I give him the name *Whiter*, I intimate some other thing: in both cases my Thought is led to something beyond Cajus, and there are two things brought into consideration.[103]

Relations, however, will only be established when both objects exist together, in some sense. For example, if one of the objects are removed or cease to exist, then the relation ceases: "And if either of those things be removed, or cease to be, the Relation ceases, and the Denomination consequent to it, though the other receive in itself no alteration at all. v.g. *Cajus*, whom I consider to-day as a Father, ceases to be so to morrow, only by the death of his Son, without any alteration made in himself."[104]

Working from this basic understanding of what a relation is, Locke argues for four points about relations. First, there is no simple idea, substance, mode, or relation, which is not capable of almost an infinite number of relations in reference to other things. For example,

One single Man may at once be concerned in, and sustain all these following *Relations*, and many more, *viz.* Father, Brother, Son, Grandfather, Grandson, Father-in-law, Son-in-law, Husband, Friend, Enemy, Subject, General, Judge, Patron, Client, Professor, European, English-man, Islander, Servant, Master, Possessor, Captain, Superior, Inferior, Bigger, Less, Older, Younger, Contemporary, Like, Unlike, *etc.* to an almost infinite number. . . .[105]

Locke's second point is contained in the following passage: "This farther may be considered concerning *Relation*, That though it be not contained in the real existence of Things, but something extraneous, and superinduced: yet the *Ideas* which relative Words stand for, are often clearer, and more distinct, than of those Substances to which they do belong."[106] What I take Locke to be arguing here is that, as ideas go, we can have a full and evident perception of relations; additionally, this type of perception is somehow related to a metaphysical point that Locke wants to make, viz., that relations do not exist independently of the operation of the mind.

Locke appears to make a similar point in II. xii of the *Essay*. Here Locke discusses what he takes to be three different kinds of complex ideas that we have, viz., complex ideas of modes, substances, and relations. Of complex ideas, in general, Locke writes that it is a power the mind has to "put together those *Ideas* it has, [i.e. simple ideas which it passively receives] and *make new complex ones*, which it never received so united."[107] This means that most of the complex ideas we have are ideas, which we create. This is particularly true of mixed modes and relations. Of mixed modes and relations, Locke writes:

> [*S*]*econdly, Mixed Modes and Relations*, having no other *reality*, but what they have in the Minds of Men, there is nothing more required to this kind of *Ideas*, to make them *real*, but that they be so framed, that there be a possibility of existing conformable to them.[108]

In contrast to this, Locke discusses the way complex ideas of substances are formed. For example, whereas mixed modes and relations are "voluntary Collections of simple *Ideas*, which the mind puts together, without any reference to any real Archetypes, or standing Patterns, existing anywhere. . . ,"[109] our complex ideas of substances are created with the intention to represent actual things:

> [*T*]*hirdly*, Our *complex* Ideas *of Substances*, being made all of them in reference to Things existing without us, and intended to be Representations of Substances, as they really are, are no farther *real*, than as they are such Combinations of simple *Ideas*, as are really united, and co-exist in Things without us.[110]

Herein lies the difference in clearness between our ideas of mixed modes and relations and our complex ideas of substances. Mixed modes and relations contain within them the possibility of being clearer than our complex ideas of substances because mixed modes and relations have in them "that combination of *Ideas*, and thereby that perfection which the Mind intended they should: So that the Mind acquiesces in them, and can find nothing wanting."[111] Our complex ideas of substances are otherwise:

> For their desiring to copy Things, as they really do exist; and to represent to our selves that Constitution, on which all their Properties depend, we perceive our *Ideas* attain not that Perfection we intend: We find they still want something, we should be glad were in them; and so are all *inadequate*.[112]

Scholars have worried about Locke's views of relations. This is so because Locke seems to be committed to a kind of radical subjectivism about relations. That is, it might commit Locke to saying that Cajus ceases to be a father only if I (or we) cease to consider him as a father![113] However, R. I. Aaron writes that while it is tempting to interpret Locke, in the light of the passages above, as holding to the thesis of the unreality of relations, he suggests that there is nonetheless in Locke's thinking "a foundation for the relation in reality."[114] Douglas Odegard notes this curious view of Locke and points out that this view of relations creates a number of problems for the coherence of Locke's views. For example, one problem is that Locke seems to be denying that there are any relations between the primary qualities of substances and the secondary qualities that they support: if the idea of substance is the idea of an unknown something which is related to qualities by "supporting" them, then it is curious to suggest that no relations exist while substances do exist.[115] Another problem is that this "interpretation requires saying that, e.g., husbands do not exist in the same sense as men."[116]

Odegard suggests that one way around this problem is to provide an alternative interpretation. He suggests that Locke's views of the denial of the reality of relations "is a comment on the manner of their existence, not a rejection of their existence."[117] This means that, on the one hand, Locke believes that relations are properties that objects and people possess in virtue of how the correlates of the relation stand to another. On the other hand, as I interpret Odegard, relations are "unreal" in the sense that these are not properties, which objects and persons possess regardless of other things. Real properties are properties, Odegard explains, that "exist in things regardless (conceptually) of other things."[118]

Odegard's insistence that a new alternative interpretation is needed is correct. In one sense, Locke does believe that some relations are real, i.e., some exist independently of the operation of the mind. For example, at a certain level of existence, which Locke said was (albeit temporarily) unknowable, there exists a necessary, causal relationship between primary qualities of objects and the secondary qualities of objects. Locke said that if we could know what the primary qualities of objects were, we would also know the causal relationships that they have. Knowing both of these things would give us the power, among other things, to predict every sort of secondary property that it could support. Our ideas of these relations are like substances, viz., ectypes, which are made with reference to archetypes or standing patterns.

There is, however, a second thesis about relations that Locke maintains. Odegard describes them as unreal; unfortunately, the term "unreal" does not seem to square well with Locke's views. The reason is that relations do not appear to be entirely unrelated to what is considered real. Instead, I prefer to call this other class of relations "conventional relations." The term "conventional" is better because this class of relations depends partly upon the operation of the mind. Take, for example, the relational term "father." On the one hand, to be a father, two correlates must actually be in place, viz., a man and a child he has either adopted or born from his fertilization of an ovum. However, the existence of such an association does not guarantee that the male parent is a father. The reason is that the term "father" indicates (at least in our culture) something above the correlate of the male parent, e.g., the role, which a male parent can play and psychological states associated with such a role. The concept of 'father', then, unlike our concepts of substances and real relations, are not ectypes because they are partially put together by the mind without reference to any archetypes or standing patterns.[119]

Third, Locke writes that relations, like all other ideas, ultimately make reference to simple ideas either of sensation or reflection:

> Though there be a great number of Considerations, wherein Things may be compared one with another, and so a multitude of *Relations*, yet they *all terminate in*, and are concerned about those *simple Ideas*, either of Sensation or Reflection; which I think to be the whole Materials of all our Knowledge.[120]

Relations, like any complex idea for Locke, are partially created by the mind by means of combining simple ideas together, which do not normally exist together in nature. Therefore to find where our ideas of relations begin, we must look to the simple ideas out of which they are made.

Finally, the words, which we use to express relations and indicate or denominate roles that an individual or thing can have, imply properties that are not really properties of the individual or thing:

> [F]ourthly, That *Relation* being the consideration of one thing with another, which is extrinsical to it, it is evident, that all Words, that necessarily lead the Mind to any other *Ideas*, than are supposed really to exist in that thing, to which the Word are applied, are *relative Words*: v.g. A *Man Black, Merry, Thoughtful, Thirsty, Angry, Extended*; these, and the like, are all absolute, because they neither sig-

nify nor intimate any thing but what does, or is supposed really to exist in the Man thus denominated: But *Father, Brother, King, Husband, Blacker,* Merrier, *etc.* are Words which, together with the thing they denominate, imply also something else separate, and exterior to the existence of that thing.[121]

In conclusion, Locke ends this brief discussion of the general nature of relations with a promise "to shew . . . how all the *Ideas* we have of *Relation*, are made up, as the others are, only of simple *Ideas*; and that they all, how refined, or remote from Sense soever they seem, terminate at last in simple *Ideas*."[122] He turns the discussion to the considerations of cause and effect, and ultimately to the nature of goodness and moral goodness, which, as I will shortly, show are both relations. Some things to keep in mind about relations within this context is that they are voluntary collections of simple ideas, which the mind partially puts together, without any reference to any real archetypes, or standing patterns, existing anywhere, and in virtue of this, they are considered by Locke to be extraneous and superinduced.

The Nature of Good and Evil

To understand the nature of good and evil (i.e., to understand that they are relations) as it is presented in the *Essay*, we must understand the relationship happiness and misery have to our notions of good and evil. There are three points to discuss: why humans pursue happiness, why happiness for humans is relative to each individual, and the relationship of happiness and misery to the terms, good and evil.

First, as Locke expounds, happiness is pursued by all humans, and by implication, pleasure, because of the nature of pain.[123] For example, when someone is in pain because of disease, or an injury, it consumes his life, and mars everything that he took to be good and enjoyable. Moreover, pain can even turn someone away from a life of virtue, piety and religion:

> we being capable but of one determination of the will to one action at once, the present *uneasiness,* that we are under, does naturally determine the will, in order to that happiness which we all aim at in all our actions: For, as much as whilst we are under any *uneasiness,* we cannot apprehend our selves happy, or in the way to it. Pain and *uneasiness* being, by every one, concluded, and felt, to be inconsistent with happiness; spoiling the relish, even of those good things which we have: a little pain serving to mar all the pleasure we rejoiced in.[124]

Next, even though pain plays an important part in the motivational life of humans, and when humans are in pain they are consumed by a desire to get rid of it, humans do not flee from pain to the same things, which promise to make them happy. In fact, as the quotation indicates, happiness is relative to each individual, which means that happiness is not the same thing for everyone:

> [F]rom what has been said, it is easie to give an account, how it comes to pass, that though all Men desire Happiness, yet their *wills carry them so contrarily*, and consequently some of them to what is Evil. And to this I say, that the various and contrary choices, that Men make in the World, do not argue, that they do not all pursue Good; but that the same thing is not good to every Man alike. This variety of pursuits shews, that every one does not place his happiness in the same thing, or chuse the same way to it.[125]

The suggestion of relativism here is now stronger and reinforced:

> The Mind has a different relish, as well as the palate; and you will as fruitlessly endeavour to delight all Men with Riches or Glory, (which yet some Men place their Happiness in,) as you would to satisfy all Men's Hunger with Cheese or Lobsters; which, though very agreeable and delicious fare to some, are to others extremely nauseous and offensive. . . . Hence it was, I think, that the Philosophers of old did in vain inquire, whether *Summum bonum* consisted in Riches, or bodily Delights, or Virtue, or Contemplation: And they might have as reasonably disputed, whether the best Relish were to be found in Apples, Plums, or Nuts; and have divided themselves into Sects upon it. For as pleasant Tastes depend not on the things themselves, but on their agreeableness to this or that particular Palate, wherein there is great variety: So the greatest Happiness consists, in the having those things, which produce the greatest Pleasure; and in the absence of those, which cause any disturbance, any pain. Now these, to different Men, are very different things.[126]

Locke's view so far is that even though happiness is something greater than pleasure, he describes happiness as something that humans take to be just the most pleasure that they can have while they are alive on the earth. As a consequence of this view, because humans pursue those things which cause pleasure and avoid those things which cause pain, and because men differ from one another with regard to what gives them pleasure and gives them pain, it is natural to conclude that among men there will be no *summum bonum* of happiness which everyone will pursue. That is, there does not appear to be anything, which causes the same kind of pleasure in all men, i.e., pleasant things are different to different men.

Even though things that cause pleasure and pain are relative to different men, Locke writes:

> what has an aptness to produce Pleasure in us, is that we call *Good*, and what is apt to produce Pain in us, we call *Evil*, for no other reason, but for its aptness to produce Pleasure and Pain in us, wherein consists our *Happiness* and *Misery*.[127]

But what does "aptness" mean? What Locke means is that there are objects, which, whenever they operate on our minds or our bodies, are apt, i.e., have a natural tendency, or are inclined, to either produce pleasure or pain. This means that these things will cause pleasure or pain for many, but not all, who they bump up against. These are the things which are called good or evil, as the case may be, even though, as Locke points out earlier in II. xxi. 55 of the *Essay*, that the same thing is not good to every man alike.

Now it seems clear that Locke is expounding here a view about the relationship of nonmoral value (since he only uses the terms good and evil without making specific reference to moral goodness or moral evil) and certain kinds of nonmoral facts, i.e., facts which cause either pleasure or pain. But what sort of relationship is Locke introducing here? The suggestion is that certain kinds of facts (or fact as the case may be) of the world can be so arranged (whether intentionally or not) to produce or to confer nonmoral value. In other words, what Locke is saying is that if we say, e.g., that something, i.e., an object or person, or an act, is good or evil, then the characteristic by virtue of which that object, person, or act is good or evil is a characteristic of causing pleasure or pain in us.

Such a view presupposes certain elements. First, it presupposes that the object, person, or act which is called good or evil, i.e., the object, person, or act which causes pleasure or pain, can be described in nonvalue, neutral terms. Second, it presupposes that every object, person, or act, which produces pleasure or pain, is called good or evil by virtue of causing pleasure or pain. Third, such a view presupposes that weights can be associated with the objects, person, or act which cause pleasure and pain so that the possibility exists that some objects, persons, or acts may be assigned a greater degree of goodness or evilness depending on how much pleasure and pain it causes. All three elements, which I have described and which appear to be presupposed by such a view, are in the text.

Concerning the first point, before Locke points out what we call good or evil, he makes clear what it is that he is referring to. He writes that it is "by the operation of certain objects, either on our minds or our bodies, and in different degrees"[128] which have an aptness to produce either pleasure or pain. But what kind of object is Locke referring to? In order for this view to work, it would have to be a sensible object which has the power to produce certain kinds of ideas in us and which can be described in purely nonethical terms. The kind of object that Locke is referring to is anything which can cause the simple idea of pleasure or pain in our bodies: "By *Pleasure* and *Pain*, I would be understood to signifie, whatsoever delights or molests us; whether it arises from the thoughts of our Minds, or anything operating on our Bodies."[129] Locke describes these objects simply as objects which have the power to produce either pleasure or pain in our bodies, or even both depending on what it is. For example, Locke describes the power something like heat has to produce both the ideas of pain and pleasure in our bodies at different times:

> Only this is worth our consideration, That *Pain is often produced by the same Objects and* Ideas, that *produce Pleasure* in us. This their near Conjunction, which makes us often feel pain in the sensations where we expected pleasure, gives us new occasion of admiring the Wisdom and Goodness of our Maker, who designing the preservation of our Being, has annexed Pain to the application of many things to our Bodies, to warn us of the harm that they will do; and advises us to withdraw from them. But he, not designing our preservation barely, but the preservation of every part and organ in its perfection, hath, in many cases, annexed pain to those very *Ideas*, which delight us. Thus Heat, that is very agreeable to us in one degree, by a little greater increase of it, proves no ordinary torment: and the most pleasant of all sensible Objects, Light it self, if there be too much of it, if increased beyond a due proportion to our Eyes, causes a very painful sensation.[130]

Although the text in II. xxi. 43 of the *Essay* can be interpreted in such a way to show that the objects which cause pleasure and pain are sensible objects which are describable in purely nonvalue, neutral terms, does the text in II. xxi. 43 support the second presupposition, viz., that every object, person, or act which produces pleasure or pain is called good or evil in virtue of causing pleasure or pain? What Locke writes appears to answer this question directly, viz., "therefore, what has an aptness to produce Pleasure in us, is that we call *Good*, and what is apt to produce Pain in us, we call *Evil*, for no other reason, but for its aptness to produce Pleasure and Pain in us, wherein consists our *Happiness* and *Misery*." Locke writes that we call those objects good or evil by virtue of their aptness to produces pleasure or pain, but, as is evident in the text, he adds immediately that we call them good or evil for *no other reason* but this aptness.

Finally, the text supports the third presupposition, i.e., weights can be associated with the objects, person, or act which cause pleasure and pain so that the possibility exists that some objects, persons, or acts may be assigned a greater degree of goodness or evil depending on how much pleasure and pain it causes. Locke in II. xxi. 42 of the *Essay* supports this view when he writes that:

> yet it often happens, that we do not call it so, when it comes in competition with a greater of its sort; because when they come in competition the degrees also of Pleasure and Pain have justly a preference. So that if we will rightly estimate what we call *Good* and *Evil*, we shall find it lies much in comparison: For the cause of every less degree of Pain, as well as every greater degree of pleasure has the nature of *good*, and *vice versa*.

Locke appears to be saying two different but related things here. The first is that even though there are times where we might call something good or evil by virtue of the pleasure or pain it causes, we have to keep something in mind when we do this, viz., that we are making a kind of comparison. That is, what we call good or evil now by virtue of the pleasure or pain it causes, may not be called as such if the pain or pleasure of the object increases or as Locke describes it, competes with the initial pleasure or pain. So, if an object causes pleasure or pain at a certain time we may call it good or evil as the case may be. But if that same object, or perhaps another like it, on another separate occasion causes additional pleasure or pain, we may conclude that this is also good or evil, but that it involves a greater good or evil than the last.

The second point is implied by the first. If it is true that what we call good "lies much in comparison," as Locke says it does, then it stands to reason that weights, if you will, can be assigned to the objects which cause greater or less pain. So, for example, if someone with callused hands lightly rubs the top of my hand, I may feel a certain amount of pleasure if any at all. However, if someone with uncallused hands lightly rubs my hand, I may experience a greater degree of pleasure with the touch of the latter hand. Moreover, if this is true, then some objects, persons, or acts may be assigned a greater degree of goodness or evilness depending on how much pleasure and pain it causes. This is what Locke appears to be saying when he writes that "every less degree of Pain, as well as every greater degree of Pleasure has the nature of *good*, and *vice versa*." That is, the degree of goodness or evilness goes up or down, as the case may be, with the degree of the amount of pain or pleasure present.

But now I must return to my initial view. I claimed early that what Locke means by the term "aptness" in II. xxi. 42 of the *Essay* is that there are objects, which, whenever they operate on our minds or our bodies, are apt, i.e., have a natural tendency to produce pleasure or pain in us. The reason is found in the difference between the things that cause pain and the things that cause pleasure. Locke, as I pointed out in a passage above, believes that there are objects, which have the powers to produce pleasure in us. But, as far as pleasure is concerned, this appears to be the strongest claim we can make so that what we call good (at least for humans here on earth) refers to those things, which tend to, but not always, produce pleasure in our minds and bodies.

The nature of pain, at least for Locke, is not quite as elusive. Although Locke recognizes that pain is somewhat relative to each individual, we know that there are certain things, which will and do cause pain for all normal humans. For example, Locke frequently makes reference to the rack, a device used in his time to exact confessions. Locke seems to be pretty convinced that if this device is used on any human body, it will produce pain. Therefore, whereas it might be hard to say that there are objects, which will produce pleasure in everyone, it is not quite as hard to say this about pain. That is, there are some objects, which will always cause pain.

It might, however, be objected that my interpretation of Locke is mistaken on the grounds that the objects, etc., that cause pleasure or pain do, in fact, possess the intrinsic property (or quality) of goodness or evil, i.e., these objects are in themselves good or evil or have the nature of goodness or evil and possess goodness or evil quite apart from what we might believe about it.[131] Locke allegedly indicates such a view in this passage: "Farther, though what is apt to produce any degree of Pleasure, be in itself *good*; and what is apt to produce any degree of Pain, be evil."[132] Moreover, he adds in the very last sentence of II. xxi. 42 of the *Essay* that "every greater degree of Pleasure, has the nature of *good*." This is a very different view from the one I take Locke to be arguing for, since it appears to make goodness or evil an intrinsic property; whereas, I hold that Locke views goodness or evil as a conventional relation between persons which can feel pain or pleasure and objects which have the power to cause pleasure and pain. Moreover, since goodness and evil are conventional relations, there is no such instrinsic property (or quality), archetype, or standing pattern, which completely answers our ideas of goodness or evilness.[133]

There are a number of responses to this problem. First, Locke could mean just what he appears to say, and then my interpretation will be wrong. That is, what Locke really means (a) is that the objects, which cause pleasure and pain have the nature of goodness or evil and are in themselves good or evil. Or perhaps Locke could have just (b) made a mistake here when he added the phrases, *in itself*, and *has the nature of good*. Or perhaps what Locke has said is short for something else (c), viz., that what is apt to produce any degree of pleasure be in itself good for us in the sense that something that causes pleasure may have some sort of instrumental value. The same could also be said about the last phrase. Perhaps what Locke means is that every object which is good in itself or has the nature of goodness is good in the sense that (d) it possesses some kind of pleasure causing power such that every object like it is good or "tends to be good." That is, by using those phrases, Locke should not be interpreted as saying that goodness is an intrinsic property. All that he is doing is simply providing criteria for applying the terms good and evil.

My answer to this problem is that (d) is the correct interpretation. Thus, (a) is wrong because Locke maintains a clear distinction between the objects that cause pleasure and pain, and what we call good and evil. Moreover, claiming that there are moral facts in the world would be inconsistent with what both John Colman and I call, Locke's ontological beginning point of the *Essay*, viz., all things that exist are particular things. It is inconsistent because in Boyle's description of the universe, there are no universal natures or mind-independent properties of goodness. This beginning point is a presupposition of the *Essay*, which, as I pointed out in the first section of this chapter, Locke borrows from Robert Boyle. Furthermore, (b) is wrong because I think that it is an uncharitable reading of the text even though he was not as clear as he could have been. Finally, (c) is wrong because the context does not seem to warrant such a view. In this passage Locke is only introducing the relationship between the words "good" and "evil" and the criteria for what we call good and evil. Up to this point in the Power chapter of the *Essay*, even though Locke mentions the use of absent goods which we pursue for a greater end, viz., our happiness, he never talks at length about the utility of pain and pleasure.

I take it, then, that (d) is the right interpretation (of course pending some other better interpretation). In other words, the terms "goodness" or "evil" are conventional relations that rest partially upon the correlates of an object with the powers to cause pleasure and pain and upon the body of some person designed to feel that pleasure or pain. However, since they are both conventional relations, then there is no archetype or standing pattern that completely answers those terms. By describing "goodness" and "evil" this way, Locke is not defining what those terms are, but he is simply providing the criteria for applying both of these terms.[134] Before I discuss what moral goodness is, there are two further points that Locke makes about nonmoral goodness and evil, viz., that what we call good or evil will not move us to pursue or flee unless it is taken to be a necessary part of our happiness, and finally what we call good can later become something that we call evil and visa versa.

Locke clearly articulates in the *Essay* that whenever someone is presently in the grip of some sort of pleasure or pain, he naturally either pursues the pleasure or flees from the pain (as was pointed out in II. xxi. 36 of the *Essay*). Locke also adds that if the objects, which are apt to produce pleasure and pain, are not presently causing pleasure and pain, these objects, which are called good and evil because of their aptness to produce pleasure or pain, will not necessarily engage the desire of a human:

> [T]hough this be that, which is called *good* and *evil*; and all good be the proper object of Desire in general; yet all good, even seen, and confessed to be so, does not necessarily move every particular man's *desire*; but only that part, or so much of it, as is consider'd, and taken to make a necessary part of his happiness. All other good, however great in reality, or appearance, excites not a Man's *desires*, who looks not on it to make a part of that happiness, wherewith he, in his present thoughts, can satisfie himself. *Happiness*, under this view, every one constantly pursues, and *desires* what makes any part of it: Other things, acknowledged to be good, he can look upon without *desire*; pass by, and be content without.[135]

Locke's point in this passage is to explicate how far all men are really at liberty concerning their own actions. He argues men are free even to the point of being able to resist what is in reality good for them, even those goods which are seen and confessed to be so by them. Locke adds that these goods will not be pursued until the agent himself engages his own desires. This is a point that Locke made earlier in the Power chapter that nothing can determine the will except the agent's own desires:

> [A]nother reason why 'tis *uneasiness* alone determines the will, may be this. Because that alone is present, and 'tis against the nature of things, that what is absent should operate, where it is not. It may be said, that absent good may by contemplation be brought home to the mind, and made present. The *Idea* of it indeed may be in the mind, and view'd as present there: but nothing will be in the mind as a present good, able to counter-balance the removal of any *uneasiness*, which we are under, till it raises our desire, and the *uneasiness* of that has the prevalency in determining the *will*. Till then the *Idea* in the mind of whatever is good, is there only like other *Ideas*, the object of bare inactive speculation; but operates not on the will, nor sets us on work. . . .[136]

But the desires of an individual are not engaged after some sort of good, as Locke points out, until a judgment is made about it, viz., it is necessary for my happiness, or it will, in some sense, ruin my happiness. Until this happens, the idea will not move the will.[137]

The final point to consider is also one point that Locke ends the Power chapter with. Locke writes that the unpleasantness or pleasantness associated with any sort of action, i.e., the characteristics which we use to show that an action is good or bad, may change. This implies that on a certain occasion some action may be called good by someone. Later, however, that same action may be called bad by the same person:

> [T]he last inquiry, therefore, concerning this matter is, Whether it be in a Man's power to change the pleasantness, and unpleasantness, that accompanies any sort of action? and as to that, it is plain in many cases he can. Men may and should correct their palates, and give relish to what either has, or they suppose has none. The relish of the mind is as various as that of the Body, and like that too may be alter'd; and 'tis a mistake to think, that Men cannot change the displeasingness, or indifferency, that is in actions, into pleasure and desire, if they will do but what is in their power.[138]

Locke adds, in the same passage, that here are two closely related reasons for such a phenomenon. First, the appetites men use to make judgments about things, persons, or actions, are closely analogous to their culinary appetites. People have different tastes for different types of pleasure and pain. The second related reason is a little more complicated:

> any action is rendered more or less pleasing, only by the contemplation of the end, and the being more or less persuaded of its tendency to it, or necessary connexion with it: But the pleasure of the action it self is best acquir'd, or increased, by use and practice. Trials often reconcile us to that, which at a distance we looked on with aversion; and by repetitions wear us into a liking, of what possibly, in the first essay, displeased us. Habits have powerful charms, and put so strong attractions of easiness and pleasure into what we accustom our selves to, that we cannot forbear to do, or at least be easy in the omission of, actions, which habitual practice has suited, and thereby recommends to us.

First, as Locke appears to expound, an action can be depicted or represented as pleasing in our minds when it is estimated that it either has a tendency to lead to our happiness or has a necessary connection with our happiness. However, the best cause of why some actions in themselves cause pleasure and some cause pain is habit. Repetitive and recurrent actions often establish dispositions of the mind or character so strong that, as Locke reveals, "we cannot forbear to do, or at least be easy in the omission of, actions, which habitual practice has suited, and thereby recommends to us." However, Locke does add that these habits can be broken when we are faced with trials, i.e., some sort of state of pain or anguish that tests patience, endurance, or belief. For example, suppose that there is a person who for most of his life has spent it being fairly inactive. In fact, he despises being active because of the pain that it causes in his muscles. One day because of sluggishness and overeating, he has a heart attack. The doctor orders, among other things, exercise. The trial of the heart attack, which includes a brush with death, powerfully motivates him to change the kind of lifestyle that he had formally loved so much. Now, unlike his former lifestyle, he watches what he eats and exercises daily. In fact, even though exercising is still just as painful as it was before the heart attack, he likes it because now it makes him feel better, and he knows that exercising and a low fat diet will contribute towards his happiness.

The Nature of Moral Goodness and Evil

It is necessary to understand the nature of good and evil in order to understand what Locke says of the nature of moral good and evil. However, if this is true, it will lead to conclusions which may be surprising to those scholars who believe that what Locke wrote in the *Essay* supports or is logically consistent with a single, ultimate, criterion of morality. The evidence for this view is found in the following passage:

> [G]ood and Evil, as hath been shown, B.II.Ch. XX.2, and Ch. XXI.42,) are nothing but Pleasure or Pain, or that which occasions, or procures Pleasure or Pain to us. *Moral good and evil* then, is only the Conformity or Disagreement of our voluntary Actions to some Law, whereby Good or Evil is drawn on us, from the Will and Power of the Law-maker; which Good and Evil, Pleasure or Pain, attending our observance, or breach of the Law, by the Decree of the Law-maker, is that we call *Reward* and *Punishment*.[139]

Locke writes that moral goodness and evil are only the conformity or disagreement of our voluntary actions to some law.[140] This is a very curious way of describing moral goodness and evil. What does he want us to understand about moral goodness and evil? A voluntary action may conform or agree with a law in the sense that a description of the action may correspond to what the law says is obligatory. Likewise, a voluntary action may not agree with some law just in case it does not correspond to what the law says is obligatory. But even though there may or may not be an agreement between a voluntary action and a law, where does moral goodness and evil fit in? Locke says that moral goodness is just that conformity, and moral evil is just that disagreement. But to say that moral goodness is conformity seems to be saying that it is a relation that exists between two things, viz., the action and the rule.[141] In fact, this is just what Locke says in II. xxviii. 4 of the *Essay*:

> There is another sort of Relation, which is the Conformity, or Disagreement, Men's voluntary Actions have to a Rule, to which they are referred, and by which they are judge of: which, I think, may be called Moral Relation; as being that, which denominates our moral actions. . . .

But what does it mean to say that moral goodness and evil are relations? What is morally good and evil appears to be identical to the conclusion that we make about the comparison of an action and a law. That is, it is identical to the conclusion that is made whenever someone looks beyond the action in order to see how it stands in relation to a law. This is accomplished primarily whenever there is a basic similarity between the description of the action and the law, i.e., the mind looks beyond the action to a rule in which there is a basic correspondence between the action and the description of the action which is obligatory or forbidden.

However, since moral goodness is a relation, then there appear to be other things that are relevant, especially concerning where moral goodness and evil exist and the source of moral goodness and evil. First, how does Locke want us to understand moral relations: are they real or conventional? If they are real, then our ideas of moral goodness would be like our ideas that we have of substances. This would mean, then, that our complex ideas of moral goodness and evil would be created with the intention to represent something existing without us. If conventional, then even though moral goodness and evil will rest partially upon two correlates, they are largely a voluntary collection of simple ideas that the mind puts together without reference to any real archetypes or standing patterns. Locke does not understand moral relations as real and, therefore, views them as conventional. This is so because moral relations are not created with the intention to represent something existing without us. Instead, Locke makes clear that conventional relations terminate and are ultimately founded on our simple ideas of sensation and reflection that the mind (partially) puts together, and are intended to denominate or classify actions.[142]

A second related point is that since moral goodness is a voluntary collection of simple ideas, which the mind puts together, then it appears to be something that does not exist independently of what we believe about it, or as Locke might put it, moral goodness and evil are not contained in the real existence of things. Instead, moral goodness and evil, by virtue of being conventional relations, are something "extraneous and superinduced," which means that moral goodness and evil are largely created by us and imposed upon the world in the sense that it is a means of categorizing the world.

Now that we have a better understanding of what Locke means when he writes that moral goodness and evil are only the conformity or disagreement of our voluntary actions to some law, I can expound why he believes that this view follows from the claim that good and evil are nothing but pleasure and pain. His relational view of moral goodness and evil follows because of the way Locke describes what is good and evil. Like moral goodness and evil, what is good and evil (in a non-moral sense) is also a conventional relation. But there is also another reason. This reason modifies his notion of what is morally good and evil. The consequence also follows by virtue of the fact that, as Locke relates this, pleasure and pain are also associated with moral goodness and evil. Locke adds, "whereby Good or Evil is drawn on us, from the Will and Power of the Law-maker; which Good and Evil, Pleasure or Pain, attending our observance, or breach of the Law, by the Decree of the Law-maker, is that we call *Reward* and *Punishment*."[143] This means that there are basically two different conditions that Locke gives for us to apply the terms moral goodness and evil. That is, if we say of some particular act that it is morally good or evil, and if we are prepared to defend this claim, then we should be prepared to appeal to two different sorts of characteristics. First, we have to show that the voluntary action, which was performed, was either consistent or inconsistent with some sort of rule, a rule determined by God, the civil authority, or the moral community. Second, we also have to show that there is a possibility of pleasure or pain attending the observance of the rule or the breach of the law, which can be drawn upon us from the will and power of the lawmaker.

Having now discussed, in some detail, what Locke means by the terms "good" and "evil," and the terms "moral good" and "moral evil," before I close this chapter I would like to make one last comment about this position. A suggestion, perhaps, may be ventured that Locke's view of moral good and evil is logically inconsistent with the view that there is a single, ultimate, moral standard. I cannot help to think that such an outlook is too unlikely. The reason is that most scholars argue that either Locke is still committed to a natural law view, or that he is committed to some sort of hedonistic utilitarianism. Although I examine both opinions in the next chapter (and find them both lacking), the following discussion may suffice to show that this outlook is not altogether a too extravagant doctrine.

Now why is Locke's view of moral goodness logically inconsistent with a single, ultimate, moral standard? Before I answer this question, I would like to put this issue in more general terms. Instead of assuming that this is Locke's view, let us suppose for the moment that moral goodness has the same sort of relational characteristics that Locke discusses. Again, as I maintain, why would such a view be inconsistent with absolutism? A contemporary scholar, Fred Feldman, talks at length about this issue. His discussion, in brief, is as follows.[144]

In its simplest terms, the defense of absolutism involves arguing that there is a significant moral criterion stating the necessary and sufficient conditions for an act to possess the property of rightness. Additionally, he discusses a kind of *moral relativism* inconsistent with absolutism that he calls *conceptual relativism*. This is the view that there is no such property as rightness, or in other terms, rightness is a relation between acts and societies. Both views are logically inconsistent because if it is true that there is no property such as rightness, then there cannot be a significant criterion stating the necessary and sufficient conditions for an act to have the property of rightness.[145]

But, now, how does Locke's view measure up to the existence of a single, ultimate, moral standard? First, Locke does conceive of what is good and hence what is morally good as a conventional relation. For example, what we call "good" ends up being a conventional relation between two objects that are related in a certain way, viz., that one body has, at least, the capacity to feel pleasure or pain, and the other object has, at least, the power to cause pain. Moreover, what we call "morally good" also ends up being a conventional relation between two objects that are related in a certain way, viz., between a voluntary action which is either consistent or inconsistent with a rule. But this is not all, as I understand Locke, the rule that is in place must have pleasure and pain associated with either the observance or the breach of some action.

Second, since Locke conceives of moral goodness as a conventional relation, then it stands to reason, given that he does call moral goodness a moral relation, and given all that he says about the nature of conventional relations, goodness and even moral goodness do not exist independently of what we believe about them and therefore cannot be the property of an action nor can they be thought to have a nature that exists independently of our beliefs.[146] In fact, as such reasoning goes, moral goodness and goodness in general are the results of our collecting simple ideas together without any reference to anything existing anywhere. This truly seems to be the kind of conclusion Feldman might sugguest[147] and the observation that Locke wants us draw since he was so specific about the nature of conventional relations. Therefore, Locke's view of moral goodness is inconsistent with the view that there is a single, ultimate, moral standard.

Notes

1 Locke, *Essay*, I. i. 3. Locke's third purpose in the *Essay* is to make an "Enquiry into the Nature and Grounds of Faith, or Opinion" (Ibid.).

2 John W. Yolton, *John Locke and the Way of Ideas* (Oxford: Oxford University Press, 1956), 1-71.

3 Ibid., 39.

4 Thomas Burnet, *Remarks Upon An Essay Concerning Human Understanding: Five Tracts*, ed. Peter A. Schouls (New York: Garland Publishing, Inc.).

5 Burnet, "Third Remark Upon *An Essay Concerning Human Understanding*," in *Remarks Upon An Essay Concerning Human Understanding: Five Tracts*, ed. Peter A. Schouls (New York: Garland Publishing, Inc.), 7.

6 Ibid., 6.

7 Peter A. Schouls, *Reasoned Freedom: John Locke and Enlightment* (Ithaca: Cornell University Press, 1992), 28.

8 J. B. Schneewind, "Locke's Moral Philosophy," in *The Cambridge Companion to Locke*, ed. Vere Chappell (Cambridge: Cambridge University Press, 1994), 200.

9 John W. Yolton, *Locke and the Compass of Human Understanding* (Cambridge: Cambridge University Press, 1970), 173.

10 Yolton, *John Locke and the Way of Ideas*, 30-71.

11 J. L. Mackie, *Problems from Locke* (Oxford: Oxford University Press, 1976), 207.

12 R. I. Aaron, *John Locke* (Oxford: Clarendon Press, 1965), 94.

13 Colman, *John Locke's Moral Philosophy*, 51.

14 John Marshall, *John Locke: Resistance, Religion and Responsibility* (Cambridge: Cambridge University Press, 1994), 30.

15 Ibid.

16 Locke, *Essay*, I. ii. 2.

17 Ibid., I. ii. 4-14.

18 Ibid., I. ii. 14 ff.

19 Locke begins his attack against the view that there are universally agreed speculative principles by arguing that this view is false because "'tis evident, that all *Children*, and *Ideots*, have not the least Apprehension or Thought of them: and the want of that is enough to destroy that universal Assent, which must needs be the necessary concomitant of all innate Truths. . . ." (Ibid., I. ii. 5). The reason (which is also a reason he gives in the *Essays*) why he believes this is that "If therefore Children and *Ideots* have Souls, have Minds, with those Impressions upon them, they must unavoidably perceive them, and necessarily know and assent to these Truths, which since they do not, it is evident that there are no such Impressions" (Ibid.).

Locke proceeds to consider objections to his views. He writes: "[T]o avoid this, 'tis usually answered, that all Men know and *assent* to them, *when they come to the use of Reason*, and this enough to prove them innate" (Ibid., I. ii. 6). Locke responds by to this by stating that the phrase "when they come to the use of reason" can mean one of two things: "either, That as soon as Men come to the use of Reason, these supposed native Inscriptions come to be known, and observed by them: Or else, that the Use and Exercise of Men's Reason, assists them in the Discovery of these Principles, and certainly make them known to them" (Ibid., II. ii. 7). Locke characteristically argues that neither meaning of the phrase will support the existence of innate ideas. For example, if we assume the latter meaning is correct, Locke argues that, in the end, we will not be able to distinguish between truths thought to be innate, e.g., the maxims of mathematicians, and other truths that are not thought to be candidates of innateness. If we assume that the former is correct, Locke argues that even though it is necessary "that Men should come to the use of Reason, before they get the Knowledge of those general Truths" (Ibid., II. ii. 12), i.e., the principle of identity and the Law of Non-contradiction, there is evidence that many individuals who are many years past their age of becoming rational who do not know either principle:

> How many instances of the use of Reason may we observe in Children, a long time before they have any Knowledge of this Maxim, That it is impossible for the same thing to be and not to be? and a great part of illiterate People, and Savages, pass many Years, even of their rational Age, without ever thinking on this, and the like general Propositions. (Ibid.)

Locke's argumentation shifts for the rest of this chapter. Instead, what he argues is that even if we assume for the sake of argument that it is true that both laws are known and assented to when the use of reason comes about, it still does not prove that these law are innate. The reason is that there is another more plausible explanation for why knowledge and assent are given to these laws by those who first acquire their use of reason. This explanation is a familiar one which he later expands in detail in the other chapters of the *Essay*, viz., before the use of reason, individuals, whose senses are working properly, let in ideas into the mind which some are stored in the memory. The mind grows by degrees familiar with these ideas and their names. Later the mind begins to abstract these ideas and learns the use of general names. Locke writes that as soon as he understands the abstract terms involved in each law, the truth of each law will appear to him. In fact it will be self-evidently true to them. But, as Lock relates, this is no different than when this same individual understands using the same method that a rod and a cherry are not the same thing (Ibid., II. ii. 16). Locke adds that even though he realizes that these laws are self-evident because they are in fact assented to upon the hearing and understanding of the terms, self-evidence does not indicate innateness either. The reason he gives is that there are claims which individuals understand in the same way which are not typical candidates for innateness, e.g., red is not blue (Ibid., II. ii. 20).

20 Ibid., I. iii. 1.
21 Ibid.
22 Ibid., I. iii. 4.
23 Ibid.
24 Ibid. Here we see a brief glimpse of what later Locke attempts to for-

mulate in more precise terms in the third and fourth chapters of the *Essay*, viz., Locke's view that morality is capable of demonstration. Interestingly enough, however, we see in the paragraph immediately following this the way this demonstration begins:

> [T]hat men should keep their Compacts, is certainly a great and un-deniable Rule in Morality: But yet, if a Christian, who has the view of Happiness and Misery in another Life, be asked why a Man must keep his Word, he will *give* this as a *Reason*: Because God, who has the Power of eternal Life and Death, requires it of us. But if an Hob-bist be asked why; he will answer: Because the Publick requires it, and the *Leviathan* will punish you, if you do not. And if one of the old *Heathen* Philosophers had been asked, he would have answer'd: Because it was dishonest, below the Dignity of a Man, and opposite to Vertue, the highest Perfection of humane Nature, to do otherwise. (Ibid., I. iii. 5)

The demonstration, as Locke points out, could be from one of three presupposi-tions (which he, of course, later in book 2 explains why) and then, as the para-graph prior to this adds, proceeds by deduction.

25 Ibid., I. iii. 6.
26 Ibid.
27 Ibid., I. iii. 7.
28 Ibid.
29 Ibid., I. iii. 8.
30 Ibid.
31 Ibid., I. iii. 9.
32 Ibid.
33 Ibid., I. iii. 11.
34 Ibid., I. iii. 12.
35 To this same discussion Locke adds the practice of exposing unwanted children, the various acts of patricide, and the various tribes which make it a practice of eating their children and the children of their enemies (Ibid., I. iii. 9).
36 Ibid., I. iii. 12.
37 Locke's point that all things that exist are particular things is a point that Locke borrows from Boyle and the Corpuscularian Philosophy. In the *Es-say*, however, Locke never attempts to defend this claim. He merely assumes it.
38 Ibid., III. iii. 1.
39 Of the chief end of language, Locke writes later, "the *ends of Language in our Discourse with others*, being chiefly these three: *First, To make known* one Man's Thoughts or *Ideas* to another. *Secondly*, To do it *with* as much ease and *quickness*, as is possible; and *Thirdly*, Thereby *to convey* the *Knowledge* of Things" (Ibid., III. x. 23).
40 Ibid., III. iii. 2-4.
41 Ibid., III. iii. 6.

42 This distinction is also made by R. S. Woolhouse. However, Wool-house uses a different way to describe Locke's view. He describes Locke's view of the ground of general words as Conceptualism (R. S. Woolhouse, *Locke's Philosophy of Science and Knowledge* [New York: Barnes and Noble, 1971], 96). This is the view that "the ground on which a general word is applied to a thing, the ground on which a thing is said to be of a certain sort or to have a certain property is that it is *related in a certain way to a mental entity, a Concept*" (Ibid., 77). This view stands at odds with a view that Woolhouse makes clear that Locke attacks, viz., Realism (Ibid., 99). According to Wool-house, Realism is the view that "the ground on which a general word is applied to a thing—the ground on which it is said to be of a certain sort or to have a certain property—is that it manifests a universal" (Ibid., 77).

43 Locke, *Essay*, III. iii. 7.

44 Ibid.

45 Ibid., III. iii. 11.

46 Ibid., III. iii. 9.

47 Ibid., III. ii. 12.

48 Ibid. Locke also makes the same point just in the same section: "the abstract *Idea*, for which the name stands, and the Essence of the Species, is one and the same."

49 Ibid.

50 Ibid.

51 According to the Scholastics, the statement of the essence of something is made up of two terms, one which expresses the genus, i.e., the term which states what things the subject is like, and the other which expresses the difference, i.e., the term which states what things the subject is different from. Thus when we say that "man is a rational animal," the term "animal" expresses the determinable part a man's essence, i.e., man's genus, and the term "rational" expresses the determining or differentiating part of man's essence.

52 What I take Locke to mean by this second premise is this, viz., that when we analyze both what the Scholastics call the essence of a species and our abstract ideas that general words signify, we realize that their natures are quali-tatively the same. That is, both Locke and the Scholastics agree that general ideas are complex abstract ideas and omit the individuality that particular ideas possess. Since there is no qualitative difference concerning the nature of these abstract ideas, Locke draws the inference that the essence of sorts or species must also be formed the same way that he thinks abstract ideas are formed.

53 Woolhouse, *Locke's Philosophy of Science and Knowledge*, 105.

54 Ibid., 83.

55 Ibid., 105.

56 Locke, *Essay*, III. iii. 13.

57 Boyle, *The Origin of Forms and Qualities According to the Corpuscu-lar Philosophy*, 40.

58 Locke, *Essay*, III. iii. 14.

59 I should point out that Locke is using a moral term in this example. This is significant because it gives a glimpse of his understanding of the justifi-

cation of morality. I will return to this point later.

60 Locke here is referring to severely deformed fetuses, a sight he was probably privilege to on numerous occasions.

61 Although Locke never discusses why he moves from talking about the concept of covetousness to the concept of man, such a move would, of course, irritate the Scholastics and the Schools. First, Locke attacks their view of morality. There are no essences that determine moral concepts. This is irritating enough. But, now, he attacks their view of man: man the crown of creation and the highest being of existence! Such an attack would be interpreted by the Scholastics as not just a strike against Aquinas and Aristotle, but an assault against God.

62 Locke, *Essay*, III. iii. 14. See also Woolhouse's discussion of this argument (*Locke's Philosophy of Science and Knowledge*, 103).

63 Locke, *Essay*, III. iii. 15.

64 Although Locke argues that the real constitution of a substance is unknowable, it is my sense that Locke believes that the unknowability is relative to the state of technology. The following passage seems to indicate such a view:

> [I] deny not, but a Man, accustomed to rational and regular Experiments shall be able to see farther into the Nature of Bodies, and guess righter at their yet unknown Properties, than one, that is a Stranger to them: But yet, as I have said, this is but Judgment and Opinion, not Knowledge and Certainty. This *way* of getting, and *improving our Knowledge in Substances only by Experience* and History, which is all that the weakness of our Faculties in this State of *Mediocrity*, which we are in this World, can attain to, makes me suspect, that natural Philosophy is not capable of being made a Science. (IV. xii. 10; cf. IV. iv. 13)

65 Ibid., III. iii. 16.

66 Ibid., III. iii. 17.

67 Boyle, *The Origin of Forms and Qualities According to the Corpuscular Philosophy*, 53-54.

68 Ibid., 56.

69 Ibid.

70 Ibid.

71 Ibid., 56-57.

72 Ibid., 54.

73 Boyle, *The Origin of Forms and Qualities According to the Corpuscular Philosophy*, 69.

74 Ibid., 50.

75 There is a controversy that surrounds this passage. On the one hand, the point I make about the imperceivability of corpuscles is generally accepted by other scholars, e.g., Woolhouse, *Locke's Philosophy of Science and Knowledge*, 113; Laudan, "The Nature and Sources of Locke's Views on Hypothe-

ses," 217; Mandelbaum, *Philosophy, Science, and Sense Perception*, 16; and, R. M. Yost, "Locke's Rejection of Hypotheses About Sub-Microscopic Events," *Journal of the History of Ideas* 12 (1951): 123. On the other hand, the conclusion that Locke thought that corpuscular explanations were useful is disputed. For example, Yost attempts to defend the view that Locke rejected the usefulness of such explanations in the discovery of scientific practice (Ibid., 125-6). My view is that Locke accepts such explanations in terms of explaining how objects interact with our senses. It is also my view that since Boyle thought such explanations were needed and useful (and I give such examples of explanations in the text that follows) and since the *Essay* was an attempt to work out many of the views of Boyle's corpuscularism, I think that it is more probable to believe that Locke thought so himself than to think that he did not. Such a conclusion is also defended by Mandelbaum, *Philosophy, Science, and Sense Perception*, 11-4, Laudan, "The Nature and Sources of Locke's Views on Hypotheses," 220, and Woolhouse, *Locke's Philosophy of Science and Knowledge*, 114.

76 Locke, *Essay*, III. iii. 17.

77 A closed laboratory vessel with an outlet tube, used for distillation, sublimation, or decomposition by heat.   .

78 Boyle, *The Origin of Forms and Qualities According to the Corpuscular Philosophy*, 96.

79 Ibid., 90.

80 It is a thin volatile essential oil, $C_{10}H_{16}$, obtained by steam distillation or other means from the wood or exudate of certain pine trees. It is used as a paint thinner and a solvent, but in Locke's day it was also used medicinally as a liniment.

81 Boyle, *The Origin of Forms and Qualities According to the Corpuscular Philosophy*, 90.

82 Locke, *Essay*, III. iii. 17.

83 Ibid., II. viii. 23.

84 Ibid., II. viii. 22.

85 Locke underscores my point in the following passage:

For though Fire be call'd painful to the Touch, whereby is signified the power of producing in us the *Idea* of Pain; yet it is denominated also Light, and Hot; as if Light and Heat, were really something in the Fire, more than a power to excite these *Ideas* in us; and therefore are called *Qualities* in, or of the Fire. But these being nothing, in truth, but powers to excite such *Ideas* in us, I must, in that sense, be understood, when I speak of secondary *Qualities*, as being in Things; or of their *Ideas*, as being in the Objects, that excite them in us. Such ways of speaking, though accommodated to the vulgar Notions, without which, one cannot be well understood; yet truly signify nothing, but those Powers, which are in Things, to excite certain Sensations or *Ideas* in us. Since were there no fit Organs to receive the impressions Fire makes on the Sight and Touch; nor a Mind joined to those Organs to receive the *Ideas* of Light and Heat, by those impressions from the Fire, or the Sun, there would yet be no more Light, or Heat in the World, than there would be Pain if there were no sensible Creature to feel it, though the Sun should continue just as it is now, and Mount *Aetna* flame higher than ever it did. (II. xxxi. 2)

86 Ibid., III. iii. 17.

87 See also Woolhouse's discussion of both of these arguments (Woolhouse, *Locke's Philosophy of Science and Knowledge*, 103-3).

88 Locke, *Essay*, III. iii. 19.

89 Aristotle, *Metaphysics*, 1043b 15-20.

90 Ibid., 1071a 28-9.

91 I am indebted to Fred D. Miller, Jr. for the following discussion.

92 See W. D. Ross on this point (W. D. Ross, *Aristotle* [London: Methuen and Co., Ltd., 1923], 74).

93 Ibid.

94 Locke, *Essay*, III. iii. 19.

95 Ibid., III. iii. 18.

96 The reason is that Locke never talks in terms of simple ideas as being essences. Nor does he ever talk about why the nominal and real essence of simple ideas are the same. In fact, as far as I can tell, Locke never makes this point. This makes sense because simple ideas have no hidden constitution.

97 Ibid., II. xxii. 1.

98 See Locke's point about this at II. v: Of *simple* Ideas *of divers Senses*.

99 Ibid., III. iii. 18.

100 Ibid., IV. iii. 11.

101 Ibid., III. iv. 20.

102 Ibid., II. xxv. 5.

103 Ibid., II. xxv. 1.

104 Ibid., II. xxv. 5.

105 Ibid., II. xxv. 7.

106 Ibid., II. xxv. 8.

107 Ibid., II. xii. 2; Brackets are mine.

108 Ibid., II. xxx. 4.

109 Ibid., II. xxxi. 3.

110 Ibid., II. xxx. 5.

111 Ibid., II. xxxi. 3.

112 Ibid.

113 I am indebted to Fred D. Miller, Jr. for bringing this point to my attention.

114 Aaron, *John Locke*, 181.

115 Douglas Odegard, "Locke and the Unreality of Relations," *Theoria* 35 (1969): 148.

116 Ibid.

117 Ibid., 150.

118 Ibid., 149.

119 Michael Ayers also writes something similar: "Yet Locke's conclusion that the real object of the concept of *father* is an abstract relation, not the substantial bearer of the predicate, the thing related, is not entirely implausible. The study of *policemen* can be thought of as the study of a role, rather than the study of a sub-class of the species *man*, or the study of *man* in a certain state" (Michael Ayers, *Locke* [London: Routledge, 1991], 2: 95).

Later in the next two sections I will make use of Locke's view of relations when I talk about his view of nonmoral goodness and moral goodness. Locke conceives of both as logical relations, and therefore neither one can be said to have a completely separate metaphysical existence; instead, they are both partially created by us and used a certain way to class and categorize the world.

120 Locke, *Essay*, II. xxv. 9.

121 Ibid., II. xxv. 10.

122 Ibid., II. xxv. 11.

123 In II. vii, Locke discusses the origin of our ideas of pleasure and pain: they are simple ideas conveyed into the mind by means of sensation and reflection. On the one hand, to say that they are simple ideas conveyed by means of sensation means that pleasure and pain are uncompounded perceptions which occur in the mind whenever an external object makes some sort of causal impression on one or more of our senses (II. ii. 1). For example, if an object causes an impression on a sense, which is an agreeable impression, then the mind perceives the simple idea of pleasure. If an object causes an impression on a sense, which is not an agreeable impression, then the mind often perceives the simple idea of pain. On the other hand, to say that pleasure and pain are simple ideas conveyed by means of reflection means something slightly different. What Locke wants us to understand is that as the mind turns in on itself and its operations of thinking and willing, each simple idea, which arises, brings about, in some sense and in some way, the uncompounded ideas of pleasure and pain. In fact, like sensation, "there is scarce . . . any retired thought of our Mind within, which is not able to produce in us *pleasure* and *pain*" (II. vii. 2).

124 Ibid., II. xxi. 36; cf. II. xxi. 46.

125 Ibid., II. xxi. 54.

126 Ibid., II. xxi. 55.

127 Ibid., II. xxi. 42. Hobbes also writes something close to this in the *Leviathan*: "But whatsoever is the object of any man's appetite or desire, that is it which he for his part calleth good: and the object of his hate and aversion, evil; and of his contempt, vile and inconsiderable" (Hobbes, *Leviathan*, 48).

128 Locke, *Essay*, II. xxi. 42.

129 Ibid., II. vii. 2.

130 Ibid., II. vii. 4.

131 It appears to be reminiscent of some of Locke's contemporaries who held that goodness and evil are properties of the nature of persons and actions in the same way that hardness is a property of the leg of a wooden chair.

132 Ibid., II. xxi. 42.

133 Hobbes also adds that the words of good, evil, and contemptible: "are ever used with relation to the person that useth them: there being nothing simply and absolutely so; nor any common rule of good and evil, to be taken from the nature of the objects themselves; but from the person or the man, where there is no commonwealth; or, in a commonwealth, from an arbitrator or judge, whom men disagreeing shall by consent set up, and make his sentence the rule thereof" (Hobbes, *Leviathan*, 48-9).

134 Although Locke is providing a criterion for us to apply the term good and evil to objects, actions, and people, I do not think that Locke should be interpreted as providing both necessary and sufficient conditions for the term good or evil. This is based on all that Locke says about the relativity of pleasure and pain, and the relativity of happiness. What Locke has provided us with by appealing to the existence of pleasure and pain is a contingent condition for what we call good or evil. The reason that pleasure and pain are contingent conditions for what we call good and evil is that we have the power to resist the effects of pleasure and (certain kinds) of pain because what we call good can later under different circumstances become evil to us and vice versa.

135 Ibid., II. xxi. 43.

136 Ibid., II. xxi. 37.

137 Another reason Locke gives for this point appears to be that if we argue that the perceived greatest good always determines our actions, it will lead to untoward consequences:

> If it were so, that the greater good in view determines the *will*, so great a good once propos'd, could not but seize the *will*, and hold it fast to the pursuit of this infinitely greatest good, without ever letting it go again: For the *will* having a power over, and directing the thoughts, as well as other actions, would, if it were so, hold the contemplation of the mind fixed to that good. (II. xxi. 38)

The consequence would be that given the way the will is determined by desire, the will would never let go of what it takes to be the greatest good. But this is not the case because experience has shown that people take up and lay down those things they desire.

138 Ibid., II. xxi. 69.

139 Ibid., II. xxviii. 5.

140 By "voluntary action" Locke refers to any action in which the agent was not determined in either the forbearance or performance of that action, consequent to ordering of the action by the agent (Ibid., II. xxviii.3). By 'law' Locke means any kind of rule which men judge the rectitude or pravity of their actions (II. xxviii.6).

141 This is also the interpretation S. Alexander gives to the very same passage: "Moral good or evil is thus a relation of human actions, which are modes, to other modes which are rules of action" (S. Alexander, *Locke* [Port Washington, NY: Kennikat Press, 1908], 69).

142 Locke, *Essay*, II. xxviii. 14.

143 Ibid., II. xxviii. 5.

144 Fred Feldman, *Introduction to Ethics* (Englewood Cliffs, NJ: Prentice Hall, Inc., 1978), 167-170.

145 W. T. Stace also describes the debate between the moral absolutist and the ethical relativist in very similar terms: although the moral absolutist asserts that there is a single universal moral standard, the ethical relativism "denies that there is single moral standard which is equally applicable to all men at all times" ([1996], 200). Gilbert Harman also describes this debate in the same terms (Gilbert Harmon and Judith Jarvis Thomson, *Moral Relativism and Moral Objectivity* [Cambridge: Blackwell Publishers, Inc., 1996], 8).

146 Ralph Cudworth apparently seems to have this very same view in mind when he turns his critical eye toward it:

And since a thing cannot be made any thing by mere will without a being or nature, every thing must be necessarily and immutably determined by its own nature, and the nature of things be that which it is, and nothing else. For though the will and power of God have an absolute, infinite and unlimited command upon the existences of all created things to make them to be, or not to be, at pleasure; yet when things exist, they are what they are, this or that, absolutely or relatively, not by will or arbitrary command, but by the necessity of their own nature. There is no such thing as an arbitrarious essence, mode or relation, that may be made indifferently any thing at pleasure: for an arbitrarious essence is a being without a nature, a contradiction, therefore a non-entity. Wherefore the natures of justice and injustice cannot be arbitrarious things, that may be applicable by will indifferently to any actions or dispositions whatsoever. For the modes of all subsistent beings, and the relation of things to one another, and immutably and necessarily what they are, and not arbitrary, being not by will but by nature. (Ralph Cudworth, *A Treatise Concerning Eternal and Immutable Morality*, in *British Moralists 1650-1800*, ed. D. D. Raphael [Oxford; Oxford University Press, 1969], 1: 105-119).

In contrast to this, Locke also states a similar point again in the following passage taken from "Of Ethics in General" concerning the nature of goodness:

For happiness and misery consisting only in pleasure and pain, either of mind or body, or both, according to the interpretation I have given above of those words, nothing can be good or bad to any one but as it tends to their happiness or misery, as it serves to produce in them pleasure or pain: for good and bad, being relative terms, do not denote anything in the nature of a thing, but only the relation it bears to another, in its aptness and tendency to produce in it pleasure and pain; and thus we see and say, that which is good for one man is bad for another. (John Locke, "Of Ethics In General," in *Life and Letters of John Locke*, ed. Lord King [New York: Burt Franklin, 1972], 310-11)

It should be noted that "Of Ethics in General" was to be chapter 21 of book 4 of the *Essay*. For a discussion of this document, see von Leyden, "Introduction," in *Essays On the Law of Nature* (Oxford: Clarendon Press, 1954), 69-75.

147 I say Feldman might suggest this because he talks about the property of rightness as a relation between acts and societies. Of course, anyone who has benefited from the works of R. M. Hare will understand that the terms "good" and "right" do not mean the same thing in every context. However, as Hare illustrates, there are contexts in which the terms "good" and "right" have the same prescriptive function (R. M. Hare, *The Language of Morals* [Oxford: Oxford University Press, 1952], 151-152). For my purposes, then, even though we shall expect to find differences in the meaning and function of these words, I will assume for the sake of argument that the meaning and function are the same.

4
The Irreconciliation of the *Essays* and the *Essay*[1]

Introduction

Of John Locke's philosophy, Peter Laslett writes, "Locke is, perhaps, the least consistent of all the great philosophers, and pointing out the contradictions either within any of his works or between them is no difficult task."[2] He argues that the inconsistency extends especially to his moral views.[3] John Colman writes:

> Locke's significance in the history of philosophy is a sufficient reason for a study of the relationship between his general epistemology and the ethical views expressed in the *Essay* and other of his writings; and a major aim of the present work is to show that, contrary to what has often been supposed, he does produce a consistent moral theory.[4]

Such divergent views about Locke puzzle the mind and demand thoughtful attention. In an attempt to partially solve this mystery, I will argue that, contrary to Colman, there is an important break in Locke's moral views between the *Essays On the Law of Nature* and in the *Essay Concerning Human Understanding*. I will also argue, contrary to Laslett, that Locke's views are not inconsistent because he has created problems for himself he could not solve.[5] Instead, I will argue that the incompatibility of his views stems from the different presuppositions from which he begins each work.

John Colman On the Reconciliation of the *Essays* and *Essay*

John Colman attempts to defend a view that I call "the reconcilability thesis." The reconcilability thesis is (partly) the claim that Locke's theory of moral knowledge in the *Essay* is compatible with the theory of natural law propounded in the *Essays*.[6] There are, however, three objections to this thesis: First, the *Essay* is at odds with the *Essays* because Locke rejects the essentialism of the *Essays*, and instead, accepts a corpuscular view of the world in the *Essay*. Second, Locke departs in the *Essay* from the natural law tradition in his treatment of good and evil. Third, Locke abandons the moral absolutism of the *Essays* for a version of ethical relativism in the *Essay*. John Colman has offered replies to each of these objections. As I pointed out in the Introduction, a number of scholars tend to agree with Colman. Nevertheless, I will argue that Colman's replies fail, and that the three objections stand.

Colman examines the objections that Locke is not a natural law philosopher because he rejects substantial forms in favor of corpuscularian essences.[7] Substantial forms (whether universal kinds or essences) are important to a natural law view of morality because without them we cannot know the law that governs the proper development of man.

Colman's response to this objection is essentially this. First, he simply admits that in the *Essay* Locke does reject substantial forms and embraces corpuscularism. Corpuscularism favors scientific explanations in terms of efficient causes. However, Colman argues that even though this is true, this does not entail the banishment of final or teleological explanations. This is so because it is possible for us to know the mechanical operations of things in terms of their final causes as God has assigned them. In fact, as Colman correctly points out, this is Robert Boyle's view.[8] Colman appeals to Boyle because, as I documented in chapter 1 and 3, Boyle was Locke's major source for these corpuscular views. In addition to this, Colman adds that since Locke, in the *Essay*, does not explicitly reject his own natural law views expounded in the *Essays*, Locke remains true to his natural law ethic in the *Essay* since his position in the *Essay* is at least compatible with Boyle's views concerning final causes.

My response underscores the difficulties that the text of the *Essay* creates for Colman's line of reasoning. What Locke says in the *Essay* is incompatible with his views in the *Essays* because as I argued in chapter 3 not only does he reject the existence of substantial forms but he also rejects scientific explanations in terms of final causes.[9] If I am right, then this lends strong evidence to the view that Locke rejects his natural law views in the *Essays* by rejecting substantial forms that are needed to defend such a view. Therefore, Colman fails to maintain his own position concerning Locke's early and later views of essences.

The second objection Colman considers concerns Locke's treatment of good and evil: Locke is not a natural law philosopher because he advocates in the *Essay* a subjectivistic and relativistic account of good and evil.[10] If this is true, then such a view is inconsistent with a natural law view because without an objective content to human happiness, there can be no general agreement concerning the good of humans.

Colman argues, however, that Locke's subjectivistic and relativistic account of good and evil in the *Essay* can be reconciled with his views in the *Essays*. Although his reasoning is complicated, Colman's argument is essentially this: even though Locke's views of the subjectivity and relativity of pleasure in the *Essay* will cause him trouble deriving some of the content of the law of nature, Locke's views of pain will not. This is so because certain sorts of pain will not vary much from human to human. Colman calls this Locke's negative hedonism.[11] Therefore, Locke can provide a rational foundation for a minimal content of the law of nature.

My argument against Colman proceeds in two different ways. First, in the *Essay*, not only does Locke argue that there is no general agreement as to what the proper good of man is, but he also argues that there is no proper good for man.[12] Such a point is inconsistent with a natural law theory because natural law stresses the point that there is a proper good for man, i.e., a good that is proper for his nature.

Next, Colman undermines his own position by maintaining that Locke is a negative hedonist in the *Essay* because this view is inconsistent with his moral theory in the *Essays*. This is so because negative hedonism would commit Locke to maintaining that certain types of pain are the key factor in the determination of the normativity of actions. However, in the *Essays*, Locke never gives pain, or pleasure for the matter, such a central focus and role. Instead, the normativity of actions is determined by the natural law, which prescribes modes of action suited to our nature.

Additionally, if we assume that Locke is a negative hedonist, it will commit him to a kind of ethical naturalism. Maintaining such a view commits Locke to the intrinsic existence of the property of goodness. However, there is evidence in both the *Essay* and in his essay, "Of Ethics in General," which was to be the last chapter of the *Essay,* that Locke is no longer committed to such an intrinsic property of goodness or moral goodness.[13]

In the light of both of my arguments against Colman's views of good and evil in the *Essay*, I conclude that he fails to maintain his own position. The consequence of such a failure lends more evidence that Locke is no longer committed to a natural law formulation of moral knowledge.

The final objection that Colman examines argues that Locke's philosophy in the *Essay* is contrary to natural law doctrine. This is so because Locke embraces some sort of cultural moral relativism. That is, Locke believes in the *Essay* that the variable law of opinion determines solely the moral goodness or wrongness of an action.[14] Colman attacks this view by arguing that Locke does not settle for ethical relativism in these terms. Instead, as Colman maintains, Locke advocates the view in *Essay*, as well as in the *Essays*, that the true touchstone of moral rectitude is the unvarying divine law, viz., the law of nature, standing behind the law of opinion or tradition. Tradition or the law of opinion, therefore, becomes the main source of knowledge of the law of nature.

First, even though I agree with Colman that the third objection he considers is flawed, Colman's understanding of why it is wrong is flawed itself. This is true because Locke advocates the view in neither the *Essays* nor the *Essay* that tradition is a source of true moral beliefs about the law of nature. Next, there is no real textual evidence in the *Essay* that Locke understands the divine law mentioned in the *Essay* in terms of the law of nature.

Although showing that Colman fails again on this last point is enough to prove that Locke's views cannot be reconciled, I believe that there is a way of salvaging this third objection he attacks. There is a version of moral relativism that Locke does hold that would put his views in the *Essay* further at odds with the *Questions*. As I discussed in the last chapter, this viewpoint is found in the *Essay* in his section on relations: *moral goodness is a relation between an act and one of three laws found in society.* As I argued in the last chapter, such a view is logically inconsistent with moral absolutism generally conceived and, therefore, logically inconsistent with his natural law views in the *Essays* because such a view is one version of moral absolutism.

Unfortunately, a problem still remains for my interpretation of the *Essay* and my thesis. There is a passage in the *Essay* where Locke appears to undermine everything I have said:

> The ideas of a supreme Being, infinite in power, goodness, and wisdom, whose workmanship we are, and on whom we depend; and the ideas of ourselves, as understanding, rational creatures, being such as are clear in us, would, I suppose, if duly considered and pursued afford such foundations of our duty and rules of action as might place morality amongst the sciences capable of demonstration: wherein I doubt not but from self-evident propositions, by necessary consequences, as incontestable as those in mathematics, the measures of right and wrong might be made out, to any one that will apply himself with the same indifferency and attention to the one as he does to the other of the sciences.[15]

Many scholars believe that this passage is indicative of Locke's commitment to a demonstrative system of morals. This means that Locke is, as Colman puts it, "committed to the view that the precepts of morality can be found out by unaided human reason,"[16] and that Locke himself understands this demonstrative attempt within a natural law framework.[17] This especially comes out in Locke's, *On the Reasonableness of Christianity.*[18]

But the passage above does not have to be interpreted in light of a commitment to the law of nature. First, this is so because, as I have argued, Locke's formulation of the account of morality in the *Essay* is inconsistent with his account in the *Essays*. Second, and this is a point that must be underscored, the passages at II. xxviii. 5 and at IV. iii. 18 are consistent. This is true because nothing in the text at IV. iii. 18 (or anywhere in the *Essay* for that matter) indicates that Locke is committed to the discovery of an eternally true, system of morality. Additionally, both passages are consistent because the definitions of the concepts of demonstration and self-evidence mentioned in IV. iii. 18 have no resemblance to what they normally mean in this kind of discussion. Finally, both passages are consistent because the foundationalism mentioned at IV. iii. 18 is not formulated to derive the nature of goodness or the nature of moral goodness. Instead, Locke's discussion at IV. iii. 18 makes clear his commitment to the nonfoundational nature of moral rules (and moral claims in general) and to how the justification of moral rules terminates in foundational nonmoral claims.

Now part of what Locke says at IV. iii. 18 becomes clearer in the light of the passage at II. xxviii. 5 and in the pages following this passage especially at II. xxviii. 6 and beyond (and visa versa). That is, at least with reference to the divine rules, Locke seems to think that men judge their actions against the divine rule "which God has set to the actions of men—whether promulgated to them by the light of nature, or the voice of revelation."[19] That is, our source of divine rules can either come from the voice of revelation, i.e., the Christian Scriptures, or it can from the light of nature, i.e., by means of the kind of foundationalism spoken of in the passage at IV. iii. 18.[20]

Perhaps there is still a problem. Maybe someone could object that Locke is committed in some sense to building an eternally true system of morals. This is so because of the important comparison he makes between moral knowledge and mathematical knowledge. For example, Locke writes, "*moral Knowledge* is as *capable of real Certainty*, as Mathematicks."[21] The assumption behind this view rests upon the position that since the ground of the certainty of mathematics is universal and eternal truth, then the ground of the certainty of morality must be the same. This is, in fact, the position Leibnitz maintains against Locke.[22] However, in the same passage just quoted above, Locke discusses the ground of both kinds of knowledge. In fact, as Locke argues, the ground is nothing but, and goes no deeper than, the perception of the agreement or disagreement of our ideas.[23] Locke understands the implication of his own view and writes the same:

> [B]ut it will here be said, that if *moral Knowledge* be placed in the contemplation of our own *moral ideas*, and those, as other Modes, be of our own making, What strange Notions will there be of *Justice* and *Temperance*? What confusion of Vertues and Vices, if every one may make what *Ideas* of them he pleases?[24]

Locke's answer to such a problem comes a few lines later, viz., that "'tis bare impropriety of speech to apply them [i.e., moral terms] contrary to the common usage of the Country."[25]

There is one final objection that I will discuss. The problem, as I see it for my interpretation (or if my interpretation is right, then a logical consistency problem for Locke's own position), rests upon the view that when Locke talks about the different kinds of moral rules or laws, he talks at length about the divine law. This is a problem because unlike the other rules which Locke discusses, viz., the Civil Law and the Law of Opinion and Reputation, the Divine Law, which he describes as the only true touchstone of moral rectitude, implies the existence of a single, ultimate, moral standard.

Perhaps one way to smooth out the problem is to reject my interpretation, specifically the part that emphasizes that moral goodness is a relation and, hence, does not exist independently of what we believe about it. But doing this would seem to fly in the face of certain texts in which Locke clearly states that moral goodness is a relation, not to mention the texts in which Locke discusses the nature of these kind of relations.[26] Moreover, if we reject my interpretation, then what are we to do about the Civil Law and the Law of Opinion? Locke clearly implies that the rules upon which moral goodness depends can be based on any one of the three that he mentions.[27]

If my interpretation is not to be rejected (at least not without ignoring important and clear passages), then there might be some way of reconciling the fact that Locke seems to hold simultaneously some sort of theistic absolutist view, and moral goodness is merely a conventional relation.

One way we might resolve this problem points to the fact that Locke may have come under pressure from his critics to say something more of the role that the Divine Law plays in all of this. In fact, this is documented in the Preface of the 4th Edition.[28] For example, Locke responds to an attack from James Lowde. Lowde (rightly) accuses Locke, after his reading of the passages at II. xxviii. 5-20, of making the Law of Opinion the sole source of virtue and vice. An implication of this position, Lowde (correctly) thinks, is that this makes virtue vice and vice virtue, for each society calls virtue those actions that they praise, and vice those of which they disapprove. Additionally, what one society calls a virtuous act another may call a vicious act. Locke responds to Lowde by arguing that his purpose is not to argue that these are the right sources, but only that they are possible sources that men use and can use.

Locke also adds that if Lowde would have taken the time to reflect more clearly upon what he said in the *Essay*, specifically II. xxviii. 5-20, even though virtue and praise are united closely, and even "though, perhaps, by the different Temper, Education, Fashion, Maxims, or Interest of different sorts of men it fell out, that what was thought Praiseworthy in one Place, escaped not censure in another; and so in different Societies, *Vertues* and *Vices* were changed,"[29] we must remember that what societies praise and blame are "for the most part kept the same every where."[30]

In what appears to be an attempt to clarify what he said and to set at ease Lowde's suspicions, Locke adds two sentences to his description of the Divine Law which appeared in the second edition of the

Essay (which was published in 1694), viz., "[*F*]*irst*, The *Divine* Law, whereby I mean, that Law which God has set to the actions of Men, whether promulgated to them by the light of Nature, or the voice of Revelation" and "This is the only true touchstone of *moral Rectitude.*"[31]

But even after these additions in the second edition, Locke's critics were not satisfied.[32] For example, after reading the same section of the *Essay*,[33] viz., II. xxviii. 8ff, Leibnitz (correctly) responds to Locke's relational view of moral goodness and virtue by pointing out that his view implies that the "one and the same act would be morally good and morally bad at the same time under different legislators."[34] Leibnitz adds that, since this is not "the ordinary sense that is given to morally good and virtuous acts, I prefer for myself, to take as the measure of moral good and of virtue the invariable rule of reason which God is charged with maintaining."[35]

Therefore, one way of making sense of what is going on here is to point out that Locke initially conceived of the Divine Law as one of three laws men can use to measure moral goodness. But by doing this, the Divine Law is put on an equal footing in its status and value with the other two laws.[36] This kind of lowering of the Divine Law appears to have worried many scholars including Lowde and Leibnitz. The implication of such a move raises the suspicion that the Divine Law is not a central doctrine in Locke's thinking and it does not have any sort of privileged metaphysical or epistemic position. However, to avoid any additional criticism, Locke adjusted the text of the *Essay* to read as orthodox as he could have.

Although this explanation makes sense of what Locke did, the logical problems still remain. Again, the logical problem rests upon the apparent fact that Locke simultaneously holds two inconsistent outlooks: a theistic absolutist view about morality and moral goodness and a relationally-based notion of moral goodness. Unfortunately, I do not think that this problem can be adequately solved. I do have, however, one other idea of how to make sense out of this.

Let me recast this discussion in a slightly different way. From my reading of the *Essay*, I see Locke attempting (partly) to reconcile the following problems. First, how do we account for moral goodness and evil in a world that denies the metaphysical machinery to support it, e.g., the universal Law of Nature? That is, how do we account for moral goodness and evil beginning from the presupposition of corpuscularism and its main assumption, viz., that there are only atoms in motion? This problem raises another interesting issue as well. What are we to do about the existence of God? How does He fit into this discussion? But, even more importantly, how are we to talk about God and the rules He has for our lives? These questions seem to be at the heart of Locke's worries.

One possible way of making sense out of this would be to suppose and to argue that Locke internalized Boyle's corpuscular view. In addition to this, we may suppose that this internalization led him to do two things. First, this led him to reject theism altogether. Second, since he did not want to abandon morality altogether, he created a relativistic conception of morality. This explains why he conceived of the three rules in the way that he did. However, when scholars like Lowde and others began to see the true nature of his discussion, Locke adjusted the text to make it read more like the currently accepted opinions of the Church. Therefore, what we see in the *Essay* is a philosopher resigning himself to the fact that corpuscularism makes it too difficult to believe in God. Additionally, if there is any room for morality, then we are left with only a relativistic conception of moral goodness and evil.

This view has certain advantages. It squares well with his relational view of moral goodness and evil. It also fits well with his rejection of moral properties. Additionally, it squares well with why he did not articulate a (solely) theistic view of morality. That is, God, like the civil servant who creates laws for society, has only his own will to consult. It also makes sense out of why Locke adjusted the text to read less like a heretical document (mentioned earlier), which created the logical problem in the first place. That is, he wanted (perhaps) to hide his radical departure from the normal way of discussing morality. Finally, this view sits consistently with his relational view of virtue and vice that many scholars worried about at II. xxviii. 10-12.

Now, while this view makes sense out of a lot of different strands of thinking in the *Essay*, it is far too radical. First, this is so because it does not square well with Locke's own life. He seemed to be a sincerely committed Christian. Locke's sincerity is also supported by his remarks in the *Reasonableness of Christianity*.[37] Second, such a view does not square well either with the text of the *Essay*. For example, Locke argues for the existence of God at IV. x and seems to think that certain attributes of God are foundationally basic for the deduction of nonbasic, moral rules mentioned at IV. iii. 18. Finally, such an interpretation does not sit well with the experimental flavor of the *Essay*. That is, as many scholars argue, the *Essay* appears to be Locke's attempt to mainly explore the implication of the presupposition of the new science.[38]

Another person might attempt to support a Laslett–like interpretation of the *Essay*. In other words, someone might argue that Locke (while maintaining his own theistic outlook) was, if not unconscious of the radical implications of his views he created, at least incapable of managing his views. This includes the implications of resting morality upon a relation and emptying the content of virtue and vice. It also includes not giving the Divine Rules a privileged status among the rules he discusses. While this point does not resolve the logical problem created by Locke in the second edition of the *Essay*, we may understand that he only made things worse for himself when he changed the text in the second edition. That is, we may understand that, when Lowde and Tyrrell made Locke aware of criticisms, he attempted (mistakenly) to fix the problem by introducing his own beliefs into the text of the *Essay*.

Such a view does have its advantages. It squares well with the text of the *Essay* generally, including the way he attempted to adjust it in the second edition. Moreover, it fits well with his response to James Lowde.[39] It also supports the kinds of problems that other scholars raised about the text of the *Essay*.

However, this interpretation seems problematic as well. This is so because Locke seems conscious of his own views and the implications of his views.[40] Additionally, while we can imagine that all the views and doctrines in the *Essay* might be terribly difficult to manage, Locke's overall intelligence stands against the view that he could not logically manage his own views. Finally, even if we suppose that there may be logical inconsistencies within the text of the *Essay*, they are not so overt as to deserve the kind of criticism Laslett provokes against Locke. I dare say that many of the problems found in the text of *Essay* are problems that only emerge after better ways are discovered to approach the kind of issues Locke discusses.

Finally, one might also attempt to pull together both strands in the following way. Locke embraces theism (personally and philosophically), but he does not embrace the moral relativism he attempts to defend in the *Essay*. However, after working out the implications of Boyle's corpuscularism, he thought that moral relativism is a natural consequence of corpuscularism. In fact, Locke argues for the relativity of moral goodness because, other than totally abandoning morality altogether, what else is left to talk about regarding the nature of moral goodness and evil? This view of morality ultimately led him, in good relativistic fashion, to list that by which people normally judge actions. However, when the text of the *Essay* came under the scrutiny of other scholars, Locke scrambled to adjust the text to assure others of his orthodox position. Therefore, what we see in the *Essay* is Locke's attempt to work out the implications of the new science beginning from the presupposition of corpuscularism and the constraints it imposes for our knowledge of moral goodness and evil.

Such a view has many advantages. First, it squares well with his rejection of the existence of moral properties and his argument for the relativity of moral goodness and evil. It also works well with his placement of the Divine Rule on an equal footing with the other rules. This interpretation also fits well with his personal views of Christianity and why he attempted to adjust the text to avoid trouble. Finally, this last view draws together his views of virtue and vice and the experimental flavor of the *Essay*.

In the end, I think the last interpretation has the best chance of making sense of why Locke ended up talking about morality and God the way he did. It was, perhaps, the only way he could talk about both given the constraints of corpuscularism.

Peter Laslett On the Irreconcilability of the *Essays* and the *Essay*

Peter Laslett attempts to defend a thesis that I call "the irreconcilability thesis." The irreconcilability thesis is (partly) the claim that Locke's views in the *Essay* are incompatible with (especially) his theory of natural law propounded in the *Essays*.[41] In fact, as Laslett points out: "The *Essay* has no room for natural law."[42] However, even though I agree with Laslett that there is no room for natural law in the *Essay*, I disagree with his reason for the incompatibility. Laslett argues that Locke's divergent views are a matter of his inability to manage his own views. I disagree with Laslett's reason because there is a better explanation for understanding the incompatibility of these two works. That is, the incompatibility rests upon the different starting points from which he begins both works. Let me attempt to make my point a little clearer.

As I pointed out in chapter 2, Locke attempts to demonstrate the existence of the law of nature in the *Essays*. The first question in the *Essays* is dedicated to that endeavor. The third argument of this question is of special importance for the present discussion. From this argument for the existence of the law of nature, we see Locke's reliance upon an Aristotelian outlook of the world, including his reliance upon universal kinds and essences. This outlook paints a picture of the universe where every particular thing, whether it is a physical object or some sort of living organism, has an essence or a form or a fixed nature that is determined by a universal kind. The essence of a particular determines basically two things. First, it determines the growth and identity of an individual object. Second it also determines the particular's function within the universe, i.e., it determines, as Locke writes, its "form and manner and measure of working."[43] It is this second aspect that interests here because the essence of a human guides it to become an animal with special kinds of capacities, capacities that distinguish it from all other beings and animals. Some of these capacities are mentioned in this quotation:

> for it does not seem to fit in with the wisdom of the Creator to form an animal that is most perfect and ever active, and to endow it abundantly above all others with a mind, intellect, reason, and all the requisites for working, and yet not assign to it any work, or again to make man alone susceptible of law precisely in order that he may submit to none.[44]

Although Locke begins the *Essays* with a number of presuppositions about the universe, viz., a Christian-Aristotelian outlook with its emphasis on universal kinds and essences, how does this square with his starting point in the *Essay*? The answer is plain: it does not square at all. Locke begins the *Essay* with a totally different presupposition. I would now like to turn to that discussion.

Locke's presupposition for the *Essay* stems from his reason for writing the *Essay*. As I pointed out in chapter 1, it is typically thought that the origin of the *Essay* grew out of a desire of a number of individuals (e.g., Boyle, Newton), and in particular Locke himself, to formulate in greater detail the epistemological basis of the knowledge of the law of nature that Locke had begun in the *Essays*. I have argued that the evidence does not support such an opinion. Instead, internal considerations of the *Essay* show Locke's staying force of concerns brought over from Boyle. In fact, many scholars argue that the amount of intellectual energy Locke put into the effort to find a philosophy of knowledge on par with Boyle's views, points to the stance that the *Essay* was primarily an attempt to bridge the gap between Boyle's corpuscular views and traditional philosophy.

Assuming that such a view is true, what does it mean to conceive the universe in corpuscular terms, and what kind of implications does this have for morality and especially natural law?

Conceiving the universe in terms of a corpuscular philosophy means (among other things) assuming that all things that exist are particular things. One significant implication of this assumption is the denial of universals or universal natures including universals conceived of as properties (e.g., virtue, shape or color), natural kinds (e.g., the various biological species and genera) and relations (e.g., being one apart or being next to). However, the proponents of universals argue that being able to talk about properties, kinds and relations is important. This is so because the existence of universals explains attribute agreement, the phenomena of subject predicate discourse, and the use of abstract or general terms. How does it differ from those who deny the existence of universals?

Those who deny the existence of universals argue (minimally) that in every instance mentioned above, universals are explanatorily irrelevant. Locke is no exception. For example, as I argued earlier, Locke denies the existence of all the metaphysical machinery to conceive of natural kinds as universals. In fact, he is well known for this. For example, Locke argues that appeal to universals (especially substantial forms or Aristotelian essences) to ground the formation of kinds is explanatorily irrelevant. Instead, natural kinds are put together and formed by us when we have a need to classify things into groups. Locke makes clear that there is nothing metaphysically deep about such classifications. It is just a way of speaking. The same holds true for even our ideas of substances in general.

Although Locke denies the existence of substantial forms and Aristotelian essences and all the metaphysical machinery to support such a view, what implications does this have for natural law? Let us suppose for the sake of argument that, in the *Essay*, Locke is committed in some sense to the existence of the law of nature. Also, let's place him with a specific natural law tradition: one that stems back at least to Aquinas. What kind of metaphysical machinery should be in place? Again, minimally, scholars from this tradition maintain a commitment to a certain kind of (repeatable) universal kind and an essence or substantial form.

But now we can ask the following question: what bearing does this have for Laslett's outlook of the *Essay* and *Essays*? What this shows is that although (as Laslett maintains) there is no room for the law of nature in the *Essay*, the reason is not that Locke was unable to consistently maintain his opinions. On the contrary, the reason is that Locke begins both books from completely different standpoints. The *Essays* presuppose a Christian/Aristotelian outlook, and the *Essay* begins from the assumption of corpuscles.

In this chapter, I describe and examine two different theses: the reconcilability thesis and the irreconcilability thesis. The reconcilability thesis is (partly) the claim that Locke's theory of moral knowledge in the *Essay* is compatible with the theory of natural law propounded in the *Questions*. John Colman attempts to defend the reconcilability thesis. I argue that Colman's views fail.

Peter Laslett attempts to defend the irreconcilability thesis. He argues that there is an inconsistency between the *Essay* and *Essays* because Locke created problems for himself that he could not manage. I argue against Laslett that Locke's views are not inconsistent because he created problems for himself that he could not solve. Instead, I argue that the inconsistency can be explained by making clear the different starting points from which he begins both works.

Finally, as I briefly discussed earlier, the positions of both Colman and Laslett also encompass the interpretation of the *Treatises*. For example, Colman argues that Locke's commitment to the law of nature can be traced from the *Essays*, through the *Essay*, and all the way to the *Treaties*. In addition to this, Laslett maintains his own thesis with reference to the *Treatises*. He argues that Locke's inability to maintain his own views extends into the *Treatises*.

In the next chapter, I argue against both views. Against Colman, I argue that Locke's commitment to the law of nature begins and ends the *Essays*. Against Laslett I maintain that the *Essay* and the *Treatises* are consistent. What emerges then is the following view: The *Essay* and the *Essays* are inconsistent, *and* the *Essay* and the *Treatises* are consistent.

Notes

1 The following discussion was initially published under the title, "Locke's Moral Revolution: From Natural Law to Moral Relativism," *The Locke Newsletter* 31 (2000): 79-114. The author would like to thank Professor Roland Hall, editor of *The Locke Newsletter* (now known as *Locke Studies*) for his permission to use the article in this book.

2 Laslett, "introduction to the *Two Treatises of Government*," 82.

3 Ibid.

4 Colman, *John Locke's Moral Philosophy*, 5.

5 Laslett, "introduction to the *Two Treatises of Government*," 82.

6 I say "partly" because Colman maintains that the consistency of Locke's views is traceable from the *Essays* through to the *Treatises*. I take Colman to defend the following thesis: The *Essays* and the *Essay* are consistent, *and* the *Essay* and the *Treatises* are consistent. In this chapter, I examine the first part, and in the next chapter, I examine the second part.

7 Colman, *John Locke's Moral Philosophy*, 240-2.

8 Robert Boyle, "A Disquisition about the Final Causes of Natural Things," in Thomas Birch (ed.), *The Works of the Honourable Robert Boyle* (London, 1772), 5: 392-452.

9 Locke, *Essay*, III. iii. 15-17.

10 Colman, *John Locke's Moral Philosophy*, 242-3.

11 Pamela Kraus also defends such an interpretation. See her essay, "Locke's Negative Hedonism," *The Locke Newsletter* 15 (1984): 43-63.

12 Locke, *Essay*, II. xxi. 55-56.

13 John Locke, "Of Ethics in General," 308-325.

14 Colman, *John Locke's Moral Philosophy*, 238.

15 Locke, *Essay*, IV. iii. 18.

16 Colman, *John Locke's Moral Philosophy*, 139.

17 Of course, this is the view that Colman advocates. But there are other scholars who also understand this passage in this way, e.g., Simmons, *The Lockean Theory of Rights*, 19; Grant, *John Locke's Liberalism*, 25-6; Rapaczynski, *Nature and Politics: Liberalism in the Philosophies of Hobbes, Locke, Rousseau*, 150; von Leyden, "Introduction to the *Essays On the Law of Nature*," 77; Aaron, *John Locke*, 266; Yolton, *Locke and the Compass of Human Understanding*, 170-2; S. Alexander, *Locke*, 71; J. D. Mabbot, *John Locke* (The Macmillan Co. 1973), pp. 116-121; and Thomas Burnett, "Second Remark upon an *Essay Concerning Human Understanding*: in a letter address'd to the author," in Peter A. Schouls (ed.), *Remarks upon an Essay Concerning Human Understanding: Five Tracts* (Garland Publishing, Inc. 1984), 20-1.

18 John Locke, *On the Reasonableness of Christianity*, ed. I. T. Ramsey (Standford, CA: Standford University Press, 1958), 64-68.

19 Locke, *Essay*, II. xxviii. 8.

20 The only other commentator on Locke who makes the same connection between the passages at II. xxviii. 5 and IV. iii. 18 is S. Alexander, *Locke*, 69-70.

21 Locke, *Essay*, IV. iv. 7.

22 Gottried Wilhelm Leibnitz, *New Essays Concerning Human Understanding*, tr. Alfred Gideon Langley (Open Court Publishing Co., 1949), bk IV, ch. iv, sec. 1-10.

23 Locke, *Essay*, IV. iv. 6-7.

24 Ibid., IV. iv. 9.

25 Ibid., IV. iv. 10; Brackets are mine.

26 Ibid., II. xxviii. 4-5 and II. xxv. 1-11.

27 Ibid., II. xxviii. 6.

28 See the first footnote on page 354 of Nidditch's edition of the *Essay*.

29 Locke, *Essay*, II. xxviii. 11.

30 Ibid.

31 Ibid., II. xxviii. 8. See the textual notes supplied by Nidditch on page 352 of the *Essay*.

32 This same passage also worried other scholars at Oxford. For example, James Tyrrell urged Locke several times to make clear what he means in this passage because "some thinkeing men at Oxford" think what he says "seems to come very near what is so much cryed out upon in Mr: Hobs; when he asserts that in the state of nature and out of a commonwealth, there is no moral good or evil: vertue, or vice but in respect of those persons, that practice [it or] thinke it so. if you please to tell me what I shall say to those that [make] this objection you will doe your self right" (James Tyrrell to Locke, 30 June 1690, in E. S. De Beer (ed.), *The Correspondence of John Locke* Vols. 1-8 [Oxford, 1979], 4: 100-2).

33 Leibniz read the French translation of the *Essay* published by Pierre Coste in 1700. Coste's translation is based upon the Fourth Edition of the *Essay* published also in 1700 and contained all the additions which Locke had made to the previous editions. For a discussion of this point, see Alfred G. Langley's comments in his translation of Leibnitz's, *New Essays Concerning Human Understanding*, 3-12.

34 Leibnitz, *New Essays Concerning Human Understanding*, Bk. II, ch. xxviii, sec. 5.

35 Ibid. Alfred G. Langley also writes concerning Leibnitz's view: "Leibnitz maintains, as against Locke's theory of relativity, the absolute and objective character of Moral Law. It is objective and universal, not subjective and particular; not dependent upon the opinions of men, but grounded in the 'the general institution of God,' and ultimately in his infinitely perfect moral nature, and is thus valid for and binding upon all moral beings as such. This Moral Law absolute and ideal which changes not; it is progressively and approximately attained or realized in the history of the individual and the race according to men's apprehension of its nature and requirements and their strength of purpose and effort in its pursuit" (*New Essays Concerning Human Understanding*, FN 1, 262).

36 von Leyden also makes a similar point: "For the purpose of an examination like this [i.e., Locke's project in the *Essay*] God's revealed law and the law of nature occupied no higher rank than any other of such rules nor did divine sanctions carry a greater force than those attached to the civil law or the

law of reputation. Within the scheme of the *Essay* Locke's intention was not to deal with the absolute and universal grounds of morality but with the variable moral ideas in men's minds and the several origins of their individual consciences" (von Leyden, "introduction to the *Essays On the Law of Nature*, 78; brackets are mine).

37 Locke, *On The Reasonableness of Christianity*, 43-44.

38 For example, Yolton writes, "Locke sought to elaborate an account of human understanding which would make sense of the new science of nature" (*Locke and the Compass of Human Understanding*, 16).

39 See footnote in Nidditch's edition of the *Essay*, 354-5.

40 See Locke's discussion of the comparison of moral knowledge and mathematical knowledge (IV. iv. 9) and his discussion of the nature of morality (II. xxviii. 4, 15).

41 The irreconcilability thesis also maintains the inconsistency of Locke's moral views in the *Essay* and Locke's moral views in the *Treatises*. Laslett spends most of his time discussing the relationship between the *Essay* and *Treatises* (Laslett, "introduction to the *Two Treatises of Government*," 79-92). I examine this view in the next chapter.

42 Ibid., 93.

43 Locke, *Essays*, 117; f. 18.

44 Ibid.

5
The Reconciliation of the *Essay* and the *Treatises*

Introduction

In the last chapter, I identified two different approaches that scholars take to work out the development of Locke's moral viewpoint. Again, one method emphasizes that Locke's moral outlook in the *Essay* and the *Essays*, especially with his reliance in the *Essays* upon the law of nature, can be reconciled. I argued that ultimately this stance fails because the *Essay* does not contain the metaphysical machinery needed to support the existence of the law of nature. As Laslett maintains: "The *Essay* has no room for natural law."[1]

The other approach sets out to defend the irreconcilability of Locke's moral perspective. Although I agree with this point of view, I took issue with the reason for the difference. Locke's moral perspectives are not different because he was unable to manage his own views; on the contrary, the difference is best explained by the different presuppositions from which he begins both works.

In this chapter, I concentrate on the ramifications of my arguments found in chapter 4 for some of the fundamental issues in the understanding of Locke's political philosophy found in the *Treatises*. Let me illustrate my point.

It is currently thought by many scholars that Locke's *Treatises* relate far more closely to the *Essays* than to the *Essay* because of the role of the law of nature in the first and second and its incompatibility with the third. If this is true, then Locke's approach to political matters in the

Treatises has the same and deep-rooted justification as his approach in the *Essays*. However, in this chapter, I outline a paradoxical alternative: an individual can but rub his eyes in amazement when he learns that even though it appears that the *Essays* and the *Treatises* are conceptually linked by virtue of the use of the term "law of nature," but when we look closer at Locke's reasoning, we see that the link is between the *Essay* and the *Treatises*.

No doubt, if my thesis is correct, an individual familiar with this literature will immediately see the ramifications for Locke's political views. Notwithstanding this point, it is still a line of reasoning worth rehearsing. I will begin with Colman.

John Colman On the Reconciliation of the *Essay* and the *Treaties*

Colman articulates, and no doubt reasonably defends, the position that there is a consistent strain of thinking that Locke attempts to defend in the *Essays*, continues to bolster in the *Essay*, and applies in the *Treatises*. This strain of thinking is, as Colman argues, Locke's loyalty to the law of nature. In addition to this, it must be pointed out that, at least from Colman's point of view, Locke's allegiance to the law of nature is one with deep metaphysical roots. That is, as I pointed out in chapter 2, (the early) Locke articulates for all intents and purposes a Christian/Aristotelian outlook of the world including a commitment to universal kinds and essences. But what exactly does Colman's thesis come to? Apparently to this: the Locke of the *Essays* is the same as the (later) Locke of the *Treatises*. That is, Locke's conception of the law of nature with its function in the state of nature, his reliance upon it to organize civil society, and, if Richard H. Cox[2] is correct, its role in the governance of the relations between nations, is the same as his use of the law nature in the *Essays*.

Despite the lucidity of Colman's reconcilability thesis, there are problems with it as I have analyzed it. To sum up, Colman's position is this: the *Essays* and *Essay* are reconcilable, *and* the *Essay* and *Treatises* are consistent as well. However, against Colman, I made a case in chapter 4 that the *Essays* and the *Essay* are not reconcilable. If I am correct, then I have shown that the reconcilability thesis is false because, from a (purely) truth-functional point of view, all I have to do is show that one side of the conjunction is false to show that the whole assertion is false. Therefore, I conclude that the reconcilability thesis is false.

Dispensing with Laslett's position is another matter. The reason is that our positions hitherto are, from a truth-functional point of view, essentially the same. We both conclude that there is no room for law of nature in the *Essay*, and as a consequence, the *Essays* and the *Essay* are not reconcilable. As I tried to show in chapter 4, the crucial difference between Laslett's and my standpoint are the reasons for the irreconcilability of both books. But how then shall I proceed to show that Laslett's thesis is false? My challenge is as follows. Laslett maintains not only that the *Essays* and the *Essay* are irreconcilable, *but* also that the *Essay* and the *Treatises* are not reconcilable. But now my present purpose is in focus: I must aim my arrows on the latter claim. To show that the latter claim is false is to confirm Laslett's irreconcilability thesis is false. That's the golden mark I seek to hit.

Peter Laslett on the Irreconcilability of the *Essay* and *Treatises*.

My attack of Laslett's position shall proceed in two ways. First, I reproduce and evaluate Laslett's arguments for the irreconcilability of the *Essay* and the *Treatises*. After finding fault with his arguments, I then give an (albeit brief) account of the *Treatises* and the role that the law of nature has in it.

Laslett begins the defense of his position by raising a mystery similar to the one I began with in my introduction.[3] The puzzle is this: why did Locke initially refuse to make known that he was the author of the *Treatises*? According to Laslett, one plausible explanation (and perhaps the most likely one) appears to be that Locke did not want scholars to compare his ideas of natural law in the *Treatises* with his ideas of natural law in the *Essay*. But why would Locke worry about that? Apparently, the answer has something to do with the negative attention Locke received about the *Essay* from "some thinking men at Oxford." In fact, these scholars at Oxford had discovered what I showed in chapter 4: The *Essay* has no room for natural law. In the end, as Laslett makes clear, Locke did not want the statements on natural law set alongside those statements in the *Essay* because the accounts are sharply at odds.[4] Fortunately, Laslett does not leave us in the dark about this problem, so I will turn to this discussion.

Laslett's method begins and proceeds in the following way. He attempts to convince us that Locke cannot consistently maintain his viewpoint between the *Essay* and the *Treatises* because the *Treatises* contains, for all intents and purposes, an orthodox view of the natural law.[5] In other words, as I understand Laslett, the view of the law of nature in the *Treatises* has its historical roots in that tradition which accepts the objective existence of the law of natural including the metaphysical machinery to support the natural law. In fact, as Laslett makes plain, this point serves to distance Locke from Thomas Hobbes (and, if he is right, Locke's own nominalist viewpoint in the *Essay* I outlined in chapter 4) in so many ways that it needs no great play of imagination to see the differences.[6] In fact, a mere cursory examination of the *Treatises* and the *Leviathan* will make his point clear.

With this idea in mind (one which I shall challenge momentarily), Laslett gives us an open, aboveboard, and explicit discussion of the major differences between the *Treatises* and the *Essay*. I will summarize and concentrate primarily on his major argument.

The major line of thought, in brief, is as follows. As Laslett points out, throughout the *Treatises* we are left with no misapprehensions about the existence of the law of nature:

> The *State of Nature* has a Law of Nature to govern it, which obliges every one: And Reason, which is that Law, teaches all Mankind, who will but consult it, that being all equal and independent, no one ought to harm another in his Life, Health, Liberty, or Possessions.[7]

However, in the *Essay*, the vivid portrayal of the law of nature is missing. In fact, as Laslett makes clear,[8] when Locke discusses the rules, which men refer their actions to, the law of nature is entirely missing:

> [T]he *Laws* that Men generally refer their Actions to, to judge of their Rectitude, or Obliquity, seem to me to be these three. 1. The *Divine* Law. 2. The *Civil* Law. 3. The Law of *Opinion* or *Reputation*, if I may so call it.[9]

Before I proceed with the examination of Laslett's argument, a couple of comments about this passage in the *Essay* are in order. First, as I discussed in chapter 4, this passage simplifies everything enormously when it comes to understanding the change in Locke's mind in the *Essay* and his reliance upon the law of nature. Additionally, as I argued in chapter 4, this passage (and the passages prior to this one, viz., II. xxviii. 5 and 6) provides substantial evidence of Locke's moral theory in the *Essay* and his commitment to moral relativisim.

I bring up these comments to underscore the importance of Laslett's position. Certainly, Laslett and I see eye to eye entirely concerning the first point. Obviously, Laslett never makes the second and more controversial point (and I doubt he would agree with it). Nevertheless, Laslett has mapped out with rigid precision the problem that I must investigate. I will now turn to that discussion.

My focus against Laslett will proceed by casting shadows of uncertainty on the idea that the law of nature mentioned in the *Treatises* is cut from the same cloth as the orthodox position of the law of nature. To do this, I will bring forward the following case: I will contend that Locke's description of the *state of nature* sets him at odds with the orthodox tradition. Next, I will argue that his description of the *individuals* in the state of nature does the same thing. After this, I will argue that much of what Locke discusses in the *Essays* is not brought forward into his discussion found in the *Treatises*. Finally, I will end this chapter with a brief alternative way of looking at the second part of the *Treatises*. It is my view that these facts bear sufficient evidence that, like the *Essay*, the *Treatises* have no room for natural law.

Locke's Account of the State of Nature

One of the fundament tenants of the *Treatises* is Locke's use of the state of nature. It is a concept that Locke employs no fewer than thirty eight times in the second part of the *Treatises*. Although the state of nature is not typically the center of discussions within the natural law tradition, it is a concept employed by those within the Christian/Aristotelian tradition, especially Hooker. On the latter account, man was originally in a state of innocence. Additionally, because of the introduction of sin and the consequent expulsion of Adam and Eve, they were thrust, so to speak, into a state of nature. (It should be noted that the passage Locke quotes from Hooker describes something like the state of nature even though Hooker does not explicitly use the term state of nature.)[10] Finally, because of the inconveniences of the state of nature, i.e., because of the nuisance of living alone even though it is relatively peaceful existence, humans, compelled by their natural propensity to seek the companionship with other humans, leave the prepolitical state to form a political civil society.[11]

Having briefly spelled out the role that the state of nature plays within the orthodox natural law tradition, what, if anything, do we want to make about such a point? The main line of thought, in brief, is as follows. One hallmark of an orthodox natural law view employs a specific account of the state of nature. In this view, the state of nature is a rather harmonious time period. Cox develops this point at length,[12] and it makes sense to think this is correct. The reason is that, as I pointed out in chapter 2, individuals possess certain properties that contribute to the overall peacefulness of the pre-civil society. That is, individuals within this tradition are basically rational and possess the fundamental predispositions to live according the law of nature. So if the *Treatises* contain an orthodox discussion of the natural law, as Laslett and Colman contend, then we would expect Locke to carve out an account of the state of nature in line with the Christian/Aristotelian tradition. But does he do this? Cox argues that this central theme is entirely missing from the *Treatises*:

> [M]y detailed argument in support of this interpretation of Locke's intention is divided into two parts; each centers upon one of two basically different usages which Locke makes of the term 'state of nature', but each converges on the conclusion that Locke's underlying view is that the original condition of man is one of 'pure anarchy', or that the state of nature, far from being a state of peace, harmony, and plenty, is in reality, one of war, enmity, and misery, in which the law of nature, so far from being effective, is not even known.[13]

I will now turn to consider Cox' reasons for thinking that Locke's account of the state of nature in the *Treatises* is outside of the orthodox tradition. The reasons Cox brings forward fall, in many ways, like a thunderclap. What I mean is this: the evidence that he brings forward is so compelling that it startles one out of the typical hermeneutical slumber so often reserved for the *Treatises*. Basically, Cox makes two points. First, Cox argues that although Locke begins the second part of the *Treatises* with a traditional description of the state of nature, what we notice is that Locke carefully modifies this description as he proceeds with his discussion. In fact, according to Cox, when we tease out all the passages that depict the state of nature, there is a striking parallel between Locke's state of nature and Hobbes' state of nature. Second, Cox makes a remarkable case that the state of nature and Locke's discussion of the state of war, normally thought to be conceptually distinct by Lockean scholars, in fact, are identical states.

To understand the point Cox attempts to make about Locke's depiction of the state of nature, it is not necessary to examine every pas-

sage at which the term "state of nature" occurs. Instead, I will only focus only on two references to the state of nature.

Locke essentially begins the second part of the *Treatises* with a
discussion about the state of nature.[14] Prior to the origins of civil society, all individual people are in a state of nature. This means that this is
time when there are no established civil laws, no recognized and indifferent judges with the authority to hear disputes between individuals,
and no common authorities to enforce the civil laws. Secondly, in reference to one another, all people are in a natural state of freedom and
equality. Since all people in a state of nature are free and equal, Locke
argues that no one ought to harm another person in his life, health, liberty, or possession.

Although Locke discusses what individuals may do in order to restrain others from violating the rights of others, what is typically missing is an explicit statement by Locke that indicates what he thinks
about this time period. Is it like Hobbes' state of nature? Is it short,
nasty and brutish? Is it a time of hardship and want? Or is it a time of
relative peace and harmony? Whatever it is, Locke leaves us with precious little to go on. Nevertheless, as Cox points out, one gets a general
impression that Locke has something like the latter point of view in
mind. Although this is not conclusive, this appears to be what Locke
wants us to understand two reasons. First, from his discussion of what
rights individuals have to defend themselves and (more importantly) to
what extent they may go to protect their own lives, one gets the impression that in the state of nature, ordinary prudence would (or should)
suggest that criminal activity is not worth the risk. Additionally, at the
end of his discussion of the state of nature, Locke includes a quote from
Hooker. Again, one is left with the feeling that the real reason that individuals form a political society is not because of insecurity, fear, dan-
ger, or want. On the contrary, as Hooker makes clear, individuals leave
the state of nature because they are tired of living alone.

As significant as raised letters to the blind, Locke changes the
mood of the state of nature in a later passage:

> [I]f Man in the State of Nature be so free, as has been said; If he be
> absolute Lord of his own Person and Possessions, equal to the great-
> est, and subject to no Body, why will he part with his Freedom? Why
> will he give up this Empire, and subject himself to the Dominion and
> Controul of any other Power? To which 'tis obvious to Answer, that
> though in the state of Nature he hath such a right, yet the Enjoyment
> of it is very uncertain, and constantly exposed to the Invasion of oth-
> ers. For all being Kings as much as he, every Man his Equal, and the

greater part no strict Observers of Equity and Justice, the enjoyment of the property he has in this state is very unsafe, very unsecure. This makes him willing to quit this Condition, which however free, is full of fears and continual dangers. . . .[15]

What are we to make of such a dramatic change? Cox argues that what we have here is a developing turnaround of Locke's early portrayal of the state of nature.[16] But let us get clear what this means. What we have here is not a reversal in the sense that Locke has changed his mind. Nor is it a reversal in the dreary sense that Laslett complains, viz., Locke is unable to manage his views. On the contrary, what we have here is a scholar, with an intuitive sense of affairs, slowly revealing what he eventually wants the astute reader to comprehend.

But if Cox is right about this point, why would Locke want to do this? Specifically, why would Locke want to give us an impression at the beginning of the second part of the *Treatises* that the state of nature is an era of good feeling and then change it into a time in which the milk of human kindness had turned sour? Although I do not think a conclusive answer is forthcoming, Cox gives a plausible explanation that Locke did not want his understanding of the state of nature associated with the state of nature describe by Hobbes. The reason is that, besides the obvious risks to his career and reputation, nothing was more inimical to society and to the true faith than the ideas of Hobbes. To light such a fuse would invite dangerous political ramifications.

Although, not having a conclusive answer may make one hesitate in making this point too positive, it does not impair the usefulness of what Cox wants to show. That is to say, Locke's progressive reversal serves to distance him from an orthodox view of the law of nature. There is another reason to think that Locke's state of nature is more akin to the state of nature discussed by Hobbes. According to Cox, although Locke writes as if the state of nature is different than the state of war, a closer reading reveals that they are the same. I will now turn briefly to that topic.

Another reason why readers of the *Treatises* have thought that Locke is closer in his outlook to a traditional account of the law of nature is that Locke makes a crucial distinction between the state of nature and the state of war. The discussions appear to be kept conceptually distinct by Locke. Hobbes, of course, collapses them together:

[H]ereby it is manifest that during the time men live without a common power to keep them all in awe, they are in that condition which is called war, and such a war as is of every man against every man.

For War consisteth not in battle only, or the act of fighting, but in a tract of time wherein the will to contend by battle is sufficiently known. And therefore, the notion of time is to be considered in the nature of war, as it is in the nature of weather. For as the nature of foul weather lieth not in a shower or two of rain, but in an inclination thereto of many days together, so the nature of war consisteth not in actual fighting, but I the known disposition thereto during all the time there is no assurance to the contrary.[17]

Locke's discussion of the state of war initially resists such a collapse. The reason is that whereas Hobbes delineates the state of war as a time where there is a chronic distrust and the lurking suspicion of immanent violence, Locke characterizes the state of war in dissimilar terms.[18] In fact, as Locke discusses very early in the second part of the *Treatises*, a state of war is not just a time where individuals are tortured by their own suspicions of each other. On the contrary, a state of war is created when one individual declares either by word or action that he intends to destroy the life of another. Locke remarks that such a declaration is not just a comment made in the heat of a quarrel (neither is it, I would add, a careless colloquialism); instead, what Locke has in mind is "a sedate setled Design" that is revealed by an announcement or by an action.[19] So, while a war may take place in the state of nature, one feels reluctant to see them as identical states. Unfortunately, as Cox points out, Locke's initial discourse "tends, naturally, to induce a framework in the reader's mind which is not easily disturbed thereafter."[20]

The question now is whether these states are truly kept separate in the second part of the *Treatises*. Again, as in the last section, Locke initially appears to set us upon a certain path only to clarify his meaning later. This issue is no different and is illustrated by three passages in question found toward the end of the *Second Treatise*, §§ 225-227.

The passages are part of Locke's examination of the dissolution of government. Specifically, the context concerns just how secure the foundation of a government is when it is based upon the consent of its citizens. Can such a republic stand upon such a flimsy base? Will not such an arrangement inevitably give way to frequent rebellion? Locke's carefully crafts his answer in three replies of which the second reply (§ 225) and third reply (§ 226) add to our understanding of the state of nature. The last section (§ 227) reinforces both replies made earlier.

In the second reply, Locke makes clear that although civil society rests upon consent of its members, the citizens of this republic are not so easily persuaded to give in to the temptation of revolution or rebellion. Perhaps from his own experience (Locke lived through the England's civil war), Locke remarks that citizens often put up with many abuses and mistakes with great patience. However, he does mention that there are extreme conditions in which the citizens will not placidly bear the strain of a corrupt government. Instead, these same citizens will endeavor to put the rule of the government back into the proper hands "to secure to them the ends for which Government was at first erected: and without which, ancient Names, and specious Forms, are so far from being better, that they are much worse, than the state of Nature, or pure Anarchy; the inconveniencies being all as great and as near, but the remedy farther off and more difficult."[21]

Here, reminiscent of Hobbes, Locke clearly describes the state of nature as a time of pure anarchy. But what are we to make of such a point? Cox uses this point to set the wedge deeper between Locke's true (but sometimes hidden) views and the traditional understanding of Locke's commitment to an orthodox understanding of the law of nature.[22] The point Cox makes is certainly interesting because although the state of nature described at the beginning of the *Second Treatises* is a time without civil laws, one does not come away with the impression that it is time of anarchy, i.e., something close to a time of chaos, enmity, and confusion. Although if this is not enough to convince someone that Laslett is wrong, perhaps the third reply will drive the wedge deep enough to push Locke away from a traditional outlook of the state of nature, to push him into the open arms of Thomas Hobbes, and ultimately away from the tearful eyes of Thomas Aquinas and Aristotle.

Although in the second reply Locke attempts to play down, so to speak, the potential for rebellion among the citizens of a government formed primarily by consent, in the third reply (§ 226) Locke makes the potential for rebellion a deep virtue for such a republic. Locke reasons that the leaders of society and civil government will think twice before making the situation too miserable for its citizens because the citizens know what is at stake: "For when Men by entering into Society and Civil Government, have excluded force, and introduced Laws for the preservation of Property, Peace, and Unity amongst themselves; those who set up force again in opposition to the Laws, do *Rebellare*, that is, bring back again the state of War, and are properly Rebels."[23]

Like the passage at § 225 discussed earlier, Locke appears to make a case that once the foundations of civil society are sufficiently undermined, the state of nature *and* a state of war is automatically reintroduced. At least for Cox, both states are coextensive. This is certainly one reasonable interpretation. But there is a problem that Cox appears to miss. Cox does not seem to understand that the passages at § 225 and § 226 discuss a specific example. That is, Locke specifically concentrates on what happens to a civil society that is successfully destabilized by *violent* means. Thus it would make sense to pronounce that a state of war (or a state of anarchy) is introduced because of the sedate and settled design of the rebels. But does this have to imply that the state of nature and the state of war are the same? I do not think so. Again, as I understand Locke's initial account of the state of war at the beginning of the *Second Treatise* (§§ 16-21), a state of war is introduced by specific criteria. It is not, as Hobbes contends, a time of fear and suspicion. What we need is a statement by Locke that makes clear that *any sort of dissolution* of the civil society introduces not just a state of nature, but also a state of war. Although I do not think such a passage is forthcoming, § 277 comes pretty close to what we need.

Locke begins § 227 in the following way: "In both the forementioned Cases, when either the Legislative is changed, or the Legislators act contrary to the end for which they were constituted; those who are guilty are guilty of Relbellion." The following point may be noticed at once. The quotation lists, what appears to be, two different conditions. The government can be dissolved when the Legislative is changed (without the consent of its citizens) or it can be dissolved when the members of the Legislative branch of the government act in some way that undermines the government. My intuitions, at this point, tell me that the distinction is important. The point, in short, is this. A civil government can be changed by non-violent or by violent means. But does the text support such a distinction? If it does, then we may have nearly resolute evidence for collapsing the state of nature and the state of war together. In fact, in the rest of the passage, Locke states the same. In short, the argument is this.

First, in the same paragraph (§ 227), Locke discusses separately both conditions I just mentioned. This means, at least, that he has in mind that a government may be dissolved in different ways. Second, when he discusses the first condition, he appears to have something close to what I have articulated. "They, who remove, or change the Legislative, take away this decisive power, which no Body can have, but by the appointment and consent of the People." Whatever change Locke has in mind, it appears he does not mean a violent overthrow. But here is the upshot. He concludes that "introducing a Power, which the People hath not authoriz'd, they actually *introduce a state of War*, which is that of Force without Authority: And thus by removing the

Legislative establish'd by the Society . . . they unty the Knot, and *expose the People a new to the state of War.*"

Finally, in the same passage, Locke discusses the second condition. Here it is clear that, unlike the first condition, Locke has in mind the violent dissolution of a civil government. "And if those, who by force take away the Legislative, are Rebels, the Legislators themselves, as has been shewn, can be no less esteemed so; when they, who were set up for the protection, and preservation of the People, their Liberties and Properties, shall by force invade, and indeavour to take them away; and so they putting themselves into a state of War with those, who made them the Protectors and Guardians of their Peace. . . .""

Taken together these passages appear to paint a different outlook of Locke's state of nature. The state of war is not just a possible intermittent, temporary time during the state of nature, it appears to be coextensive with the state of nature. Nevertheless, Cox anticipates skeptics at this point and adds the following thought for our consideration: "what can Locke mean by the expressions 'bring back *again* the state of war' and 'expose the people *anew* to the state of war except that the state prior to or without government *is* the state of war?"[24]

Locke's Account of the Nature of Individuals in the State of Nature

So far the facts bear sufficient witness that the second part of the *Treatises* cannot be treated simply as a document that takes its authority from the natural law tradition. To strengthen his point further, Cox brings into our view another aspect of the *Second Treatise* similar to the last point. Cox concentrates on Locke's description of human nature. Again, as he points out, Locke begins with a portrayal of human nature that is akin to a traditional viewpoint of the nature law. Later, however, Locke either changes his mind, or if Cox is right, Locke's true belief emerges—a view, no doubt, that is more in line with Hobbesian idea of human nature.

This discussion begins with Locke's statement concerning men's knowledge of the law of nature and the possibility of adherence to the law of nature in the state of nature.[25] Without a doubt, the story is familiar to anyone with even a cursory knowledge of the *Second Treatise*: "The *State of Nature* has a Law of Nature to govern it, which obliges every one: And Reason, which is that Law, teaches all Mankind, who will but consult it, that being all equal and independent, no one ought to harm another in his Life, Health, Liberty, or Possessions."[26] We may also add another passage to this one. In this passage, Locke attempts to speak to the extent punishment is allowable in the state of nature: "for though it would be besides my present purpose, to enter here into the particulars of the Law of Nature, or its *measure of punishment*; yet, it is certain there is such a Law, and that too, as intelligible and plain to a rational Creature, and a Studier of that Law, as the positive Laws of Common-wealths, nay possibly plainer. . . ."[27]

After reading these passages (and others not mentioned), one is left with two plain unvarnished facts. The knowledge of the law of nature requires no extraordinary perception to discern, *and* the informing light of the law of nature upon the minds of all mankind produces a very clear conviction to follow the precepts of the law of nature. Nevertheless, Cox points out that later on in the *Second Treatise* Locke appears to be in no way prepared to assume the responsibility of this viewpoint.[28] On the contrary, Locke veers to the other extreme, which makes him look like he is infected with the disease of indirection (no doubt a view Laslett might maintain). But is this really the case? Perhaps a discussion of the texts in question can settle this point.

The passages in question are II. §§ 124-127. Here Locke's discussion focuses primarily on why men leave the state of nature and form a government. His conclusion is one of Locke's most telling strokes: "The great and *chief end* therefore, of Mens uniting into Common-wealths, and putting themselves under Government, *is the Preservation of their Property*. To which in the state of Nature there are many things wanting."[29] But what is even more telling are the reasons he gives, and it is here that Cox makes his case.

First, the individuals, who live in the state of nature, leave the state of nature because there is no "*establish'd*, settled, known *Law*, received and allowed by common consent to be the Standard of Right and Wrong, and the common measure to decide all Controversies between them."[30] Of course, that is right. But what about the role of the law of nature? Does it not play a role in the guidance of those in the state of nature? Locke seems to articulate that it does in the first part of the *Second Treatise*, §§ 4-15. But the following text indicates something different: "For though the Law of Nature be plain and intelligible to all rational Creatures; yet Men being biased by their Interest, as well as ignorant for want of study of it, are not apt to allow of it as a Law binding to them in the application of it to their particular Cases."[31]

The following two points may be noticed at once. First, individuals in the state of nature do not perceive the law of nature because each individual is intoxicated with pride and possesses a lack reverence for the authority of the law of nature. Second, each individual of the state of nature appears to ignore the evidence of the existence of the law of nature, which is conclusive to all fair-minded men. In other words, individuals in the state of nature appear to be utterly heedless of the teachings of the law of nature.

The next section in the *Second Treatise* (§ 125) adds no less authority to the position Cox defends. The urge to leave the state of nature is aggravated by the fact that "there wants *a known and indifferent Judge*, with Authority to determine all differences according to the established Law."[32] Initially, when Locke discusses this point in the first part of the *Second Treatise*, even though the law of nature authorizes each person to be a judge in his own case (and in the case of others unjustly attacked) with the additional last word to be executioner of the law of nature, Locke makes clear that the apprehension of the law of nature constrains extreme responses. But now Locke appears to alter his views: "For every one in that state being both Judge and Executioner of the Law of Nature, Men being partial to themselves, Passion and Revenge is very apt to carry them too far, and with too much heat, in their own Cases; as well as negligence, and unconcernedness, to make them too remiss, in other Mens."[33]

Locke adds one more point in § 126 before summarizing his thoughts in § 127 about the urgency of the formation of civil society. It is similar to the last point in § 125. Again, men leave the state of nature because of the lack of legal system. As a result when an injustice occurs, the heat of passion and revenge are likely to overshoot the mark of a reasonable compensatory calculation and levelheaded punitive measures. Now Locke adds a remarkable statement. Normally, after one reads §§ 4-15, one is left with the impression that in the state of nature since every man has the authority to be judge and executioner of the law of nature, an equilibrium would naturally result between those bent on evil and those who only desire to a live a wholesome life. As a result, one is left with the impression that the state of nature is a relatively safe time period. But now Locke appears to modify that viewpoint. There is no equilibrium; instead, evil enjoys the advantage because, as Locke makes clear, "They who by an Injustice offended, will seldom fail, where they are able, by force to make good their Injustice: such resistance many times makes the punishment dangerous, and frequently destructive, to those who attempt it." In other words, in the state of nature, justice is a goal far more remote that we had supposed it to be, and those who seek justice often pay the cost with the pangs of keenest misery.

There is one last point in § 127 that must be mentioned. Again, after one reads Locke's initial statements on the law of nature, one is left with an air of quiet, unaffected assurance that although men were motivated eventually to create civil society, there was, nevertheless, an atmosphere of reluctance to lose the freedom and equality guaranteed by the law of nature. But such an interpretation should be met by a flat refusal. Locke plainly states that the conditions mentioned early do not make people *merely* reluctant to leave the state of nature; on the contrary, the environment of the state of nature gives rise to the tremendous earnestness to leave the state of nature. In fact, Locke adds something even more remarkable: because the state of nature is so inconvenient "we seldom find any number of Men live any time together in this State."[34]

Although the shadows of uncertainty should be dark enough to blur the position that the law of nature mentioned in the *Treatises* is cut from the same cloth as the orthodox position of the law of nature, the vigorous school of necessity demands that I proceed to give more evidence less the opposition, in their infatiguable defense of Laslett's position, convince themselves that my position relies too heavily on the views of Cox, or as is commonly enunciated in scholarly circles, my position lacks depth, or it is too shallow. Therefore, to weaken the persistently hostile stance taken against alternative interpretations of the *Second Treatises*, I will finish chapter 5 with additional substantial evidence that proves that I have no less authority to maintain that the *Second Treatise* does not derive its authority from the orthodox natural law tradition, nor does it obtain its authority from the domination of Laslett's influence by the sheer force of his personality.

A Brief Comparison of the *Essays* and the *Second Treatise*

Cox correctly points out that Locke's law of nature "bears practically no resemblance, except in name, to what was meant by most of his contemporaries, and certainly can in no way be reconciled with what his seeming authority, Richard Hooker, meant by the natural law."[35] Cox argues persuasively that an internal examination of the *Treatises* reveals that Locke's commitment to the law of nature is more akin to Thomas Hobbes' view of the law of nature. I would also add that it certainly bears no resemblance to even Locke's own early 1664 views of the law of nature in his *Essays*. I will now turn to this discussion.

As I mentioned earlier, Laslett maintains not only that the *Essays* and the *Essay* are irreconcilable, *but* also that the *Essay* and the *Treatises* are not reconcilable. So far I have tried to bring forth well-authenticated testimony in such a way as to raise a suspicion that the *Essay* and the *Treatises* are reconcilable. To do this, however, is as difficult as untangling a length of yarn that runs into knots continually. Although Cox demonstrates persuasively that Locke's use of the law of nature is not consistent with the traditional outlook of the law of nature, his examination has not been accompanied by irrevocable guarantees that this is so. If I am right, the need is urgent that I bring forth additional indisputable and overwhelming evidence that the *Essay* and the *Treaties* are reconcilable. Athough I do not think such a position is ultimately defensible, I am steadfast that my position is equally credible as Laslett's thinking and, therefore, just as respectable for scholarly society.

In the rest of this chapter I am going to do two things. Although Cox distances Locke from the natural law tradition, he does not detach Locke from his own natural law roots. As I discussed in chapter 2, Locke articulates, for all intents and purposes, in the *Essays On the Law of Nature*, a traditional natural law viewpoint.[36] Therefore, I will briefly match the *Essays* up to the *Second Treatise* in order to make it clear that Laslett's interpretation is not the only adequate reading of the *Second Treatise*. After that I am going to address specifically the issue of the consistency between the *Essay* and the *Second Treatise*. I will try to show that the conclusions I derive in chapter 4 can find a home in the *Second Treatise*: a home that will not create more hermeneutical problems than it tries to solve.

Let me begin with my assessment. I will focus primarily on those features employed by Locke in the *Essays* that make him a natural law theorist, and then I will argue that these features are missing in the *Second Treatise*. But what features are necessary to be characterized in this way? As I mentioned earlier in chapter 2 and in chapter 4, the following concepts are most of the fundamental tenants for a natural law theory worth its salt: there must be a commitment to the existence of universal kinds, of essences, a human function, a human good, and virtues that aim at the good.[37] Of course, Locke explicitly denies the existence of each one in the *Essay*. But what about the *Second Treatise*? Anyone familiar with the *Second Treatise* understands that there is no discussion of any of these concepts.[38] In fact, when it may have been advantageous to discuss these topics (and our most sanguine hopes exceeded), Locke apparently sidesteps the issue because it would be an unnecessary distraction. Notwithstanding this last point, why does Locke avoid discussing these points? I think there are a number of plausible interpretations, and so I will turn now to consider which one is the best explanation.

The first account is the one that both Cox and I explicitly reject. That is, the first rationalization is that Locke is in fact committed to a natural law outlook in the *Second Treatise*. On this view, Locke avoids discussing the rudiments of the natural law because it is genuinely beside his point. And, of course, such an explanation is entirely plausible because the *Second Treatise* is Locke's reflections about political philosophy and not about the metaphysical underpinning of his thoughts.

This position certainly has the tide of victory in its favor because in the *Second Treatise* Locke uses the lingo of a natural law theorist. He refers to the natural law several times and employs it in ways similar to other accepted natural law theorists. Unfortunately, I do not think such a view can pass through the fires of affliction. First, I think Cox makes a good case that Locke has in mind something different than just articulating an orthodox outlook. An internal examination of the *Second Treatise* reveals that Locke begins with views similar to those in the natural law body of literature only to undermine the account. Second, such an understanding of the *Second Treatise* does not take into the historical context surrounding Locke's intellectual development discussed in chapter 1 and chapter 4. That is, it does not take into account Boyle's influence on Locke and the major project that consumed Locke at the same he was writing the *Second Treatise,* viz., Locke's attempt to work out the implications of the new science beginning from the presupposition of corpuscularism and the constraints it imposes on our knowledge of moral goodness and evil.

The second narrative I take to be just as equally plausible to the one above. Locke does not discuss the metaphysical underpinnings of the law of nature because although he uses the term "natural law" he is no longer committed to its existence. The strength of this view rests upon the historical evidence mentioned above. I also want to add one more point that, as far as I know, has not been brought forward for debate. Again, there is pretty good evidence that Locke's most important goal for writing the *Essay* was simply and solely for the purpose of reconciling corpuscularism and the possibility of moral knowledge. Unfortunately, what is overlooked is whether Locke had other addition goals for the *Essay*? There is *prima facie* evidence that the answer is yes. The support is actually brought forward by Laslett, but surprisingly unnoticed. Here is how I understand this point.

As I pointed out earlier, Laslett complains that the *Essay* and *Treatises* cannot be seen as an integrated body of work.[39] The basic reason is that Locke never analyses concepts in the *Treatises* in the way he does in the *Essay*.[40] Or the problem can be put in this way. Locke's methodology is significantly different in the *Treatises* than his style in the *Essay*. Of course, Laslett is precisely right. Locke never scrutinizes his political concepts in the *Treatises in the same way* he breakdowns his moral concepts in the *Essay*. But what eludes me is why Laslett does not seem to appreciate the examples Locke uses in the passage where Locke discusses the demonstration of morality.[41] His demonstration employs political concepts. In fact, they are the very same concepts employed in the *Second Treatise*. But what does this detail demonstrate? This attests to the observation that the problem has now to be envisaged from a wider angle. Here is the point. Just because Locke does not utilize the same methodology in the *Treatises* as he brings into play in the *Essay* does not mean that there still is not a conceptual link.

Can this latter interpretation stand the test of scrutiny expected by the scholarly community or will it be laughed out the court? No doubt there are weaknesses. The most obvious one is that I have not proven Laslett's standpoint incontrovertibly false. Although that is ultimately the mark I would like to shoot for, my goal for this chapter is something less than that. In its place, I want to show that I have no less authority for the claim that the *Second Treatise* is not a natural law document. In other words, the *Treatises* do not need to be seen as another tedious and twice-told tale about the authority of the law of nature so popular during Locke's day. I think the *Treatises* has something more drastic and far sweeping than that, and so I will turn to that discussion.

A Corpuscularian Account of the *Second Treatise*

The unyielding quality of Laslett's position rests largely on the apparently settled differences between the *Essay* and the *Treatises*. I have sought to give a clear and vigorous presentation that the dissimilarities are not as obvious as Laslett suggests. Nevertheless, there still remains an issue that hitherto has not been discussed. Like Laslett, I agree that there is no room for natural law in the *Essay*. At the bottom of this assertion are the concerns that Locke brings forth from Boyle and corpuscularism. But if, as I maintain against Laslett, the *Essay* and *Treatises* are consistent, then some attempt should be made to account for the consistency, an account that redefines and recasts the *Second Treatise* in a different light. Although such an endeavor would be too large for this chapter, there is still a way of making clear what it would look like. The focus, as I see it, has to be on the argument Locke gives at the beginning of the *Second Treatise*.[42] It is that argument with its alignment to the law of nature that is taken as the touchstone for the interpretation of the *Second Treatises*. Therefore, in what follows, I will recast this argument in terms of a corpuscular outlook. This is where I believe the shoe pinches.

In order to challenge the abiding significance of Locke's perceived association with the law of nature, it is again necessary to consult the views of Cox. According to Cox, in order to understand Locke's argument in § 6 of the *Second Treatise*, we must focus on the ideas of *freedom* and *equality* first mentioned in §§ 4 and 5, and then used in his premise to derive the conclusion that no one ought to harm another. I will now turn to that discussion.

For Locke the properties of equality and freedom that he ascribes to individuals in the state of nature are inextricably tied to what he calls the precepts of the law of nature. This means that when Locke speaks of the natural properties of men he has in mind to connect them to a person's right to preserve himself and others when necessary. Cox treats these issues in the same way and collapses them together: "Men are equal with regard to their right to execute the law of nature— which, stated more candidly, means the right to do whatsoever is judged necessary to the maintenance of one's corporeal being."[43] Cox is correct, but certainly these issues can be kept separate. That is, we can describe Locke's move from the ascription of the properties of equality and freedom of individuals to the rights individuals have because of these properties. At the same time, we can also ask why Locke believes all individuals in the state of nature are equal and free as well. Of course, the answer to the second question is fundamentally important for us to know because it gives us the foundation upon which the rights of persons are based.

Cox is also after the answer to this latter question as well. Unfortunately, as Cox points out, he is well aware of the fact that Locke does not explain what this means:

> For the sum of his argument, as it appears in the chapter on the state of nature, amounts to this: Men are equal with regard to their right to execute the law of nature—which, stated more candidly, means the right to do whatsoever is judged necessary to the maintenance of one's corporeal being, including the killing of those who are a threat—because they are all 'creatures of the same species and rank, promiscuously born to all the same advantages of nature and the use

of the same faculties . . . .' This is clearly insufficient. What we want to know is what those 'faculties' are, how they are connected to the 'same advantages of nature'. Yet practically no argument or explanation on these matters is to be found at this point in the *Second Treatise*.[44]

What this quotation demonstrates is where Cox understands the answer lies: we must tease from Locke's mind his meaning behind his use of "faculties." Once we understand what this means, we will know why individuals are equal and free and then we will understand the foundation of Locke's law of nature.

Cox's summarizes two important doctrines that Locke discusses sporadically between both the treatises of the *Treatises*.[45] The doctrines in question are Locke's reliance upon self-preservation and the instrumental character of the senses and reason. Naturally, Cox concludes that these are the "faculties" mentioned earlier and the foundation of Locke's law of nature: "[T]his conception of the natural primacy of the desire for self-preservation and of the instrumental character of the senses and reason, becomes the foundation, in the *Treatises*, of what Locke chooses to call the 'law of nature.'"[46] I will now attempt to summarize his explanation.

According to Cox, the referent, so to speak, of Locke's "faculties" is Locke's commitment to the existence of a strong desire for self-preservation in man and Locke's commitment to the instrumental character of man's noetic endowment as a means to the end of self-preservation.[47] But why are these characteristics the underpinnings for his assessment of equality? Again the answer is tied to both aspects of man. The underlying line of thought, in brief, is as follows. All men have in common the strong and deep-rooted desire for self-preservation. It is a fact of tremendous significance for Locke. Cox makes this point clear: "the desire for self-preservation, which in its most natural form would be the mere spontaneous impulse to continue one's bare corporeal existence, is primordial, universally operative, and the most powerful of all desires."[48] So, Cox finds in Locke a quality that all men share, a quality that is a necessary component of the equality of all men.

The other aspect is as follows. All men are endowed with senses and reason that, as Cox elaborates, "are conceived of essentially as means to the end of preservation, which is to say as derivative of, or intended by nature to serve as instruments for, the gratification of the desires or passions."[49] Together, then, as Cox demonstrates, both act as the basis for Locke's declaration of equality.

A careful reader will no doubt understand that although Cox has reasonably illuminated Locke's notion of equality, he has left out an important aspect. That is, Cox fails to discuss Locke's use of the notion of freedom. This is a problem because Locke mentions both, and the assumption is that both are needed, at least in Locke's mind, in order to derive the rights and obligations of the law of nature (II §4 and §6). As far as I can tell, although Cox discusses the fact that Locke uses such a notion, he never discusses the foundation of the notion of freedom in Locke's *Treatises*.

This is of no little moment for Cox's position. But, perhaps, my criticism misses the mark because, as Cox or others might argue, Locke's notion of freedom is not necessary to derive the precepts of the law of nature. And yet such a outlook is mistaken because Locke's argument includes both: "The State of Nature has a Law of Nature to govern it, which obliges every one: And Reason, which is that Law, teaches all Mankind, who will but consult it, that being all equal *and independent*, no one ought to harm another in his Life, Health, Liberty, or Possessions."[50] I take Locke here to use the nouns, "independent" and "freedom," as synonyms.

Perhaps Cox may respond to my objection by admitting that he left this point out because what Locke means is utterly obvious. That is, what Locke means by a state of perfect freedom just means that all people have free will. This will not work either. First, there is no evidence in either his *Essay* or the *Treatises* that Locke articulates freedom of the will. In fact, Locke actually argues in the *Essay* that there is no such thing as freedom of the will.[51]

Second, a close scrutiny of the text in chapter II of the *Second Treatise*[52] reveals that what Locke means is something unrelated to the freedom of the will. Here I follow Laslett on this point.[53] What Locke means is that all people are *born* in a state of freedom. This meaning is also confirmed in a passage later on in the *Second Treatise*.[54] In fact, Locke argues that not only are all men born free in the state of nature, he even argues that all people are born free even when they are born in a political society. Although I will discuss Locke's meaning of the phrase "born free" momentarily, his point is clearly illustrated in this passage: "not to be subject to the arbitrary Will of another, but freely to follow his own."[55] Nevertheless, the question still remains why Locke argues this, and, as far as I can tell, Cox never discusses this point.

The straightforward meaning of the claim that all people are free in the state of nature is that all people in a state of nature are born free. Unlike a wave of the sea driven with the wind, an individual will lose this freedom only when he *consents* with others to form a common-wealth (II § 112), or if he is born in a political society, he *agrees* to be a member of a political society at the age of consent (II § 199). But still the follow question remains: what defense does Locke have that all people whether born in a state of nature or born in a political society are born free? The matter should not be permitted to go by default.

I will attempt to respond to this question by discussing two view-points that appear to be disconnected in the *Second Treatises*. In fact, Cox discusses both of these points, so for the purposes of this discussion I will rely upon his scholarship. His points, in brief, are these. First, Cox finds in Locke a reliance upon the Christian Scriptures and upon orthodox scholars like Richard Hooker[56] that gives his ideas an air of respectability. Nevertheless, as I tried to make clear earlier, Cox points out that Locke's intentions were much more complex because "it is impossible to reconcile the conditions and the powers ascribed by Locke to men in the state of nature with what his 'authorities' say about the original condition of mankind."[57] If Cox is right (and I think there is good evidence for this), what was he up to? Cox writes: "Locke, yield-ing indeed to the pressures of religious orthodoxy to the extent of ap-pearing to accept it, in fact cautiously adopts a view which is derived from an earlier philosophic (but therefore 'pagan') teaching, such as that of the ancient Stoics."[58]

Second, Cox also correctly points out that Locke's law of nature "bears practically no resemblance, except in name, to what was meant by most of his contemporaries."[59] I also add that it certainly bears no resemblance to even Locke's own early 1664 standpoint of the law of nature in his *Essays*. Cox argues persuasively that an internal examina-tion of the *Second Treatise* reveals that Locke's commitment to the law of nature is more akin to Thomas Hobbes' vision of the law of nature.

I want to argue that if we assume that Cox is right about both of these observations there is a way of connecting them both together. Additionally, the answer to how these ideas are connected is the expla-nation for why Locke believes that people are born free. Both stand-points are brought together by Locke's commitment to a metaphysical theory called nominalism. Roughly put, this is the standpoint that there are no universals. There are only particular individuals with particular properties.[60] Of course, I readily agree that such a theory is not appar-ent in the *Second Treatise*; however, a careful examination of Locke's *Essay* will reveal his commitment to nominalism.[61]

Still, I imagine that such a point is still opaque. In fact, the follow-ing questions still seem appropriate: how does his commitment to nominalism connect the viewpoints mentioned earlier, and how is this the basis for his point of view of freedom? The answer to both questions, in brief, is as follows.

A commitment to nominalism during the seventeenth century was tantamount to a commitment to atheism. This is so because it denied many beliefs held true by the Christian church. It denied the existence of innate ideas, including the innate idea of God, and it also denied a deep metaphysical justification for virtue and vice. Scholars before his death accused Locke of both standpoints.[62] A commitment to nominalism also denied the existence of the law of nature, an independent body of moral precepts contained in the natural order. If all of this is true of Locke, then he had good reasons to hide the fact that his beliefs in the *Second Treatise* were nominalistic. This could be done first by associating himself with recognized religious authorities and associating himself with orthodox doctrines such as the law of nature.

Although this explanation goes a long way to reconciling both doctrines, there is still the question of how this is connected to freedom. The connection is this: at least for Locke, his commitment to nominalism was motivated primarily by his allegiance to corpuscularism, a belief he acquired from the Royal Society and Sir Robert Boyle. It is the position that the world is ultimately made up of corpuscles or atoms and that a complete explanation of the world begins with a story about corpuscles in motion. Such a point seems innocuous (at least by our own lights); however, it leads to a radical reinterpretation of the status of humans: since all humans that are born are just clusters of spinning corpuscles, there are no primary or secondary qualities that make a human naturally subject to the rule of another. All humans are naturally unrestricted, independent, and autonomous. In other words, *all humans are free*.

We are now in a position to consider Locke's argument: "The *State of Nature* has a Law of Nature to govern it, which obliges every one: And Reason, which is that Law, teaches all Mankind, who will but consult it, that being all equal and independent, no one ought to harm another in his Life, Health, Liberty, or Possessions." A couple of comments about this line of argument are in order. First, Locke identifies the law of nature with reason. Although Locke does not make clear his meaning, it is probably close to Aristotle's notion of right reason. In other words, this is just another way of articulating that when an individual reasons this way, he is reasoning in the correct way. Certainly, this leads to the second point because immediately after this Locke identifies the right way to reason. According to Locke, once we understand that all people are equal and free, we should understand that what we might do to others is constrained by their equality and freedom.

There is a plausibility to this argument because, even as Locke points out, when one party unjustifiably harms another individual, the first party denies the freedom and equality of the second party. But why is this so? First, the first party denies the second party's equality because acting this way fails to recognize the equality making characteristics they both possess, viz., the natural primacy of the desire for self-preservation and the instrumental character of the senses and reason. The reasoning is the same for the denial of freedom. That is, when an individual unjustifiably attacks another individual, his act is tantamount to the denial that all humans are by nature unrestricted, independent, and autonomous. Locke summarizes both points in this way: the unjustifiably killing of an innocent person is an inexcusable form of subordination. But it is a subordination of the worst kind. That is, such a killing is equivalent, in some sense, to saying that the killer is *superior* to the victim and, as a result of that superiority, the killer is *authorized* to take the life of the victim. But as I insist, once we understand what Locke means by equality as unpacked by Cox, and once we understand his notion of freedom with its roots in corpuscularism, no one can possess that kind of superiority.

The conclusion of this chapter, then, is essentially this. Can we maintain with the same assurance that the *Second Treatise* finds its authority from the orthodox natural tradition? Additionally, can we maintain with the same assurance that the *Essay* and the *Treatises* are irreconcilable? I have argued that the answer is *no* to both positions. If my reasoning has been sound, a third view about the relationship between the *Essays*, *Essay*, and the *Treatises* emerges: the *Essays* and the *Essay* are irreconcilable, and the *Essay* and the *Treatise* reconcilable.

Notes

1 Laslett, introduction to the *Treatises*, 81.

2 Richard H. Cox, *Locke On War and Peace* (Oxford, 1960). I hope to publish my own critique of Cox's views in another study.

3 Laslett, introduction to the *Treatises*, 79-92.

4 Ibid., 81.

5 Ibid., 82.

6 Ibid., 83.

7 Locke, *Treatises*, II §6.

8 Laslett, introduction to the *Treatises*, 81.

9 Locke, *Essay*, II. xxviii. 7.

10 Locke, *Treatises*, II §15. I am endebited to Cox for this point. See *Locke on War and Peace*, 41.

11 Cox, *Locke on War and Peace*, 52.

12 Ibid., 73-81.

13 Ibid., 72.

14 Locke, *Treatises*, II. §§ 4-15.

15 Ibid., II. § 123.

16 Cox, *Locke on War and Peace*, 77.

17 Thomas Hobbes, *Leviathan*, ed. Edwin Curley (Indianapolis and Cambridge: Hackett Publishing Company, Inc., 1994), I. xiii. 8.

18 Locke, *Treatises*, II. §§ 16-21.

19 Ibid., II § 16.

20 Cox, *Locke on War and Peace*, 74-75.

21 Locke, *Treatises*, II. § 225.

22 Cox, *Locke on War and Peace*, 79.

23 Locke, *Treatises*, II. § 226.

24 Cox, *Locke on War and Peace*, 79.

25 Ibid.

26 Locke, *Treatises*, II. § 6.

27 Ibid., II. § 12. See also II. §§ 19, 57, 61, and 63.

28 Cox, *Locke on War and Peace*, 80.

29 Locke, *Treatises*, II. § 124.

30 Ibid.

31 Ibid.

32 Ibid., II. § 125.

33 Ibid.

34 Ibid., § 127.

35 Cox, *Locke on War and Peace*, 88-9.

36 I have also defended the same point in the following article: "The Internal Coherency of Locke's Moral Views in the *Questions Concerning the Law of Nature*," *Interpretation: A Journal of Political Philosophy* 29, no. 1 (Fall 2001): 55-73.

37 Of course, others may add the existence of God and the question of whether Locke was an theological intellectualist or a theological voluntarist. Additionally, others may want to bring up the idea of innate ideas.

38 At this point, it may be necessary to explain why I am ignoring the *First Treatise* as a source of evidence for Locke's natural law views. There are basically two reasons. First, the *First Treatise* is not so much a positive defense of position as it is negative polemic against a viewpoint. In fact, Locke provides a perfectly frank and straightforward attack of Sir Robert Filmer's *Patriarcha, or the Natural Power of Kings* that was originally published in 1680. Second, from my own reading, it is not clear that there are any passages in the *First Treatise* that may be used as evidence for Locke's allegiance to natural law. Having said this, I should not give the impression that this is impervious to argument. In fact, as Colman points out, Locke appears to embrace two characteristics often associated with the natural law tradition: the innateness and self-evidence of moral principles (*John Locke's Moral Philosophy*, 179). However, I believe a close textual analysis and comparison will reveal just the opposite. Although it would be beyond the scope of this book to delve into a line-by-line analysis of the *First Treatise's* use of the law of nature, it may be helpful to point out one of the passages.

The passage I have in mind is perhaps the most controversial. In this passage, which is too long to quote, Locke (contrary to his early views in the *Essays*) appears to embrace the innateness and self-evidence of moral principles. For example, Locke writes: "God having made Man, and planted in him, as in all other Animals, a strong desire of Self-preservation . . . ." (*Treatises*, I. § 86). Additionally, Locke writes: "For the desire, strong desire of Preserving his Life and Being having been Planted in him, as a Principle of Action by God himself, Reason, *which was the Voice of God in him*, could not but teach him and assure him, that pursing that natural Inclination he had to preserve his Being, he followed the Will of his Maker. . . ." (Ibid). The reason why this passage seems to point to the innateness and self-evidence of moral principles is this: In traditional natural law doctrine, every person is endowed with powers of reason and conscience. These powers are needed in order to distinguish certain kinds of natural impressions put in place in our nature by God, e.g., the natural inclination mentioned above in the quotation. Therefore, when the focus of these powers is turned toward our own nature, certain judgments can be made about the morality of pursuing our natural inclinations. For example, when reason apprehends the natural inclination of self-preservation, reason also apprehends at the same time that self-preservation is good and, consequently, an morally relevant goal to pursue. Therefore, the moral judgment, preserving my life is good, is innate because it rests partly upon a natural inclination and self-evidently true because reason apprehends that such a inclination is good.

I believe that such an interpretation of this passage is incorrect. This is so because an examination of the context reveals that the passage quoted above by Locke does not have anything to do with the justification of moral precepts; this passage is only concerned with explaining why all men attempt to preserve their own lives, i.e., his point in the *First Treatise* is one that concerns moral psychology or motivation. In fact, what he does say is similar to a passage in the *Essay* right before his point that no moral claims are innate or self-evident:

Nature, I confess, has put into man a desire of happiness and an aversion to misery: these indeed are innate practical principles which (as practical principles ought) do continue constantly to operate and influence all our actions without ceasing: these may be observed in all persons and all ages, steady and universal; but these are inclinations of the appetite to good, not impressions of truth on the understanding. I deny not that there are natural tendencies imprinted on the minds of men; and that from the very first instances of sense and perception, there are somethings that are grateful and other unwelcome to them; somethings that they incline to and others that they fly: but this makes nothing for innate characters on the mind, which are to be the principles of knowledge regulating our practice. (I. iii. 3)

Here in this passage, then, we see Locke's explanation for why humans seem to pursue what they take to desire and flee from what they have an aversion for; however, is not this the same kind of point that Locke makes in the *First Treatise*? It would seem so. If this is true, then I see no basis, at least for these passages, to argue for the inconsistency of the *Essay* and the *Treatises*.

Second, Locke's view of the law of nature has changed considerably in the *Treatises*, and yet maybe it remains a distinct cousin. The reason is that while there are no longer any natural propensities, there are, what Locke calls in the *Essay*, inclinations of the appetites. These appetites, including our own desire of self-preservation, operate and influence our actions without ceasing. However, Locke qualifies this point in an important way: "these are so far from being innate moral principles, that if they were left to their full swing they would carry men to the overturning of all morality" (I. iii. 13). Moral laws and rules must be created then to restrain these appetites.

39 Laslett, introduction to the *Two Treatises of Government*, 87.
40 Ibid., 84.
41 Locke, *Essay*, IV. iii. 18.
42 Locke, *Treatises*, II. § 6.
43 Cox, *Locke on War and Peace*, 85.
44 Ibid.
45 Ibid., pp. 81-88.
46 Ibid., p. 88.
47 Ibid.
48 Ibid.
49 Ibid.
50 Locke, *Treatises*, II. § 6. Italics are mine.
51 Locke, *Essay*, II. xxi. 10-20.
52 For example, see II § 4.
53 Laslett, introduction to the *Treatises*, 95.
54 See, for example, *Treatises*, II. § 61.
55 Ibid., II. § 57.

56 Richard Hooker, *Of the Laws of Ecclesiastical Polity*, ed. A. S. McGrade and Brian Vickers (New York, 1975).

57 Cox, *Locke on War and Peace*, 62.

58 Ibid.

59 Ibid., 88-9.

60 This is, of course, a specific version of Nominalism called trope nominalism. For a discussion of this version and other versions see Loux, *Metaphysics*, 53-89. Loux attributes this position to Locke's *Essay*.

61 Locke's commitment to Nominalism may be easily confirmed in the Essay. Also such an outlook is recognized by many scholars, Loux, *Metaphysics*, 80; Alan Sidelle, *Necessity, Essence, and Individualism: A Defense of Conventionalism* (Ithaca and London, 1989), 17-24; and D. M. Armstrong, *Universals: An Opinionated Introduction* (Colorado, 1989), 5-6.

62 See, for example, Thomas Burnet, "Third Remarks Upon An Essay Concerning Human Understanding," in Peter A. Schouls (ed.), *Remarks Upon An Essay Concerning Human Understanding: Five Tracts* (New York, 1984), 6-16.

Conclusion
Repositioning Locke within the History of Moral and Political Philosophy

There has been a very striking problem in the interpretation of Locke's moral and political philosophy. Since the publication of the *Essays* by von Leyden in 1954, two alternative positions seem to arise. First, one view argues that the *Essays* and the *Essay* are incompatible by virtue of role the natural law plays in the former. Peter Laslett is one proponent of this view and one reason he gives is that "The *Essay* has no room for natural law."[1] However, since the *Treatises* appear to rest in some sense on the philosophy of the *Essays* by virtue of Locke's emphasis on the law of nature, the *Treatises* and the *Essay* are also incompatible.[2] Second, another view argues that the *Essays* and *Essay* are compatible. Colman, for example, is one such proponent. He argues that the *Essay* was written as a justification for the natural law views, which appear in the *Essays*.[3] In fact, Colman argues that, even though there are problems, there remains a coherency not only between the *Essays* and the *Essay*, but also between the *Treatises* and the latter two.

My view is contrary to both positions above. First, contrary to Colman's view, I argued in chapter 4 that the *Essays* and *Essay* are inconsistent because of the material difference between both works. Although the way is not wholly smooth, the *Essay* lacks most, if not all, of the metaphysical machinery to support a view of the law of nature.

Second, contrary to the Laslett's view, I argue in chapter 5 that the *Treatises* and the *Essay* are compatible. My reasons bear a striking similitude to my arguments against Colman. That is, Locke's use of the law of nature in the *Treatises* lacks much of the philosophical underpinnings to be an orthodox natural law view. Of course, he uses the

term natural law in the *Treatises* and so this automatically lends plausibility to the position that the *Treatises* and the *Essay* are inconsistent.
However, as I try to show in chapter 5, when there is a careful examination of the text of the *Treatises*, we must place safeguards against
assuming that Locke's use of the phrase "law of nature" automatically
places him within the orthodox tradition.

The final implication that I will discuss concerns Locke's place in
the history of moral and political philosophy. On the account that I of-
fer of the relationship between the *Essay* and the *Treatises*, Locke's
stance bears a striking resemblance to the more skeptical views discussed in the twentieth century, in particular *idealism*.[4] Since such a
position, I am sure, will not sit well with many scholars, it is part of the
rational protection of my own position that I proceed without any un-
due haste because things done well, and with a care, exempt themselves
from fear.

Here is how I will proceed. First, I will describe the idealists' position that Locke's moral and political position closely resembles. After
that, I will attempt to demonstrate why Locke's point of view typifies
this similarity.

Although I contend that Locke's moral and political outlook bears
an evident similarity to idealism, he is also a *realist*. Although that
sounds suspicious, the connection can be made in this way. Idealism is
a variety of realism. Here is the link. Realism is basically the opinion
that moral claims when literally construed, are literally true or false
(cognitivism), *and* it is also the outlook that some of these moral claim
are, in fact, literally true. Idealism accepts the first thesis of realism.
But whereas the strongest version of realism defends the view that the
truth-conditions are objectivistic, idealism argues that the truth-
conditions are by virtue of someone or other's mind.

The truth-condition of idealism may be construed in one of two
ways. The first way is called *subjectivism*. This means that moral
claims are true or false relative to the desires, preferences, and goals of
an individual mind or perhaps an ideal observer. The other way is
called *intersubjectivism*. This is the belief that the truth-value of a
moral claim is relative to the conventions and practices actually in force
in the relevant society.

In the *Essay*, Locke defends idealism and specifically subjectivism
and intersubjectivism. As I argue in chapter 3, the passages at IV. iii.
18 and II. xxviii. 5-10 of the *Essay* casts an informing light on this
topic. In the first passage, we see Locke's allegiance to realism by establishing the true-conditions for moral claims. Three issues materialize

that are worth mentioning. First, Locke maintains that the demonstration of morality begins with two ideas: an idea about God and an idea about ourselves. From these self-evident propositions the truth-value of moral claims may be established. This leads to the second point: These assertions are essentially what later become called analytic truths with one qualification. Let me explain. Earlier in the *Essay*, I. iii. 1, Locke points out that although moral principles have truth-values, demonstrating the truth-values requires some exercise of the mind. So, while their truth-values may be illuminated by understanding that the predicate is contained, in some sense, in the subject, they are not so clear as simpler statements, statements like white is not black. Instead, as Locke makes clear in IV. ii. 3ff., intervening steps are needed to understand the truth-value of moral claims. Finally, although Locke argues in IV. iii. 18 that morality is capable of demonstration, the statement he demonstrates is a political claim.

Prior to IV. iii. 18, Locke discusses his own version of subjectivism and intersubjectivism in II. xxviii. 5-10. Since I have discussed these passages in detail in chapter 3, I will only briefly summarize Locke's outlook. From Locke's perspective, it is perfectly evident that what is morally good or evil is a relationship between two items: a voluntary action and a rule. However, not every rule should be used to establish the moral goodness or evil of an action. On the contrary, Locke specifically affirms that only rules that are enforced, or will be enforced eventually, may be used to determine the normative status of actions. In fact, from his perspective, there are only three sources of rules, which have this characteristic: the rules enforced by God (II. xxviii. 8), the rules enforced by the commonwealth (II. xxviii. 9), and the rules established by the moral community, which he calls the law of opinion or reputation (II. xxviii. 10).

It is from these passages that Locke's commitment to subjectivism and intersubjectivism surface. Here is why. Locke's subjectivism is most clearly demonstrated by pointing to God as one source of rule enforcement because the rules are generated by the desires, preferences, and goals of God's mind. Although it is an eventual enforcement, Locke nevertheless insists that God has establish a set of rules with enforcements, and men may use these to establish the moral good or evil of actions.[5] The other two sources of rules reflect Locke's intersubjectivism because the rules of the civil authority and the rules of moral community represent moral rules that are relative to the conventions and practices actually in force in the relevant society.

The question my analysis of Locke raises is, Where does Locke fit into the history of moral and political philosophy? First, as I argue in chapters 4 and 5, Locke should no longer be seen as someone who establishes the normative status moral and political claim with the natural law. Perhaps, we should take a cue from Cox and place Locke within the Hobbesian tradition. But that will not do either because Hobbes articulates something like an anti-realist outlook of moral claims. Maybe Locke fits into some sort of early error theory? This will not work because Locke does argue that some moral and political claims are true. Locke certainly does not represent some sort of success theory because Locke does not believe the truth-value of moral and political claims is determined by a deep metaphysical account of universals or essences. In the end, as I argued earlier and in chapter 3, Locke fits most closely within the relativist tradition. The normative element of moral and political claims go no deeper than the conventional rules established by God, the civil authority, or the moral community.

Notes

1 Laslett, introduction to the *Two Treatises of Government*, 94.

2 This question is also addressed by von Leyden. He argues that not only are the *Treatises* and *Essays* incompatible with the *Essay*, but that the *Treatises* and *Essays* are compatible because "not only about the law of nature but also other topics dealt with in the *Two Treatises*, especially in the *Second Treatise*, have their original in passages of his early essays" (von Leyden, introduction to the *Essays on the Law of Nature*, 80-2).

3 Colman, *John Locke's Moral Philosophy*, 177ff.

4 The following discussion of moral idealism relies heavily upon the article by Geoffery Sayer-McCord entitled, "The Many Moral Realism," in *Essays on Moral Realism*, ed. Geoffrey Sayre-McCord (Ithaca and London: Cornell University Press, 1988), 1-23. I am in his debt for his close analysis of the extremely confusing realist and anti-realist debate.

5 Of course, the subjectivism associated with God will only work as long as we connect to it a version of theological voluntarism. I argue that this is the only view consistent with the *Essay* because of the assumption of corpuscularism.

Appendix A
Does Locke Really Hold to an Intellectualist View of Obligation?

The intellectualist view of obligation is a view defended by the Cambridge Platonists, which includes individuals like Ralph Cudworth[1] and Samuel Clarke.[2] It is the view that the moral value of actions and moral distinctions are not created by God and by arbitrary fiat, but are fixed in the immutable nature of things.[3] In fact, not only is man's will to be determined by these, but even God cannot deviate from these precepts. As Colman relates, on this view "God is just as much a moral agent as man. . . ."[4]

As evidence for this shift in Locke, von Leyden[5] cites the following passage:

> Since therefore all men are by nature rational, and since there is a harmony between this law and the rational nature, this harmony can be known by the light of nature, it follows that all those who are endowed with a rational nature, i.e. all men in the world, are morally bound by this law. Hence, if natural law is binding on at least some men, clearly by the same right it must be binding on all men as well, because the ground of obligation is the same for all men, and also the manner of its being known and its nature are the same. In fact, this law does not depend on an unstable and changeable will, but on the eternal order of things.[6]

As an explanation for why this shift from theistic voluntarism to an intellectualism allegedly takes place in Locke's thinking von Leyden writes:

the 'voluntarist' theory carries with it an implication which Locke obviously found dissatisfying, for together with the concept of will it introduces an arbitrary element into morality. [I]n order to make his theory more perfect, Locke attempts to derive moral obligation in some other way. He does this as part of his endeavour to arrive at a purely rational foundation of ethics.[7]

This view is disputed by both John Lenz and Colman. Lenz writes that he "cannot find this cleavage in Locke's theory."[8] Lenz suggests that von Leyden's mistake is grounded upon his failure to notice a distinction that Locke makes "between the effective and terminate causes of man's obligations."[9] Colman later makes the same sort of criticism.[10] The distinction mentioned occurs in the following passage:

> [F]urther, regarding obligation, it must-be noted that some tings bind 'effectively', others only 'terminatively', i.e. by delimitation. That thing binds 'effectively' which is the prime cause of all obligation, and from which springs the formal cause of obligation, namely the will of a superior. For we are bound to something for the very reason that he, under whose rule we are, wills it. That thing binds 'terminatively', or by delimitation, which prescribes the manner and measure of an obligation and of our duty and is nothing other than the declaration of that will, and this declaration by another name we call law.[11]

According to the editors of the *Questions* (although Horwitz in his commentary ignores this problem), this is a distinction, which Locke borrowed from Robert Sanderson from his 1661 work, entitled, *De obligation Conscientiae*.[12] Locke himself is, of course, careful to point out that we are not bound by any will that is superior in the sense of having the power to coerce. On the contrary, we are bound only to those wills that are superior:

> either by natural right and the right of creation, as when all things are justly subject to that by which they have first been made and also are constantly preserved; or by the right of donation, as when God, to who all things belong, has transferred part of His dominion to someone and granted the right to give orders to the firstborn, for example, and to monarchs; or by the right of contract, as when someone has voluntarily surrendered himself to another and submitted himself to another's will.[13]

With regard to the word "terminative," Sanderson writes, "the law can be said and often is said to bind 'terminatively', that is, as the terms of the obligation and in the manner of a formal cause. . . ."[14] It appears that the terminative aspect of the law of nature is just the "terms" of the obligation. That is, it is that which is to be done or what is forbidden to be done. Sanderson goes on to say the terminative aspect is "that to which each man is bound, who operates following its prescription, just as the artisan in his work is directed by the pattern that has been set before him."[15]

To return to Locke's own account, the concept of having an obligation is explicated in the following manner. An obligation is nothing:

> other than the declaration of that will, and this declaration by another name we call law. We are indeed bound by Almighty God because He wills, but the declaration of His will delimits the obligation and the ground of our obedience; for we are not bound to anything except what a law-maker in some way has made known and proclaimed as his will.[16]

Therefore, Lenz and Colman appear to be right because, according to Locke, to say that the law of nature is binding on all men is to say that each man has a duty to discharge his own obligation to God, who is the first cause of the law of nature, and each man has a duty to discharge his obligation according to the terms of the law of nature:

> [I]n Locke's theory, then, the will of God is the form of the law of nature; it makes the directives of morality to be laws binding mankind. Human nature provides the necessary terminative element in the law of nature, for what God wills men to do is somehow incorporated in the way He has made them.[17]

Notes

1 Ralph Cudworth, *A Treatise Concerning Eternal and Immutable Morality*, 1: 105-119.

2 Samuel Clarke, *A Discourse Concerning the Unchangeable Obligations of Natural Religion, and the Truth and Certainty of the Christian Revelation*, 1: 191-225.

3 Colman, *John Locke's Moral Philosophy*, 33-35.

4 Ibid., 35.

5 von Leyden, introduction to the *Essays on the Law of Nature*, 31.

6 Locke, *Essays*, 199; fol. 99.

7 von Leyden, introduction to the *Essays on the Law of Nature*, 31.

8 John W. Lenz, "Discussion: Locke's *Essay on the Law of Nature*," *Philosophy and the Phenomenological Research* 27, no. 1 (1956): 108.

9 Ibid.

10 Colman, *John Locke's Moral Philosophy*, 41.

11 Locke, *Essays*, 185; fols. 86-87.

12 *Questions*, footnote 87, 209.

13 Locke, *Essays*, 185; fols. 85-86.

14 *Questions*, footnote 87, 209.

15 Ibid.

16 Locke, *Essays*, 185-186; fol. 87.

17 Colman, John Locke's Moral Philosophy, 42.

Appendix B
Question 4 of the *Essays Concerning the Law of Nature*

The fourth question of the *Essays* is entitled: "Can Reason Attain to the Knowledge of Natural Law through Sense-Experience? Yes."[1] To show us how we can have a knowledge of the law of nature, Locke offers the following argument: "in order that anyone may understand that he is bound by a law, he must know beforehand that there is a law-maker, i.e. some superior power to which he is rightly subject [and] that there is some will on the part of that superior power with respect to the things to be done by us."[2] Locke's proof is an argument from design. For example, he argues that it is evident from the senses that bodies exist, the visible world exists, and the visible world is framed with order.[3] This claim is true in virtue of some cause, chance, or accident. However, "it is surely undisputed that this could not have come together casually and by change into so regular and in every respect so perfect and ingeniously prepared a structure."[4] Hence the order we perceive was created by some kind of cause. Now if the world, etc., is created by some kind of cause, then the world was caused by inanimate things, animals, man, or a creator more powerful and wise than all three.[5] However, the cause cannot be inanimate things, animals, or man. Therefore, Locke concludes, "it is undoubtedly inferred that there must be a powerful and wise creator of all these things, who has made and built this whole universe and us mortals who are not the lowest part of it."[6] From here the argument turns on the meaning of an all powerful and wise creator. For example, Locke reasons that if an all-wise and powerful creator made the world, then he made the world at random, by accident, or for some purpose.[7] But it cannot be random or by accident because "it is contrary to such great wisdom to work with no fixed aim."[8] Therefore, Locke concludes that this all wise and powerful creator made the world for some purpose and that he wills man to do something.

Finally, we approach the end of Locke's argument. It is perhaps the most perplexing and interesting. It is perplexing because it is so enthymematic. It is interesting because here Locke attempts some sort of deduction of our natural law duties. Although I attempt to interpret this passage as closely to the text as possible, I interpret it in an unusual way. My view is this: Locke's argument here is a model for how we are to argue in general for these duties. Although he only argues for why man has a moral duty to preserve himself, the same sort of reasoning can be applied to all the duties. Locke even says at the very end of this passage that "there will be room perhaps elsewhere to discuss one by one these three subjects."[9] Although he never does this, let us consider the duty of self-preservation.

Locke begins the argument with this first premise: each person perceives that he is impelled by an inner instinct to preserve himself. In the same passage, Locke also mentions another instinct, viz., that instinct which impels man to enter and preserve a society with other men. Locke begins the argument in this way because, without some sort of instinct, there is no *prima facie* reason to assume that man can perform the duty. Next, in order to draw the conclusion he wants, I add the second premise that each person who perceives this inner instinct either has a moral duty to preserve himself or not. Following this, I add a third premise in order to eliminate one of the disjuncts. It can be worded in this way: if man does not have a duty to preserve himself, then preserving himself is not part of the end set out by the creator of man. Fourth, Locke denies the consequent of premise three and justifies it with some sort of empirically based justification. For example, preserving himself is part of the end set out by God because, as Locke reasons, God has made sure that by virtue of the dispositions he has placed in man "nobody can be found who does not care for himself or who disowns himself."[10] This step is crucial, as I see it, for a number of reasons. First, this step is needed in order to tie it back to the will of God concerning man. It is also needed to discover which instinct or natural propensities are either consistent or inconsistent with the will of God. It stands to reason that only those consistent with the will of God will be considered duties. Third, the empirical justification is needed in order to avoid appealing to the Scriptures. Finally, Locke draws his conclusion that man has a duty to preserve himself.

As I see it, then, all the other duties that Locke believes obtain in terms of the natural law can be argued using the formula I described above. However, describing Locke's argument this way leads to a problem. The problem I see for the argument above, and for any other like it, surrounds the empirical justification of premise four. For example, in the argument above, Locke reasons that premise four is true because "nobody can be found who does not care for himself or who disowns himself." But later, Horwitz and Zuckert point out, he gave numerous examples of individuals, which appear to contradict what he says here. (See, e.g., page 173; fol. 75). Moreover, Locke would also argue that worshipping God is part of the end set by God. But what sort of empirical reason will he use to justify this premise? Will he say that no one has been found who is careless of this duty? He also later denies this with numerous examples of people who do not seem to care about the worship of God or who do not believe in God. One response to this problem could be that such empirical justifications are only directed at normal people. So, no *normal* person has been found who is careless about himself, and no *normal* person is careless about believing in and worshipping God. However, such a move might be suspect because of the lack of textual evidence for such a modification, and because this is to assume that such a modification of the noun is guided by the intentions of our author, which are unknown. In any case, I will save this problem for another day, since I cannot see a way out this problem based on such a passage that is already too sketchy.

Notes

1 Locke, *Essays*, 147-159; fols. 47-61.
2 Ibid., 151; fol. 52.
3 Ibid., fol. 53.
4 Ibid., 153; fol. 54.
5 Ibid., fols. 54-55.
6 Ibid., fol. 54.
7 Ibid., 157; fol. 59.
8 Ibid.
9 Ibid., 159; fol. 61.
10 Ibid.

Appendix C
Locke on Innate Ideas in the
Essays Concerning the Law of Nature

In the *Essays*, the discussion of how we know the law of nature was immediately discussed after Locke discusses his arguments for the existence of the law of nature. This move is the next logical step because, according to his definition of law, we cannot say to individuals that they should obey a law that they cannot know. Locke moves to a discussion of three competing sources of knowledge of the law of nature:

> [H]owever, there are three kinds of knowledge which, without an over-careful choice of terms, I may call inscription, tradition, and sense-experience. To these may be added a fourth kind, namely supernatural and divine revelation, but this is no part of our present argument. For we do not investigate here what a man can experience who is divinely inspired, or what a man can behold who is illuminated by a light from heaven, but what a man who is endowed with understanding, reason, and sense-perception, can by the help of nature and his own sagacity search out and examine.[1]

Locke picks up the question of inscription later, however, in question 3, which is entitled, "Is the Law of Nature Inscribed in the Minds of Men? No." Its purpose is clearly stated by Locke:

> But by our inquiry whether the law of nature is written in the souls of men we mean this: namely, whether there are any moral propositions inborn in the mind and as it were engraved upon it such that they are as natural and familiar to it as its own faculties, the will, namely, and

the understanding, and whether, unchangeable as they are and always clear, they are known to us without any study or deliberate consideration.[2]

Locke immediately replies that this view is not true and that he has five arguments, which "show that there exists no such imprint of the law of nature in our hearts."[3] Locke's arguments can be summarized in the following way.

First, Locke argues that the law of nature is not inscribed in our hearts because there is no evidence for such a view, and it has never been proven by anyone:

(1) It has been only an empty assertion and no one has proved it until now, although many have laboured to this end, that the souls of men when they are born are something more than empty tablets capable of receiving all sorts of imprints but having none stamped on them by nature.[4]

Next, Locke argues that the inscription thesis cannot be true because if it were true, then there should be an immediate agreement among men about this law. However, this is not the case because:

For in respect to this law they differ so very widely, one rule of nature and right reason being proclaimed here, another there, one and the same thing being good with some people, evil with others, some recognizing a different law of nature, others none; but all see in it something obscure.[5]

Third, the inscription thesis is false because individuals who are said to live according to nature "live in such ignorance of every law, as though there were no principle of rightness and goodness to be had at all."[6] Locke argues that those closer to nature, e.g., "younger boys, illiterate people, and those primitive races,"[7] and who have no other guide than nature are those which we would expect to be less corrupted by the positive regulations of society. However, of the barbarian nations,[8] Locke writes:

But yet anyone who consults the histories both of the old and the new world, or the itineraries of travelers, will easily observe how far apart from virtue the morals of these people are, what strangers they are to any humane feelings, since nowhere else is there such doubtful honesty, so much treachery, such frightful cruelty in that they sacrifice to the gods and also to their tutelary spirit by killing people and offering kindred blood.[9]

Moreover, Locke also adds concerning the barbarous and untutored peoples that "there appears not the slightest trace or track of piety, merciful feeling, fidelity, chastity, and the rest of the virtues; but rather they spend their life wretchedly among robberies, thefts, debaucheries, and murders."[10]

Before he moves on to discuss his fourth and fifth reasons, Locke adds that although the inscription thesis is false with reference to the young, the uneducated, and the barbarians, it is also nevertheless false concerning the educated. This is true because even though there exists among the educated "some definite and undoubted views about morals [and] take these for the law of nature and believe that they are written in their hearts by nature,"[11] a better explanation is this:

> For these opinions about moral rightness and goodness which we embrace so firmly are for the most part such as, in a still tender age, before we can as yet determine anything about them or observe how they insinuate themselves, stream into our unguarded minds, and are inculcated by our parents or teachers or others with whom we live. For since these believe that such opinions are conducive to well ordering of life, and perhaps have also themselves been brought up in them in the same manner, they are inclined to inure the still fresh minds of the young to opinions of this kind, which they regard as indispensable for a good and happy life.[12]

Locke's fourth reason is similar to his third reason. The inscription thesis is false because "the foolish and insane have no knowledge of it."[13] He adds that these individuals should know the precepts of the law of nature if the inscription thesis is true because "the law is said to be stamped immediately on the soul itself and this depends very little upon the constitution and structure of the body's organs."[14]

Finally, Locke attacks the inscription thesis by arguing that if the inscription thesis is true, then "it would have to be inferred that speculative as well as practical principles are inscribed. But this seems difficult to prove."[15] One such example of a speculative principle is mentioned, viz., "it is impossible that the same thing should at the same time both be and not be."[16] Locke adds that if we carefully examine the origins of our knowledge of this principle we will see that either someone else taught it to us or "proved it to himself by induction and by observing particulars."[17]

Most, if not all, of what Locke writes against innate ideas in the *Essays* is brought forward into the *Essay*. However, there is now an important change as to the reason why innate ideas are discussed. Whereas, in the *Essays,* Locke argued against the inscription thesis as a means of knowing the existence of the law of nature, Locke now argues against the existence of innate ideas with a view to establishing a more positive thesis, viz., "how Men, barely by the Use of their natural faculties, may attain to all the Knowledge they have, without the help of any innate impressions."[18]

Notes

1 Locke, *Essays*, 123 & 125; fols. 23-24.
2 Ibid., 137; fol. 37.
3 Ibid.
4 Ibid., fol. 38.
5 Ibid., 137 & 139; fol. 38.
6 Ibid., 141; fol. 42.
7 Ibid., 139; fol. 40.
8 Locke never addresses why the young cannot be thought to have the law of nature inscribed on their hearts. Perhaps this is so because the question of the young was too obvious, and he decided to let us draw the conclusion. Of the uneducated, Locke never addresses them directly either. However, he may have thought this was also obvious, or he may have wanted us to assume what he said about the barbarians also applied to the uneducated.
9 Locke, *Essays*, 141; fol. 41.
10 Ibid., fol. 42.
11 Ibid.
12 Ibid., 141 & 143; fol. 43.
13 Ibid., 143; fol. 45.
14 Ibid.
15 Ibid., 145; fol. 45.
16 Ibid.
17 Ibid.
18 Locke, *Essay*, I. ii. 1.

BIBLIOGRAPHY

Aaron, Richard I. *John Locke*. Oxford: Clarendon Press, 1973.

Aarsleff, Hans. "Leibniz on Locke on Language." *American Philosphical Quarterly* 1, no. 3 (1964): 165-188.

Abrams, Philip. Introduction to *Two Tracts on Government*, edited by Philip Abrams, 3-111. Cambridge: Cambridge University Press, 1967.

Alexander, Peter. *Ideas, Qualities and Corpuscles*. Oxford: Oxford University Press, 1985.

Alexander, S. *Locke*. Port Washington, N. Y: Kennikat Press, 1908.

Anderson, F. II. "The Influence of Contemporary Science on Locke's Methods and Results." In *University of Toronto Studies, Philosophy*, vol. 2. Toronto, 1925

Aquinas, Thomas. *Basic Writings of Saint Thomas Aquinas*. 2 vols. Edited by Anton C. Pegis. Indianapolis and Cambridge: Hackett Publishing Co., 1997

Aristotle. *Nicomachean Ethics*. 2nd Ed. Translated by Terence Irwin. Indianapolis and Cambridge: Hackett Publishing Co., 1999.

—. *Metaphysics*, trans. by W. D. Ross. In *The Complete Works of Aristotle*, 2 vols., edited by Jonathan Barnes, 2: 1552-1728. Princeton, NJ: Princeton University Press, 1984.

—. *Politics*, trans. by B. Jowett. In *The Complete Works of Aristotle*, 2 vols., edited by Jonathan Barnes, 2: 1986-2129. Princeton, NJ: Princeton University Press, 1984.

Armstrong, D. M. *Universals: An Opinionated Introduction*. Colorado, 1989.

Ashcraft, Richard. *Revolutionary Politics and Locke's Two Treatises of Government*. Princeton: Princeton University Press, 1986.

Ayers, Michael R. *Locke*. 2 vols. London: Routledge, 1991.

Bacon, Francis. *Novum Organum*. Chicago: University of Chicago, 1952.

Berkhof, Louis. *Systematic Theology*. Grand Rapids, Michigan: Wm. B. Eerdmans Publishing Co., 1939.

Boyle, Robert. *Advice in Judging of Things said to Transcend Reason*. In *The Works of the Honourable Robert Boyle*, edited by Thomas Birch, 4: 447-469. London, 1772.

—. *A Disquistion about the Final Causes of Natural Things*. In *The Works of the Honourable Robert Boyle*, edited by Thomas Birch, 5:392-452. London, 1772.

—. *Some Considerations about the Reconcileableness of Reason and Religion*. In *The Works of the Honourable Robert Boyle*, edited by Thomas Birch, 4:151-202. London, 1772.

—. *A Discourse of Things above Reason, enquiring whether a Philosopher should admit there are any such*. In *Selected Philosophical Papers of Robert Boyle*, edited by M. A. Stewart, 209-242. Indianapolis: Hackett Publishing Company, 1991.

—. *The Origin of Forms and Qualities According to the Corpuscular Philosophy*. In *Selected Philosophical Papers of Robert Boyle*, edited by M. A. Stewart, 1-96. Indianapolis: Hackett Publishing Company, 1991.

Brody, Baruch A. *Identity and Essence*. Princeton: Princeton University Press, 1980.

Burnet, Thomas. *Remarks Upon An Essay Concerning Human Understanding: Five tracts*, edited by Peter A. Schouls. New York: Garland Publishing, Inc., 1984.

—. "Remarks Upon *An Essay Concerning Human Understanding*: In a letter address'd to the author." In *Remarks Upon An Essay Concerning Human Understanding: Five tracts,* edited by Peter A. Schouls, 3-15. New York: Garland Publishing, Inc., 1984.

—. "Second Remark Upon *An Essay Concerning Human Understanding*. In a letter address'd to the author. In *Remarks Upon An Essay Concerning Human Understanding: Five tracts*, edited by Peter A. Schouls, 1-30. New York: Garland Publishing, Inc., 1984.

—. "Third Remark Upon *An Essay Concerning Human Understanding*: In a letter to the author." In *Remarks Upon An Essay Concerning Human Understanding: Five tracts*, edited by Peter A. Schouls, 3-27. New York: Garland Publishing, Inc., 1984.

Clarke, Samuel. *A Discourse concerning the Unchangeable Obligations of Natural Religion, and the Truth and Certainty of the*

Christian Revelation. In *British Moralists 1650-1800*, edited by D. D. Raphael, 1: 191-225. Oxford: Oxford University Press, 1969.

Colman, John. *John Locke's Moral Philosophy.* Edinburgh: Edinburgh University Press, 1983.

Cox, Richard H. *Locke on War and Peace.* Oxford: Clarendon Press, 1960.

Cranston, Maurice. *John Locke: A Biography.* New York: The Macmillan Company, 1957.

Cudworth, Ralph. *A Treatise Concerning Eternal and Immutable Morality.* In *British Moralists 1650-1800*, edited by D. D. Raphael, 1: 105-119. Oxford: Oxford University Press, 1969.

Darwin, Charles. *The Descent of Man and the Selection in relation to Sex.* Chicago: Encyclopedia Britannica, Inc., 1952.

De Beer, E. S., ed. *The Correspondence of John Locke.* 8 vols. Oxford: Oxford University Press, 1979.

Descartes, Rene. *Rules for the Direction of the Mind.* In *The Philosophical Writings of Descartes*, edited and trans. by John Cottingham, Robert Stoothoff, and Dugald Murdoch, 9-78. Cambridge: Cambridge University Press, 1985.

Feldman, Fred. *Introductory Ethics.* Englewood Cliffs, New Jersey: Prentice Hall, Inc., 1978.

Frazer, Alexander Campbell, ed. *An Essay Concerning Human Understanding.* 2 vols. by John Locke. New York: Dover, 1959.

Gibson, James. *Locke's Theory of Knowledge and its Historical Relations.* Cambridge: Cambridge University Press, 1917.

Grant, Ruth W. *John Locke's Liberalism.* Chicago: University of Chicago Press, 1987.

Grotius, Hugo. *The Law of War and Peace*, trans. by Francis W. Kelsey. Oxford: Oxford University Press, 1925

Hare, R. M. *The Language of Morals.* Oxford: Oxford University Press, 1952.

Harman, Gilbert. "The Inference to the Best Explanation." *Philosophical Review* 74 (1965): 88-95.

Harman, Gilbert and Thomson, Judith Jarvis. *Moral Relativism and Moral Objectivity.* Cambridge: Blackwell Publishers, Inc., 1996.

Hill, Christopher. *Puritanism and Revolution.* New York: Schocken-Books, 1958.

Hobbes, Thomas. *Leviathan*, Edited by Edwin Curley. Indianapolis: Hackett Publishing Company, Inc., 1994.

Hooker, Richard. *Of the Laws of Ecclesiastical Polity.* Edited by A. S. McGrade and Brian Vickers. New York: St. Martin's Press, 1975.

Horwitz, Robert. Introduction to *Questions Concerning the Law of Na-
   ture*. Edited Robert Horwitz, Jenny Strauss Clay, and Diskin Clay
   and trans. by Diskin Clay. Ithaca: Cornell University Press, 1990.
—. "John Locke's *Questions Concerning the Law of Nature*: A Com-
   mentary." *Interpretation* 19, no. 3 (1992): 251-306.
Hughes, Ann, ed. *Seventeenth-century England: A Changing Culture*.
   Englewood Cliffs, New Jersey: Barnes and Noble Books, 1980.
Hume, David. *The History of England*. 6 vols. Indianapolis: Liberty
   Classics, Inc., 1983.
King, Lord, ed. *Life and letters of John Locke*. New York: Burt Frank-
   lin, 1972.
Kraus, Pamela. "Locke's Negative Hedonism." *The Locke Newsletter*
   15 (1984): 43-63.
Langley, Gideon Langley, trans. *New Essays Concerning Human Un-
   derstanding* by G. W. Leibnitz. La Salle: Open Court Publishing
   Co., 1949.
Laslett, Peter. Introduction to *Two Treatises of Government*, edited by
   Peter Laslett, 15-135. Cambridge: Cambridge University Press,
   1993.
Laudan, Laurens. "The Nature and Sources of Locke's views on Hypotheses." *Journal of the History of Ideas* 28, no. 2 (1967): 211-
   223.
Leibnitz, Gottried Wilhelm. *New Essays Concerning Human Under-
   standing*. Translated by Alfred Gideon Langley. La Salle: Open
   Court Publishing Co., 1949.
Lenz, John W. "Discussion: Locke's Essay on the Law of Nature." *Phi-
   losophy and Phenomenological Research* 27, no. 1 (1956): 105-
   113.
Locke, John. *An Essay Concerning Human Understanding*. 2 vols. Ed-
   ited by A. C. Fraser. New York: Dover, 1959.
—. *Two Treatises of Government*. Edited by Peter Laslett. Cambridge:
   Cambridge University Press, 1960.
—. *On the Reasonableness of Christianity*. Edited by I. T. Ramsey.
   Standford, CA: Stanford University Press, 1959.
—. *Essays on the Law of Nature, together with transcripts of Locke's
   shorthand in his journal of 1676*. Edited by W. von Leyden. Ox-
   ford: Clarendon Press, 1954.
—. *Two Tracts on Government*. Edited by Philip Abrams. Cambridge:
   Cambridge University Press, 1967.
—. "Of Ethics in General." In *Life and Letters of John Locke*, edited
   by Lord King, 308-325. New York: Burt Franklin, 1972.

—. *An Essay Concerning Human Understanding.* Edited by Peter H. Nidditch. Oxford: Clarendon Press, 1975.

—. *Questions Concerning the Law of Nature.* Edited Robert Horwitz, Jenny Strauss Clay, and Diskin Clay and trans. by Diskin Clay. Ithaca: Cornell University Press, 1990.

Loux, Michael J. *Metaphysics: A Contemporary Introduction.* New York: Routledge 1998.

Mabbott, J. D. *John Locke.* New York: The Macmillan Co., 1973.

Mackie, J. L. *Problems from Locke.* Oxford: Oxford University Press, 1976.

Mandelbaum, Maurice. *Philosophy, Science, and Sense Perception.* Baltimore: Johns Hopkins Press, 1964.

Marshall, John. *John Locke: Resistance, Religion and Responsibility.* Cambridge: Cambridge University Press, 1994.

Mintz, Samuel. *The Hunting of Leviathan.* Cambridge: Cambridge University Press, 1962.

Odegard, Douglas. "Locke and the Unreality of Relations." *Theoria* 35 (1969): 147-152.

Osler, Margaret J. "John Locke and the Changing Ideal of Scientific Knowledge." *Journal of the History of Ideas* 31 (1970): 3-16.

Rapaczynski, Andrzej. *Nature and Politics: Liberalism in the Philosophies of Hobbes, Locke, and Rousseau.* Cornell: Cornell University Press, 1987.

Rogers, G. A. J. "Boyle, Locke, and Reason." *Journal of the History of Ideas* 27 (1966): 205-216.

Ross, W. D. *Aristotle.* London: Methuen and Co., Ltd., 1923.

Russell, Conrad. *The Crisis of Parliament.* Oxford: Oxford University Press, 1971.

Sanderson, Robert. *De Obligatione Conscientiae.* Trans. by William Whewell. Cambridge: Cambridge University Press, 1879.

Sargent, Rose-Mary. "Learning from Experience: Boyle's Construction of an Experimental Philosophy." In *Robert Boyle Reconsidered*, edited by Michael Hunter, 60-250. Cambridge: Cambridge University Press, 1994.

Sayer-McCord, Geoffery, "Introduction: The Many Moral Realisms." In *Essays on Moral Realism*, edited by Geoffrey Sayre-McCord. Ithaca and London: Cornell University Press, 1988.

Schouls, Peter A. *The Imposition of Method: A study of Descartes and Locke.* Oxford: Oxford University Press, 1980.

Schneewind, J. B. "Locke's Moral Philosophy." In *The Cambridge Companion to Locke*, edited by Vere Chappell, 199-225. Cambridge: Cambridge University Press, 1994.

Scott, Jr., Robert B. "Five Types of Ethical Naturalism." *American Philosophical Quarterly* 17, no. 4 (1980): 261-270.

Sidelle, Alan. *Necessity, Essence, and Individualism: A Defense of Conventionalism*. Ithaca and London, 1989.

Simmons, A. John. *The Lockean Theory of Rights*. Princeton: Princeton University Press, 1992.

Stace, W. T. "Ethical Relativism." In *Philosophy and Contemporary Issues*, edited by John R. Burr and Milton Goldinger, 200-209. New Jersey: Prentice Hall, 1996.

Stewart, M. A. "Critical Notice." *The Locke Newsletter* 23 (1992): 145-165.

—. Introduction to *Selected Philosophical Papers of Robert Boyle*, edited by M. A. Stewart. Indianpolis and Cambridge: Hackett Publishing Company, 1991.

Van Fraassen, Bas C. *The Scientific Image*. Oxford: Oxford University Press, 1980.

Von Leyden, W. Introduction to *Essays On the Law of Nature, together with transcripts of Locke's shorthand in his journal of 1676*, edited W. Von Leyden, 1-92. Oxford: Clarendon Press, 1954.

—. "John Locke and Natural Law." *Philosophy* 31, no. 116 (1956): 23-35.

Woolhouse, R. S. *Locke's Philosophy of Science and Knowledge*. New York: Barnes and Noble, 1971.

Yolton, John W. *John Locke and the Way of Ideas*. Oxford: Oxford University Press, 1956.

—. *Locke and the Compass of Human Understanding*. Cambridge: Cambridge University Press, 1970.

Yost, R. M. "Locke's Rejection of Hypotheses about Sub-microscopic Events." *Journal of the History of Ideas* 12 (1951): 111-130.

Zinaich, Jr., Samuel. "Locke's Moral Revolution: from Natural Law to Moral Relativism." *The Locke Newsletter* 31 (2000): 79-114.

—. "The Internal Coherency of Locke's Moral Views in the *Questions Concerning the Law of Nature*." *Interpretation: A Journal of Political Philosophy* 29, no. 1 (Fall 2001): 55-73.

Zuckert, Michael P. "On the Lockean Project of a Natural Law Theory: Reply to Zinaich." *Interpretation: A Journal of Political Philosophy* 29, no. 1 (Fall 2001): 75-89.

—. *Natural rights and the New Republicanism*. Princeton, 1994.

Index